The Global Ethnopolis

Also by Michel S. Laguerre

AFRO-CARIBBEAN FOLK MEDICINE: The Reproduction and Practice of Healing

AMERICAN ODYSSEY: Haitians in New York City

THE COMPLETE HAITIANA: A Bibliographic Guide to the Scholarly Literature, 1900–1980 (2 vols)

DIASPORIC CITIZENSHIP: Haitian Americans in Transnational America

ETUDES SUR LE VODOU HAITIEN

THE INFORMAL CITY

THE MILITARY AND SOCIETY IN HAITI

MINORITIZED SPACE: An Inquiry into the Spatial Order of Things

URBAN LIFE IN THE CARIBBEAN: A Study of a Haitian Urban Community

URBAN POVERTY IN THE CARIBBEAN: French Martinique as a Social Laboratory

VOODOO HERITAGE

VOODOO AND POLITICS IN HAITI

The Global Ethnopolis

Chinatown, Japantown and Manilatown in American Society

Michel S. Laguerre
University of California at Berkeley

First published in Great Britain 2000 by
MACMILLAN PRESS LTD
Houndmills, Basingstoke, Hampshire RG21 6XS and London
Companies and representatives throughout the world

A catalogue record for this book is available from the British Library.

ISBN 0–333–77789–1

First published in the United States of America 2000 by
ST. MARTIN'S PRESS, INC.,
Scholarly and Reference Division,
175 Fifth Avenue, New York, N.Y. 10010

ISBN 0–312–22612–8

Library of Congress Cataloging-in-Publication Data
Laguerre, Michel S.
The global ethnopolis : Chinatown, Japantown and Manilatown in American society / Michel S. Laguerre.
p. cm.
Includes bibliographical references and index.
ISBN 0–312–22612–8 (cloth)
1. Ethnic neighborhoods—California—San Francisco. 2. Asian Americans—California—San Francisco. 3. Internationalism Case studies. 4. United States—Relations—Asia Case studies. 5. Asia––Relations—United States Case studies. I. Title.
F869.S39065 1999
307.3'362'08995073—dc21   99–31478
                                                                    CIP

© Michel S. Laguerre 2000

All rights reserved. No reproduction, copy or transmission of this publication may be made without written permission.

No paragraph of this publication may be reproduced, copied or transmitted save with written permission or in accordance with the provisions of the Copyright, Designs and Patents Act 1988, or under the terms of any licence permitting limited copying issued by the Copyright Licensing Agency, 90 Tottenham Court Road, London W1P 0LP.

Any person who does any unauthorised act in relation to this publication may be liable to criminal prosecution and civil claims for damages.

The author has asserted his right to be identified as the author of this work in accordance with the Copyright, Designs and Patents Act 1988.

This book is printed on paper suitable for recycling and made from fully managed and sustained forest sources.

10 9 8 7 6 5 4 3 2 1
09 08 07 06 05 04 03 02 01 00

Printed and bound in Great Britain by
Antony Rowe Ltd, Chippenham, Wiltshire

To the Chinese American, Japanese American, and Filipino American Communities in the San Francisco Bay Area and Silicon Valley

Contents

Preface and Acknowledgments ix

Introduction: "Little Americas" 1

1 The Global Ethnopolis 18
2 Chinatown: The Ethnopole as an Informal Capital City 28
3 Japantown: The Deglobalization of an Ethnopole 53
4 Manilatown: Global Exclusion and Global Margins 76
5 The Ethnopole as a Global City 110
6 The Global Space of the Ethnopole 129
7 The Global Ethnopole in the Global City 153

Notes and References 167
Bibliography 178
Index 187

Preface and Acknowledgments

The phenomenon of globalization, along with its attendant socio-economic and cultural ramifications, is manifest in a multiplicity of sites, processes, and structures within the confines of the American city. Globalization, in short, blows up the boundaries of the city through financial, communication, information, immigration, diasporic, and other border-crossing practices. In this widespread process of deterritorialization and reterritorialization, the ethnic enclave emerges as a privileged site for social analysis because it offers us an opportunity to decipher with precision and nuance the multifaceted aspects of *diasporic globalization*, one of the multiple forms of the globalization process. In other words, the *diasporic moment* is part and parcel of the *global moment* and the focus on the ethnic enclave is presumably an efficient way to shed light on the contents and contours of diasporic globalization.

Asian American neighborhoods – the focus of this study – which began to appear in California after the middle of the nineteenth century, were part of the outcome of the *internal orientalist project* of the United States, as Chinese, Japanese, and Filipino immigrants were brought in, segregated from the rest of society, and thereby constrained to build their enclaved neighborhoods at the physical margins of the American city. Although these communities have developed their own diasporic projects, they are nevertheless structurally located at the bottom of society because of the color-coding apparatus of the social system. Here is a clear example in which the ethnic projects, with their inherent rationale, do not completely coincide with mainstream views because of the loyalty of diasporic citizens to the homeland; their efforts to protect their long-term cultural interests; the structural constraints of the local milieu; their subaltern position in society; and the city's agenda *vis-à-vis* their integration.

Such diasporic projects find themselves embedded in the matrix of the mainstream's conflicting multicultural practices. For example, mainstream American multiculturalisms reflect *different agendas*, proceed from *different logics*, and achieve *different outcomes*.

In this rationale, *municipal multiculturalism* is practiced to produce cultural harmony among the various ethnic groups in the city, to highlight representation in the public sphere, to stress the common good over reckless individualism, and to enhance the development of good citizenship. It is achieved in the name of patriotism and for love of country.

Industrial multiculturalism follows the law of the market and is designed to please and attract a heterogeneous clientele, to spearhead competition, and to enhance economic gain. It is achieved in the name of the free market and for love of money.

Academic multiculturalism sees diversity as being good in itself because it allows different perspectives and contradictory opinions to be heard. The academy sees itself as a supermarket of ideas and a site where the integrated workforce of society is being trained in the civics of citizenship. It is achieved in the name of participatory and representative democracy and for love of freedom.

Congregational multiculturalism follows the Lord's wish and dictum that we all be brothers and sisters. Here multiculturalism is seen as the best mechanism for the formation and nurturing of a community of believers. It is achieved in the name of religious life and for love of God.

Diasporic multiculturalism as practiced by subaltern immigrant communities is seen as a mechanism to achieve parity and equality in a racialized social formation. It is achieved in the name of social justice and for love of homeland and the country of residence.

These conflicting behavioral expressions found at the local level are being exacerbated or reinforced by contradictory global practices that appear in various forms, from *ideological, strategic* to *managerial* multiculturalism.

This book does not intend to unveil a general theory of globalization, but rather has a limited goal, that is, to spell out the framework of a theory of diasporic globalization. It does so by taking into consideration central and peripheral transnational relations, border-crossing hierarchical interactions, the hybridity of temporal and spatial flows, and the positionalities of actors, institutions, and perspectives. It examines the mechanisms and parameters of the intricacies of the global process as depicted by the social transactions of ethnic enclaves with their transnational primary and secondary sites of relationship. Being the initiating, destination, or mediating site of global flows, the ethnopole provides a transnational niche in which to study aspects of the globalization of the American city and how diasporic communities have functioned as global entities.

This book also presents the idea that various institutions in the American city have their unique way of participating in and contributing to the globalization process. Fundamental ethnographies that critically examine not only these sectoral globalities, but also how the relations that these units maintain with each other and with the dominant sector of society are fashioned, are sorely needed and constitute an imperative in the process of theory building. This book is a small contribution to this collective effort as well.

The writing of a book on diasporic communities in American society is a communal project that requires the participation of many individuals precisely because the success of such an enterprise depends on one's ability to explain the collective experience of the group. To that end, several people have helped me in the preparation of this book by sharing with me their observations, reflections, and interpretations concerning a large array of issues. Foremost among these collaborators are friends and acquaintances in the Chinese, Japanese, and Filipino American communities in the San Francisco Bay Area (Gaetano Kazuo Maida, Betty Fung, Alex Ng, Nancy Tran, Elaine Wai-Ling Chu, William Chen, Richard Kono, Anni Chung, Johnny Ng, J. K. Yamamoto, Osamu Machida, Seizo Oka, Richard Wada, Kenji G. Taguma, Michiko Kimura, Tomoshige Okazaki, Kenneth Endo, Karl Kaoru Matsushita, Him Mark Lai, Al Robles, Emil DeGuzman, Frank Kong, Harvey Wong, Bullet Marasigan, Michi Onuma, Ada Chan, and others) who discussed with me some of the issues analyzed in the book. Also included in this category is a talented group of undergraduate students (Judy Chen, Charmaine Go, Tara Lai Quinlan, Margie Brown, Cheryl Locke, Siri Thanasombat, Thyrale Thai, Myoka Kim, Ann Le, Bernadette Casino, Binh Nguyen, Linda Peng, Neil Ruiz, Peter Fung, and Anna Vasquez) who were recruited for the most part through the Undergraduate Research Apprenticeship Program at the University of California at Berkeley.

I am grateful to all my colleagues and graduate students who contributed in one way or another to the completion of the book. Among them, I want to single out Him Mark Lai, Louise Hanford, Paula Lynch, Joe Fong, Nerissa Balce-Cortes, Caroline Valverde, Charles McClain, Kathleen Moran, Harry Chuck, Evelyn Nakano Glenn, Dean Carolyn Porter, Terry Strathman, Michael Omi, Jery Takahashi, Yen El Espiritu, Wei Chi Poon, David Pang, and Paul Kleyman. I am particularly indebted to Stephanie Sadre-Orafai and Smriti Rana who diligently prepared the Index.

Chapters of this book were previously read at a faculty colloquium organized by the American Studies Program at Berkeley, the annual meetings of the American Sociological Association, the annual meetings of the American Anthropological Association, an international symposium on transnational citizenship organized by the University of Quebec at Montreal, and at an international conference organized by the Italian Academy and Columbia University. I appreciate the questions, comments, and reactions of these various audiences to my ideas.

The Committee on Research of the Academic Senate, the Undergraduate Research Apprenticeship Program, and the Center for the Study of American Cultures at the University of California at Berkeley financially contributed to this research project. I appreciate Bonnie Hurd's thoughtful comments and editorial assistance. Last, but not least, I am thankful for my editors Tim Farmiloe (Macmillan), Garrett Kiely (St Martin's Press), and Keith Povey (Keith Povey Editorial Services), who have been handling with professionalism, efficiency and dedication the production of my books in the past ten years. I am grateful to them for their generosity, patience, and friendship.

Parma, Italy   MICHEL S. LAGUERRE

Introduction: "Little Americas"

When walking the streets of San Francisco, one is struck by the ethnic diversity of the urban metropolitan population. This diversity is manifested in a variety of ways: through a multiplicity of languages – Vietnamese, Cantonese, Mandarin, Spanish, Italian, Japanese, Tagalog, Russian, and French – spoken in everyday life; social services that cater to the needs of specific ethnic groups; Christian churches, Jewish synagogues, Muslim mosques, and Buddhist temples that attract worshipers of similar ethno-religious traditions; a multiformity of ethnic neighborhoods that form the infrastructural tapestry of the urban landscape; and parades and festivals that celebrate the national holidays of the homelands of residents of these cultural enclaves.

Ethnic niches thrive in several locales in the city. Some date as far back as the colonial period, some the second half of the nineteenth century, while others are of more recent origin, having emerged in the post-Civil-Rights-movement era.[1] Some of these neighborhoods, such as Chinatown, maintain a strong ethnic presence in San Francisco; others such as Japantown and Little Italy have become gentrified, a sign of their continuing integration into the larger city system. Still others, including the emerging Koreatown in the Western Addition, are presently burgeoning, either as a result of the group's recent migration to San Francisco or as a result of intra-urban migration, as in the case of the New Chinatown in the Richmond District. Finally, there are those – like the now defunct Chile Town or Manilatown – that have disappeared as ethnic neighborhoods because the ethnics no longer reside there as a group.

What also catches one's attention while strolling through San Francisco are the sobriquets that designate some of these ethnic neighborhoods. These sobriquets reflect their dominant ethnic composition and have entered the city's mainstream vocabulary, having been domesticated through discursive practices. Some neighborhoods are identified by the home countries of the diasporic residents, while others do not bear an ethnic name. For example, San Francisco's Chinese settlement is known as Chinatown, but the principal location of Mexican Americans is referred to as the Mission District, named after a settlement first established by early Spanish missionaries in order to convert the local indigenous population to Christianity. Such a name attests to the historical existence of the neighborhood prior to the arrival and settlement of the dominant and hegemonic Anglo community in San Francisco. One may recall that the various distinct minoritized ethnic neighborhoods emerged during three different periods in the history of San Francisco: namely, the period preceding the city's incorporation into the United States; the long era when racial discrimination was a genuine policy of the city; and the years after the signing of the Civil Rights Act in 1964, which made housing discrimination and segregation illegal.

The city's spatial order is encoded in the sites that comprise its morphology and is made up of mainstream neighborhoods differentiated by social class and economic status, neighborhoods currently undergoing ethnic demographic shifts and gentrification, and visibly distinct ethnic neighborhoods. This book focuses on three ethnic neighborhoods: commoditized Chinatown, gentrified Japantown, and defunct Manilatown. Examining these areas, the book seeks to decode their spatial significance, explain their insertion and incorporation into the city system, and interpret their different paths of growth. This study also examines these neighborhoods' status as capital cities for ethnic residents who live within and outside of them, and analyzes their structural position as global ethnopoles.

There is something special about the American urban landscape. Its peculiarity inheres largely in the life and death of ethnic enclaves. San Francisco is no exception to this seemingly historical phenomenon that has much to tell us about the history of immigration and the multicultural genealogy of urban America. The mainstream system seems to produce ethnic enclaves through numerous processes, and the logic of the capitalist apparatus paradoxically leads to their extinction as well. How should we explain the fact that for many years ethnic minorities have lived in specific ghettoized neighborhoods? Is it because people want to maintain an enclave that represents the national territory or capital city of their homeland? Or have racial discrimination and housing segregation confined people to these enclaves? Are they there because they are attracted by nearby industry and consequently choose to live near their places of work? Could it be that they settle in enclaves simply because housing is cheap and available, or because they lack fluency in English? In other words, do they live in these cultural enclaves because they choose to do so, or because they are subject to external factors over which they have no control?

Common wisdom has it that these enclaves exist because ethnic dwellers wish to isolate themselves voluntarily from the rest of society so that they may speak their own language, preserve their customary practices, live among other members of their group, and establish a home away from home. This interpretation is flawed in several respects. First of all, in the case of most enclaves that developed prior to the proclamation of the Civil Rights Act, the decision to live in a segregated neighborhood was not a voluntary one. Rather, the dominant system sought to prevent ethnics from living in white neighborhoods, which left them no choice but to live in ethnic enclaves.

But while racial segregation is the main factor that accounts for ethnic enclaves in urban America, poverty and wealth also help to explain the rise and decline of successive non-Anglo-European enclaves. Once the second-generation residents of these enclaves became fluent in English and were able to afford housing elsewhere, they had the option to move out and blend in with the mainstream population, which the residents of San Francisco's Little Italy did. When wealth is the primary factor in its formation, an enclave loses its segregated status once residents of other ethnic origins, but with the same class status, move in. Such was the case with San Francisco's Russian Hill, which began as a Russian enclave in the third quarter of the nineteenth century but lost its enclave's status when other groups began moving in, in about 1880.

From a morphological standpoint, ethnic enclaves have diverse origins. Enclaves, such as Chinatown in San Francisco, started at the margin of the city and then gradually became integrated into the larger city as they evolved. Other enclaves first formed on sites already occupied by other city residents and then grew over time, as in the case of Manilatown. Others came into being as the result of a resettlement scheme or intra-urban migration. For example, after the earthquake of 1906, the Japanese relocated Japantown from South Park, its initial site, to its present site in the Western Addition. In a variation on this pattern, the New Chinatown was populated first by former residents of Chinatown and then by new immigrants who came mainly from Hong Kong and Taiwan. More recently, certain ethnic enclaves have emerged within middle- or upper class white urban, and even suburban, neighborhoods. Such is the case of Little Tehran in Westwood Village in Los Angeles and Little Taipei in Monterey Park.[2]

In the course of the history of the American city, many so-called little immigrant enclaves have appeared and disappeared. Little Mexico and Chile Town, which flourished in San Francisco during the nineteenth century, are now extinct, as is Little Africa, a once vibrant African American neighborhood in New York City's Lower Manhattan. While mass migration and segregation practices may explain the emergence of most ethnic enclaves, these factors do not account for their disappearance. Although this phenomenon is not the main focus of this comparative historical analysis of San Francisco's ethnic neighborhoods, it does promise to shed new light on this neglected aspect of American history.

In San Francisco, as in the rest of the nation, an immigrant enclave is invariably referred to as a "little country," as in Little Italy; a "country-town" as in Japantown; or a "city-town," as in Manilatown. In other words, enclaves are regularly labeled in terms that suggest that they are "little" or "town" versions of countries or "town" versions of cities. Their names thus suggest that they are seen as miniature versions or replicas of the residents' old country or the capital city of their homeland. Little Italy is supposed to be a miniature and extension of the old country. In Chinatown, the old country is collapsed into an offshoot town. In the case of Manilatown, the old capital of the Philippines is duplicated as a diasporic town. These enclaves then become discrete and ethnicized little towns in the midst of an ever-expanding metropolis. But it is not always clear why they are given the status of a "little country" or "little town." Are they little *vis-à-vis* the homeland or its capital city because they are conceived as duplicates of these entities? Or are they little *vis-à-vis* the rest of the metropolis?

While there is a regular pattern in the way ethnic enclaves are named, the names of particular enclaves may nonetheless change over time. For example, in the nineteenth century, Chinatown was referred to as Little Canton or Little China, after the immigrant residents' region or country of origin. However, after the earthquake of 1906 that devastated San Francisco, Chinatown became the dominant name used by the Anglo majority to designate the neighborhood. This variation can be explained in terms of the folk status of the name. Informal names may change. Once formalized by usage, however, they are more likely to become permanent. Sometimes an ethnic enclave was officially designated as such by City Hall as a ploy to maintain or enhance the visibility of the landscape as a tourist attraction or to stabilize a business sector that provided tax revenues to the local government.

San Francisco's Japantown was revitalized in 1968 for this very purpose, as was Koreatown in Los Angeles during the Olympic Games. While we may never know who first named these enclaves, there are several hypotheses. Since they have so regularly been known as countries or towns throughout the history of the American urban landscape, it is safe to say that the enclaves were named by the mainstream population seeking to meet its own hegemonic agenda. Whether this was done by journalists or others who popularized such names, they originated as informal ways of referring to the communities of others. By the logic of the argument, the mainstream population did not consider its own area a "little" enclave.

While the mainstream named such an ethnic enclave, the residents had their own name for it. As early as 1906, in an editorial published in *Shin Sekai* (*Japanese Daily New World*), Japanese residents referred to the Japanese quarter as *Nihonjin-Machi*, that is, as "Japanese People Town." In other words, the residents' name for their neighborhood referred to the people of Japanese descent who lived there; their name for the enclave did not suggest that it was a microcosm of Japan or even refer to the country itself. Residents fought against the imposition of a name by the dominant sector of society. For many years the quarter was referred to as Japantown (Nihon-Machi) by outsiders and as Nihonjin-Machi (Japanese People Town) by insiders. The outsiders' reference to the residents' homeland was meant to belittle the residents or to underline the area's inferior status, while the reference to "Japanese People" by the residents themselves was a positive identification meant as a form of empowerment. A similar situation occurred in the Chinese enclave. The early Chinese dwellers referred to it as *babo* (Chinesetown) or *tonki* (Chinese street) and not as Chinatown.

As one older Japanese American commented,

> The Japanese in those days did not call themselves, in English, Japantown. Before the wars, from time to time I would say "Japantown" because the majority of the people started saying that, see; but I insisted on saying it was "Japanese Town." The Japanese expression would be "nihonjin" which means Japanese persons or things Japanese; "machi" is town, Japanese town. The reason for this is that Japanese people are a very sensitive people, as a whole, very sensitive compared to others.

He meant that the Japanese did not want to give the impression that they were colonizing a portion of the US landscape. Nihon Machi, however, became formalized as the official name of the enclave in 1968, when the San Francisco Redevelopment Agency and Japanese American civic leaders placed a sign of identification bearing that name at the corner of Post and Buchanan Streets.

The names of the enclaves reflect a hierarchical order projected by the mainstream on the US urban landscape. The San Francisco model is part of the larger US model. It is important to unveil the grammatical rules that prevail in this ordering system. Spatial hierarchy, or centrarchy, is made to represent the open space of the mainstream, the incarcerated space of the non-whites and non-Europeans, and the local space of the non-Anglo-Europeans. At the apex of the pyramid or at the center of the system is the new reality of the dominant sector that structures the landscape. In contrast to the ways in which minoritized quarters are stigmatized as "little" places, the mainstream refers to its space in terms of a new reality, as in "New" England, "New" Britain, "New" London, and "New" York.[3] This spatial system does not duplicate intact the spatial hierarchical order of the motherland. Rather, this new spatial order is a reversal of the old spatial order. In the New World, New England is a region and not a country. New London in Connecticut is not a capital but a secondary city of lesser importance than New York. In the United States, the old country (England) becomes a region (New England), and its capital city (London) trades its position with a secondary city (York).

In the new spatial order, the settlements of non-Anglo-Europeans are not referred to as "New," but rather as "Hill." (New Germany in Minnesota is an exception, and this for historical reasons.) In this category, one finds "Russian Hill" in San Francisco referring to both the wealth and the place of origin of its inhabitants. "French Hill" in Vermont and "Spanish Hill" in Pennsylvania reflect the same rationale. Through this distinction, the non-Anglo-Europeans are designated as being confined by design to a specific spot in town, which implies both their subaltern status and the spatial hegemony of the dominant Anglo community. The Anglos have their own hills, yet these are not obviously ethnic identifiers but rather status markers or elite enclaves; they include Nob Hill and Telegraph Hill in San Francisco, Chestnut Hill in Philadelphia, and Beacon Hill in Boston.[4]

In the third position of this spatial hierarchy are enclaves designated as towns. Already in 1683, Germantown (Philadelphia) was settled by a group of German immigrants. This designation clearly indicates its subordinate structural position *vis-à-vis* the dominant and hegemonic Anglo community, yet it refers foremost to the people who inhabited the area and only indirectly to their country of origin. The same logic explains the designation of the Greek neighborhood in Chicago as "Greektown" and the Jewish quarter or Tenth Ward in New York as "Jewtown."[5] According to Edwin Steiner, these Russian Jewish immigrants considered Rivington Street a "suburb of Minsk."[6] Thus, the designation of an enclave may refer not only to the residents' country of origin or the capital city of their homeland, but it may also refer to the "people," as in German-town. The distinction between the place of residence of the hegemonic sector and the "others" was made through the use of "city" and "town" to highlight these asymmetrical realms of power. The concept "city" designates the domain of the mainstream, while "town" refers to minoritized enclaves. For example, the old Jersey becomes "Jersey City" for the mainstream, while the old Manila becomes "Manilatown" for the Filipinos. The use of "town" rather than "city" did, however, have a specific function: it distinguished between the place of residence of the hegemonic sector and the "others," highlighting the fact of their asymmetrical power.

At the bottom of the heap are those enclaves that have been inferiorized by the mainstream by being designated as "little continents," such as Little Africa in New York City. This designation came about during the colonial era at the peak of Anglo American discrimination against both slaves and free people of color as a way to further denigrate the inhabitants of these enclaves. This practice of belittling a place was widespread in England and goes back to the era preceding the colonization period. The *Oxford English Dictionary* (2nd edition, 1989) informs us that in the social practice of that era, "Little is applied to such people as are not overstock'd with acuteness...not distinguished, inferior in rank and position." Thus, in the logic of this period, Little Africa was inhabited by inferior people. Following the same rationale, the Italian quarters in both New York and San Francisco in the nineteenth century became known as Little Italy.

In the twentieth century, ethnic enclaves continue to be designated as "little states" as in Little Michoacan; "little countries" as in Little Haiti and Little Brazil; "little capital cities" as in Little Tokyo, Little Havana, Little Taipei, Little Tehran, and Little Saigon; and "little secondary cities" as in Little Osaka and Little Bombay.[7]

In contrast, when ethnic populations name their own neighborhoods they, like mainstream populations, refer to them as "new" settlements. For example, the Chinese who live in the Richmond District of San Francisco refer to their enclave not as "Little Chinatown" because it is smaller than the old Chinatown, but rather as

"New Chinatown." In this way, they avoid the pitfall of giving the enclave a double minority status.

In general, cultural enclaves are always identified as such, and they reflect four main variables: the residents' place of origin (continent, country, state, city), their ethnic background, their status in society, and the location of their residences. The enclave names serve to identify the residents as "others" and to indicate that they are confined to a specific spatial position in the urban landscape. Customarily, space serves as a marker to locate the place of non-hegemonic groups, to identify their status in society, to delimit their sphere of interaction, and to patrol, control, and contain them in their enclaves. In the case of enclaves, space serves primarily as a mechanism of social control.

Among immigrants of the same ethnic background, a subhierarchical order prevails inside the network of enclaves. The principal enclave plays the role of capital city, while others serve as secondary towns. Manilatown in San Francisco, for example, was seen by the Filipinos as more important than Little Manila in Stockton; Little Tokyo in Los Angeles is projected as a suburb of Japantown in San Francisco, while San Francisco's Chinatown is seen as the mother of all Chinatowns in the United States. (The renaming of the former capital city in the old country does not necessarily lead to a change in the name of the diasporic town overseas. For example, Little Saigon in Westminster remains so known despite the fact that Saigon was renamed Ho Chi Minh City in 1975 and made the second most important city of communist Vietnam.)

The fact that a new community might have been named by the crown, or by a federal, state, or city government, does not change the logic behind the "new city" versus "little town" construction. The "new city" appellation elevates the status of the Anglo community, while the "little town" name downgrades the neighborhood of the ethnic minority. Furthermore, there is a logic in identifying European immigrants with the larger space and the hills, and the ethnic immigrants with flat-land enclaves. Since the minor-ity is constructed as a minor, as the name implies, its members must be placed in *little* enclaves at a *low* altitude (flat land). In other words, little people must live in little places. What is the logic of the mainstream in this apparatus? The minority enclave is supposed to be a transitional community that serves the interests of the mainstream. When it ceases to fulfill this function, it will disappear; that is, it will be pushed to another marginal corner of the city or the country (or its residents may even assimilate and lose their ethnic identity). The contrast is between the *minor* (as in minor-ity), who is compelled to live in a *little place*, at a *lower altitude*, in a *transitional* enclave with a *lower* quality of life, and the *major* (as in major-ity), who has access to a *larger* space, lives at a *higher* altitude (hills), and enjoys a *better* quality of life in a *permanent* city.[8]

Minoritized ethnic enclaves go through five phases of development in order to reach permanent fixture in the city.[9] Each phase has its own importance in terms of either strengthening or undermining the ability of the enclave to remain a viable site of settlement. It will be useful to briefly delineate here the model of their development.

The first phase, or *phase of insertion*, begins as newcomers slowly invade a site. If it happens to be a vacant site – as was the case of San Francisco's Chinatown – the residents establish their enclave and enlarge it both through biological reproduction and new immigration. If the area is inhabited, this often leads to demographic shifts as the newcomers arrive and the old-timers leave for another area, as was the case in Little Italy. It takes many years before the newcomers constitute the majority of the population in the area and change the face of the neighborhood, transforming it into their ethnic enclave.

The second phase, or *confrontation phase*, is marked by attempts by city hall, with the support of mainstream population, to dismantle the settlement. City Hall develops diverse mechanisms ranging from harassment to quarantinization to achieve this goal. And it gives diverse reasons for doing so, raising the specters of filth caused by poverty, health hazards, increased criminal activities, or whatever other factors the majority can imagine. Some enclaves lose their battles at this phase and therefore are unable to develop further and take root in the city. But short of bulldozing an enclave, which is infeasible since the city government is likely unable to relocate the people elsewhere, the city often decides to do nothing, which gives the people more time to organize their neighborhood. In this regard, the history of Manilatown, which was dismantled, differs from Japantown and Chinatown, both of which successfully completed this second phase.

The third phase, or *incorporation phase*, occurs when city hall, unwilling or unable to dismantle a settlement, decides to integrate it with the rest of the city. Some social services are then provided by the city government, licenses to build are issued, and the settlement begins to appear in both official documents and on tourist maps of the city. Incorporation, however, does not necessarily ensure recognition of enclave residents' rights, but rather makes more visible a city's racist policy of benign neglect as the city continues to provide only the bare minimum of services to the settlement. Incorporation also takes its toll on the local population in the form of tax collection and more vigorous monitoring by the police.

The fourth phase, or *maturity phase*, corresponds to the period when the neighborhood organizes its grassroots political system to interact with the formal political system of governance of the city, when residents make demands on city hall for more services, and when the enclave's business elite formalizes and institutionalizes mechanisms enabling their easy access to the movers and shakers of city hall. During this phase, social services in the neighborhood are staffed by locals, enclave residents are appointed to government agencies, and community leaders serve as advisors to the mayor's office, where they can promote community views of city policies that affect them. In this phase, the neighborhood has more power to organize itself and is a political force that can influence the outcome of city elections. Manilatown did not reach this phase, while Chinatown and Japantown have experienced different degrees of success.

The fifth phase corresponds to the *theme-parkization* of the enclave. During this phase, the neighborhood is transformed into a commoditized site for tourists' consumption. Because the city sees the enclave as equivalent to a "theme park," it routinely uses the enclave's exoticism in global publicity to attract tourists and investors, develops ordinances to reproduce its spatial peculiarity over time, and, in the process, racializes it for the benefit of city hall's coffers.

Ethnic enclaves are, in fact, always born as contested sites, contested by both the Anglo community, which does not want the ethnics to permanently occupy an area of the city, and by the enclave's residents, who do not want to be incarcerated in segregated settlements. As contested sites, they are not meant to be permanent enclaves, because their residents are constructed by the Anglos as unwelcome guests and undesirable neighbors. For their part, the residents fight for the right to live wherever they want in the city, sometimes for the sake of having free choice in selection of their place of residence, and other times for the sake of being able to send their children to Anglo-dominated schools.

Once an enclave is established, it may still remain a contested site. Anglos have, throughout the years, devised various mechanisms to get rid of enclaves, while residents have fought back. The history of the relations between both sectors has been one of boundary maintenance, transgression, contraction, and expansion. Because their boundaries are constantly challenged through embodied practices of transgression, these contested sites are routinely policed by the local Anglo residents.

Introduction: "Little Americas" 11

I have been told countless stories about Chinese Americans from San Francisco's Chinatown who were beaten by Anglos because they crossed Broadway, the line separating the two communities, and ventured into the adjacent white neighborhood.

These contested sites provide a ground for protest against one's plight in the enclave, against those responsible for this state of affairs, and against one's confinement to a specific place. But, paradoxically, since the era of the Civil Rights movements the enclave has also become the symbol of residents' acceptance of their place of confinement as a liberated turf. Instead of moving out to other quarters, some have stayed to fight for improvement of the locale. It was precisely because ethnics have been in a more or less secure environment in their enclaves that they have been able to develop strategies of resistance that prevented them from being completely assimilated into the mainstream and from totally losing their ethnic identities. Thus, enclaves are also sites where people protest city policies and the racist practices of the larger Anglo community, and make requests for city services. Moreover, they provide a niche not only for local dissent, but also for protest against policies of the homeland. They serve, too, as havens for opposition politicos and activist dissenters from the homeland, who find there a ready-made group of sympathizers who share their vision and who are able to help finance their activities.

Throughout this book I refer to the immigrant and ethnic enclave as the *ethnopolis*, a concept that stresses both the ethnic concentration and polarization of the area and its characterization as a subaltern city. The ethnopolis is here defined as an *enclave city* dominated by the hegemonic presence of one ethnic group and whose existence is tied to that of a *container city* with which it maintains multiple relations that have influenced its trajectory in many different ways. This definition not only refers to enclosure and physical boundaries, but implies the implosion of the ethnic enclave as a center to which satellite clusters of the population may be connected, and highlights a clear distinction between those ethnics who reside in the area and those who use it as a site to conduct business transactions.

The economic infrastructure of the ethnopolis is influenced by the residents, who comprise a major sector of its commercial clientele; non-residents who own and manage businesses there; those who live elsewhere but are regular clients of the enclave; tourists who buy their gifts on-site; and international business operators who invest their money there through partnerships with local firms and through establishment of their own subsidiaries. Governance of the ethnopolis is, therefore, sustained by the four sectors of the *diasporic economy* – namely, the *enclave economy*, characterized by those who own businesses in the enclave; the *ethnic economy*, which includes those who have businesses outside the enclave; the *transethnic* or *transurban* economy, which results from the interface with the *mainstream economy*, and the *transnational economy* which comprises those transactions with an overseas headquarters or subsidiary in another country and services provided by, for example, real estate agents, international trade lawyers, and the banking industry to overseas clients.

The architecture of ethnopolitan politics is made up of a formal and informal level. The formal level is enacted by elected and appointed officials who represent the enclave either as members of the group or as political operatives. They serve as a bridgehead formally linking the people to the city government and vice versa. For example, enclave officials communicate the problems of the enclave to city government officials and inform the enclave about city policies. Each of the ethnopoles under study has (or had) its own "informal mayor," known as such by the residents, to whom outsiders are often referred. At the informal level, grassroots leaders fight on behalf of the enclave for services and help establish and maintain informal connections to the mayor's office. Likewise, members of the enclave's business elite have informal connections with the mayor's office, lobbying for and advising on different ways to improve the market environment for the success of their business ventures.

In order for an ethnic enclave to achieve the status of *global ethnopolis*, it must fulfill a minimum condition: its resident population must maintain ongoing relations with the homeland and with other diasporic enclaves. By definition, the *diasporic ethnopolis* has a binational or transnational orientation. It becomes *global* when these relations encompass more than two nation-states and affect and shape in a significant way social conditions in the enclave.

The global ethnopolis maintains ongoing political and economic relations with the homeland, and, as an ethnic enclave, it may develop informal foreign policies that contradict formal external policies of the federal, state, or city government. Because of its international orientation, it provides a market for homeland goods, publishes newspapers for consumption by the homeland as well as distributing newspapers from the homeland, provides a base for dissident politicians from the homeland, and serves as a spying ground for the homeland government. Moreover, its global reach goes beyond the homeland and penetrates diasporic communities in other countries. This transnational and global dimension implies that the ethnopolis articulates itself not only with the container city but also with the cyclical structural adjustment of the homeland. In other words, its trajectory cannot be explained only in terms of its local relations with the city, but must also take into consideration extraterritorial relations, especially with the homeland.

It is important to note that not all ethnopoles are offshoot communities of an independent nation-state. For example, Manilatown developed in San Francisco before the Philippines became an independent nation-state; for the early immigrants Manila epitomized the homeland. Likewise when the first Little Italies appeared in the nineteenth century, Italy had yet to consolidate itself into the nation-state that it is today. Sometimes an ethnopole outlives the reality it is supposed to reflect, as in the case of Little Saigon in Westminster, an extension of capitalist Saigon, now Ho Chi Minh City. The transformation of the former Vietnamese capital city into a communist city has strained its relations with its capitalist offshoot.

It is also important to stress the genealogy of the meanings of these ethnopoles to show how they have evolved over time. Until the era of the Civil Rights movement, the names had negative meanings for both the mainstream Anglos and the minoritized ethnic residents because they provided a spatial basis for racial discrimination, reflected the common pattern of housing segregation, and symbolized the inferior status of the ethnics. It seemed as if stigmatization by *race* was not enough, that stigmatization by *location* as well was necessary to reinforce discrimination.[10] The negative meanings assigned to these labels did, however, lose strength over the years.

That these names have survived is partly a result of a "ghost factor" which has remained long after the purpose for which the enclaves were created. Though originally created as "guest communities," enclaves have since become "host communities." After the Civil Rights Act dismantled the architecture of housing segregation, enclave labels remained, though with somewhat different meanings. Ethnic residents now tend to view the name of their enclave as a term of "endearment" that identifies a piece of land that the group "owns" inside US territory. In this spirit, Mexican Americans now refer to their barrio in west central San José, California, as "Little Michoacan," and Japanese Americans and Chinese Americans would fight to their last breath to prevent any agency from changing the name of Japantown or Chinatown into something else.

This sort of attachment to an enclave name was obvious in an incident that occurred in 1984 in Miami's Little Havana. After some Cuban businessmen renamed, with the city's approval, a section of Little Havana calling it the Latin Quarter, working-class Cubans who lived in the enclave became very unhappy about this turn of events. The businessmen's motives had been purely commercial: they thought that the new name would reflect the diversity of the area as other Latin American immigrants were moving in, and that it would attract members of the larger Latino community to shop in the neighborhood. However, Cuban residents saw it differently and began to organize. In a highly emotional meeting with the city leadership in 1990, they demanded that "the name Latin Quarter be rescinded. To them, the name is part of a ploy ... to further deCubanize their Little Havana." As one protester put it "We deserve the name. It's ours."[11]

In the past three decades, ethnic enclaves have been projected as business centers that give commercial life to the neighborhood and as heritage places that serve as storage space for the immigrants' memories of their homelands.[12] The genealogy of these enclaves informs us about the trajectories of the enclaves, and it tells us how oppressed people have used the space of place as an instrument of their liberation struggle – how they have appropriated a negative label, turned it on its head, and used it for their own benefit.[13]

In recent years, ethnic entrepreneurs have made use of what they consider to be the positive aspect of living in a named enclave. Although they recognize that a sobriquet confers inferior status to the enclave, they nevertheless use its exoticism to turn the enclave into a viable business sector, or to maintain it as one. In one instance, Asian Indian residents in a Los Angeles suburban neighborhood consciously attempted to colonize the landscape by designating it as an enclave in order to give more visibility to their group and neutralize the presence of other people in the neighborhood. Their stated purpose was to commoditize the enclave as a commercial center. According to the *Los Angeles Times*, "When members of the Asian Indian community approached California officials [in 1991] about placing a 'Little India' sign on a freeway in Artesia, city officials objected to the idea."[14] The city wanted to prevent incoming Indian immigrants from upstaging the Anglo-American majority in particular and marginalizing longtime residents in general.

This suggests that the ethnopolis is read differently by different groups of people. For the residents, it is home: where they and their friends live and work and where the agencies that provide services to the community are located. It is also the site that reminds them daily of their homeland's social atmosphere. For first-generation immigrants, it is their new home in a foreign land or a home away from home. For the second and third generations, it is the place where they grew up, the site that holds their parents' memories about the homeland, and their space of symbolic attachment. For members of the ethnic group living outside the enclave, it is their capital city: it is the place they do their marketing for homeland products, where they visit on holidays, eat native foods, meet friends, and keep in touch with homeland traditions. For the mainstream, it is a place to buy cheap, exotic goods and bring visiting family and friends. For the mayor's office, it is an enclave with its singular set of problems as well as a site with potential voters. Finally, for tourists, it is a site of attraction, of spectacle, a living museum, and a marketplace to purchase exotic gifts.

The ethnopolis maintains a high level of subhegemonic visibility because of the concentrated ethnic population there. The community becomes visible through the site it occupies. This visibility becomes tangible because the enclave is used at times by the ethnics to stage protests against the homeland or by the local government to reach the ethnic population at large. It is the site that gives credence to the demographic importance of the ethnic community. In other words, to the uncritical mind of non-members, the ethnic population is grossly identified with the enclave.

In an effort to reproblematize, reframe, and critically explain the global dimension of these ethnopoles, I present in Chapter 1 the view that the globalization process always has a local point of reference through which it is anchored in the spatiality of everyday life and that sustains its transnational manifestation. I argue that such a process results from the implosion of the local in the global, and the global in the local, and is central in the social production of globalized locality and localized globality. In doing so, I develop a theory of globality that gives a prominent place to human agency as the embodied site of the performativity of transnational actors.

Chapter 2 analyzes the content and contours of the informal capital city concept within the context of global racism and applies it to Chinatown to show the central and symbolic importance of this ethnopole *vis-à-vis* satellite Chinese clusters in Northern California. The chapter also examines the implosion of three global events – President Nixon's visit to China in 1972, the fall of Saigon in 1975, and the return of Hong Kong to China in 1997 – and their effect on Chinatown. Furthermore, it discusses how the global selling of Chinatown to potential overseas tourists has contributed to the reproduction of the ethnopole as a racialized site.

16   *The Global Ethnopolis*

The globalized history of Japantown is addressed in Chapter 3, which explains the importance of San Francisco's three Japanese clusters after the 1906 earthquake and the ensuing leading role played by the Western Addition site. The chapter examines the local transformation and transitional evacuation of the ethnopole as a result of US–Japanese hostilities during World War II and shows how this global event was a turning point in the history of Japantown. It further explains how important it is to factor in the global dimension in the interpretation of the local reality.

Chapter 4 presents the local and global variables that led to the collapse of Manilatown as an ethnopole. Under what conditions or combined circumstances does an ethnopole cease to exist? This chapter delineates the peculiar context within which this ethnopole interacted with the local city government and the strained relations between the local residents and their homeland's national government. It demonstrates that the demise of the ethnopole was the combined result of global and local factors.

Using Japantown as a test case, in Chapter 5, I present a full argument on the ethnopole as a global city. This chapter shows how transnational actors and institutions participate in this global process, how the relations between the enclave and the mainland and other diasporic sites contribute to it, and how the ethnopole cannot be understood fully outside the framework of the global context that continually feeds both its existence and reproduction. It further delineates the various forms of globality that the ethnopole is engaged in, the mechanisms and circuits through which they are actualized, and the temporalities and spatialities of their performances.

Chapter 6 examines the global space that traverses, intersects, and reproduces the ethnopole. To do so, it analyzes the global commercial space of the ethnic "yellow pages," which provides an exemplary site for the deconstruction of this form of spatiality. These yellow pages advertise not only for local entrepreneurs but also for businesses in the homeland and other diasporic sites. The chapter demonstrates that globality has diverse spatial parameters that can be mapped out, and that the global space of the ethnopole is but one aspect of its expression. It concludes with my observation that the social production of global space sustains the ethnopole as a global city.

Chapter 7 theorizes the globality of the ethnopole within the context of the global city it is enclosed in. It argues that the ethnopole is global not only because of its transnational relations with extraterritorial sites but also because of the globalizing process of the container city it finds itself in tandem with. It argues that these two modes of globality influence and feed each other to the extent that an analyst cannot understand the complexity of one mode, except in relation to the other. It concludes that the local site of the ethnopole is an important node of global space through which the globality of the larger city is expressed.

1
The Global Ethnopolis

The city of San Francisco, with its culturally distinct neighborhoods, presents us with a telling and multifaceted laboratory where we can study the logic of how the ethnic space of difference is inserted into the vast and expanding network of the globalizing world.[15] Until recently, social scientists have studied the American city as a flat, multicultural, and stratified entity, conceiving of it for the most part as a bound locale while informally recognizing its linkage to national sites and overseas territories, especially in the case of diasporas, which maintain ongoing relations with their homelands. As a result of this narrow way of deconstructing the city, the focus of most researchers has been primarily on social interaction at the local level, whether in terms of municipal regimes, social classes, economic transactions, or ethnic niches.

In the recent past, a good deal of effort has been expended to reposition the city as a global unit of analysis. However, the various studies of globalization of the American city available are *macroperspectival*, approaching the topic through specific angles. Because of this bias or choice, the logic of a particular angle is stressed, at the expense of others.[16] But the role of the ethnic enclaves in the globalization of the city – not solely as a consequence of macroglobalization but also as an active engine of microglobalization that implodes into the macrostructure of globalization – is yet to be analyzed. Hence, I hope this study will reverse this common trend in globalization studies and in the process fill that specific void in the sociological literature.[17] In part the globalization of the city results from the fact that in the same urban environment there are various global niches that follow the logic of their global connections and local diasporic makeup. Thus, I argue that the city is global because it comprises a multiplicity of global niches in its midst that interface with and sustain each other at the local level.

A global city is any urban environment housing a multiplicity and diversity of transnational niches. This definition contrasts with the top-down approach that both privileges the centrality of business, finances, and services over human agency and de-emphasizes the role of the local community in the global process. My bottom-up approach – although it recognizes the importance and dominance of these global financial and managerial institutions – privileges human agency in these crisscrossing transnational connections. The globalization process is understood here as being fed by and produced in different niches – dominant and subjugated realms of societal practices. Further, the global process traverses the totality of society and is not simply a matter of locating and studying globalization at the top and its impact on the bottom, or vice versa. The latter formulation is not sufficient to explain the complexity of *localized globality* and *globalized locality*.[18]

In this book I will not study the phenomenon of globalization in its multifaceted aspects, nor use the dominant paradigm of the global city with its emphasis on the connecting sites of global capital, nor use a macrocomparative approach with a focus on urban sites in different countries. Rather, my approach will be *microcomparative,* with a focus on three ethnopoles in the same American city. Since I will explain globalization from an analysis of ethnic enclaves, my approach is perspectival as well. I believe that this microlevel perspective, or *microperspectival* approach, is a necessary complement to the macrolevel because both are perspectival and address different issues that are nevertheless central to understanding the multiplex content and complexity of the local and global behaviors of these ethnopoles.

Ethnopoles

The city of San Francisco, which provides the context for this study, is punctuated by a number of global poles – a concentration of local activities that are globally produced – that form the tapestry of its human infrastructure or population composition. These poles tend to have a life of their own that depends on their identities, global connections, and local articulation. Indeed, San Francisco as a *metropole* is made up of localized global poles that are visible because they are physically located there. However, they are in fact networking or transnational poles whose existence is made possible by the dispersed presence of scattered institutions and diasporic sites. The ethnic enclave – the site of a diaspora – is one example of such a global pole, and there are several such niches in the city. While the *ethnopole* is the home of a predominant diasporic group, or is at least imagined as such by the larger urban population, as in the case of Japantown, the *panethnopole* refers to a site inhabited by groups with different ethnic origins, as in the case of the Mission District. Here one finds not only Mexican-Americans but also people from El Salvador, Nicaragua, Cuba, Puerto Rico, Chile, and Peru. While the downtown area of San Francisco provides us with examples of a *technopole* (milieu of innovation) and *exopole* (edge city or milieu of services), the Castro District is a typical example of a *homopole* characterized by the sexual orientation of its population and the global network they are engaged in. While the previously mentioned poles are concentrated in specific places, the *ngopole* (non-governmental organization pole) in contrast is a cluster of sites scattered throughout the city and is active in connecting the city to overseas grassroots organizations. As *globalized local poles*, these enclaves connect the city to the rest of the world by a vast network of crisscrossing and border-crossing practices. By describing the city in terms of global poles, I emphasize the multiplicity of these transnational connections that find their point of departure, destination, and intersection in this urban environment.

These poles are not mutually exclusive, and an individual may belong to more than one – as in, for example, the case of a microchip expert who works in an exopole and lives in an ethnopole, or an activist who lives in a panethnopole and works fulltime in an ngopole. However, ethnopoles have their own corporate identities defined by the nature, multiplicity, diversity, and complexity of their global connections. Although I recognize the existence of other polar niches in the city, the object of this study is the inscription of the ethnopole in the global process.

I conceive of ethnopoles as *sites of attraction* and *sites of dispersion*. They attract newcomer residents from the homeland and encourage old-timers who live in satellite sites to return to the area for church activities, seasonal festivals, social services, and shopping. They are also sites from which people move to other residential sites in the city or the larger Bay Area. As interconnecting sites, ethnopoles are nodes in a network of sites linking the ethnopole to the homeland of its residents and to other diasporic sites as well. As hybrid sites, they serve as incubators for the diversity of ethnic traditions and intra-ethnic interaction. These are dynamic sites in which the articulation of the global with the local is materialized and can be studied because it can be identified, mapped out, and circumscribed.

The location of an ethnopole inside a global city evokes the idea that its globality cannot be understood outside the context of these intraurban relations. The ethnopole is interpreted as being global because of its transnational relations, because of its contribution to making the city in which it is located a global city, and because of its location inside a global city that sets constraints and limits to the expression of its globality. In other words, its global status is affected by its centrality as well as the centrality of the city within which it is located.

The ethnopole is global because it is reproduced as such by the relations it maintains with a container global city. Its global identity is forged and shaped by that relationship. As long as this relationship exists, the ethnopole cannot maintain an isolated existence completely outside this structure. In this relational scheme, the globality of the ethnopole contributes to the globality of the city as well.

The ethnopole is global when the community becomes involved in transnational border-crossing activities that link it to the homeland and to other extraterritorial diasporic sites as well. In this context, one may argue that temporality is a factor of globality because the intensity of the global connections is not uniform. It has its ups and downs. For example, Japantown exhibits a high level of globality during the Cherry Blossom festivals, with a sizable volume of transnational communications and the meshing of the homeland and diasporic population in attendance (Japanese from Japan, and diasporic Japanese from Peru, Brazil, Canada, and San Francisco's Japantown). The festival projects and actualizes the global aspect of the event. That high peak of globality came about because Japanese officials (the mayor of Osaka and members of the Osaka City Council), businesspeople from Tokyo, and groups of performers from Osaka participate in the festivities. Japanese businesses support and participate in it by financing floats, sending representatives from their headquarters in Japan or from subsidiaries in the United States and Canada, sponsoring events, underwriting expenses, or donating specific items such as kimonos.

The ethnopole is global because the business sector engages in transnational relations (corporate or family enterprises, import/export, subsidiary/headquarters, production/sale, marketing) and provides transnational services. An example of this is the real estate agent who helps overseas clients acquire property in the Bay Area, or the international trade lawyer who consults with and facilitates matters for foreign investors. In this case, one may speak of *sectoral globality* to indicate that a specific sector spearheads the transnational relations.

Finally, the ethnopole is global because of the movement of people, goods, capital, and communications between the diasporic and overseas sites – that is, between Japantown and Japan and between Japantown and other diasporic sites outside Japan.

As a gentrified locale, the ethnopole is global because of the diversity of its ethnic population and their transnational relations with their respective homelands. For example, inside Chinatown there are Vietnamese Americans involved in transnational relations with Ho Chi Minh City and Korean merchants who maintain ongoing relations with folks in South Korea. The multicultural globality of the ethnopole is a reflection of the multiculturality of the global city.

The ethnopole is globally linked when its globality is made possible by its connections to a third party that is itself involved in global transactions. A forward linkage occurs when the link to a satellite cluster or other institutions is made by the ethnopole in its relations with the homeland or other overseas entities. A backward linkage occurs when the link is initiated by a satellite site rather than an ethnopole, as in the case of Japanese businesspeople from Silicon Valley who use the services of banks in Japantown or who arrange for their overseas visitors to spend time in Japantown.

The dominance of the ethnopole as the central, physical, cultural, and symbolic location of the ethnic population is highlighted here. This dominance is constructed by the ethnics, as well as others, because it is the place where the community becomes more visible. Furthermore, that dominance is reproduced by the way that both sides project the community. The community serves as a central positioning site that satellite clusters may depend on to function as a symbolic capital city. It is one of several locations where transnational spatial flows are anchored in the nation-state because of the concentration of multisectoral activities it harbors.

The ethnopole grafts onto the hegemonic geography of city systems its own intrusive geography of sites that are assembled and connected to each other according to the logic of its structural location, a logic elaborated because of its external connections that work at different scales: a city scale at which it provides resources to residents of the enclave, a metropolitan scale at which it makes possible its interaction with ethnic others, a regional scale at which it transforms itself into an informal capital city, and a transnational or global scale at which the locality becomes globalized.

This geography creates a hierarchy of sites based on their connections to the center, the density of their transnational relations, and their economic importance or visibility. Independent sites may be connected or reattached to the center, creating a new dynamic in the interactive network of sites. Peripheral clusters and satellite sites are created that enhance the informal capital city status of the ethnopole. Because the satellite sites function like suburbs, these residential communities are fed by the flight of the middle class from the ethnopole.

This is a submerged or informal geography not easily detected by the mainstream, not because it is invisible or underground, but simply because it is constructed on a scale different from that of the formal or official city. It is a geography that identifies, magnifies, and privileges ethnic clusters as sites of connectivity in the ethnicized informal urban system. However, I do not want to insinuate that the ethnopolitan system parallels the formal urban system, because they interpenetrate at various levels and are intertwined in some fashion.

Thus, one may speak of a global ethnopolitan system made of diverse overseas sites, of which the global ethnopole is a node or a central node. Its importance as a global node is not simply a matter of population scale or geographical size, but rather a result of its centrality in a network of poles. The ethnopole, by the nature of its global connectivity, is located in a circuit, and its importance is highlighted by its relations with other poles in the network. The relations are denser with some poles than with others, because the ethnopole serves as a central pole *vis-à-vis* satellite clusters in the network.

The globality of the ethnopole expresses itself in different ways through individual, group, sector, and community global connections. These crisscrossed relations have different values, are denser in some cases and in certain periods of the year, and are not linked at the same level to the same country: some are sustained and permanent while others are transitional. I propose that both the global and the local are part of a continuum, and, like Game, I lean toward "an understanding of these relations in terms of 'interpenetration' rather than distinction and opposition."[19] As a continuum, they feed each other's existence.

The implosion of the global in the local

The global does not totally erase the local to the extent that we now live in a homogenized world, nor is the global separated from the local. Despite the implosion of the global in the local, and despite being nodes in a network of connectivity, localities continue to maintain their specificity and their unique character. In this light, one may advance the idea that globalization does not homogenize the global landscape but instead tends to provoke local reactions as a result of different local histories, population makeup, and political orientation. As Harvey puts it, "The collapse of spatial barriers does not mean that the significance of place is decreasing."[20] In this respect, Featherstone and Lash speak of "a global creation of locality,"[21] while Robertson proposes that "what is local is to a large degree constructed on a trans- or super-local basis" and sees the local "as an aspect of globalization."[22]

The ethnopole is a hybrid social formation and results from transnational migration and the incorporation of diasporic people in this site. This hybrid site is not the product of wholly local interaction, but the interpenetration of the global in the local. As Pieterse notes, "Global cities...and ethnic melange neighborhoods within them (such as Jackson Heights in Queens, New York) are other hybrid spaces in the global landscape."[23] A hybrid space is precisely the site where the global meets the local, or where the global shows its localized face, or simply where the global becomes visible and situated in space. By "hybrid space," I mean the site in a national landscape where the logic of the dominant sector interacts with diasporic logics that connect the landscape to other extraterritorial spaces. In other words, the hybrid space has both global and local content, two features that are essential in the making of the ethnopole.

The global implosion is again expressed in the local as the site of hybrid times. The enclave is the principal location for the public display of hybrid times. It is here that hegemonic and subaltern times meet, but the enclave is also the locale where the subaltern imposes itself by pushing over hegemonic time, so that the actual time of the enclave can be recuperated. There is an undercurrent of subaltern times in the enclave that punctuates the cultural events of the ethnopole: New Year's Day celebrations, street fairs, and festivals that link the community to the homeland. When that hybrid time manifests its globality over its locality, time within the ethnopole becomes similar to that of the homeland and dissimilar to that of the mainstream. For example, the Chinese New Year does not coincide with the mainstream American New Year. During the celebration of the Chinese New Year, Chinese Americans are at par with mainland China cultural time and are in temporal disharmony with mainstream American time. Hence, the politics of times is an important factor in the reproduction of the ethnopole.

The implosion of the local in the global

The local intervenes in various ways in the global scene as the initiating pole in transnational relations, as the receiving end of a continuum, or as a connecting or intersecting site in a crisscrossing and border-crossing network. Ethnopoles bypass state boundaries while they engage in overseas activities. For example, ethnopolitans' local initiatives with a global content take various forms, from remittances sent to parents in the homeland, to development projects sponsored by the ethnopoles, and from participating in homeland politics and maintaining relations with relatives abroad, to the development of a grassroots foreign policy agenda. Some of these relations are individual; others are household or group initiatives.

Foreign policies developed by the ethnopoles are geared toward helping the homeland, or a faction of it, and are a way of keeping relations to it alive. Depending on circumstances, a policy may counter the foreign policy of the federal government but align itself with municipal foreign policy, as was the case when Latino activists in San Francisco supported the Sandinista government during the Reagan administration;[24] or a policy may counter municipal foreign policy in accord with federal foreign policy, as in the case of the San Francisco school policy involving Japanese students during the first decade of the 20th century. Fearing a possible Japanese invasion of the United States, the federal government sided with the Japanese parents against segregation of the school system, thereby allowing Japanese students to attend white schools.[25]

Place as a location does not contain the spatial parameters of the cultural activities it generates, nor does it avoid being influenced by external cultural production. The locality is daily produced by the globality of which it is a part. As Albrow notes, "People can reside in one place and have their meaningful social relations almost entirely outside it and across the globe."[26] In this light, the ethnopole is viewed as "the localization of globality"[27] and is the incubator where "transition from identity as an island to identity as a crossroads"[28] is experienced daily by the ethnopolitans. The ethnopole is a localized global space – with its peculiar characteristics produced by border-crossing experiences and practices – that changes the nature of both societies (that is, the United States and the homeland), since it has contributed to the exploding of their artificially sealed boundaries.

The ethnopole is part of an urban system that is both national and transnational, and, in turn the order of both these national and transnational sites is influenced by their connectivity in the network. In this light, one may agree with Keeling that ethnopoles "develop hierarchical relationships that rise and fall over time according to their control and mediary functions in the system."[29] In this networked landscape, Keeling says, "interaction between and among all components is fluid, dynamic, and occurs on multiple scales."[30]

The dualism of the global–local binary when the components are seen as distinct, complementary, or in opposition to each other is inherent in the premises that present them as two different realities. Once the concepts are thus positioned, then one speaks of the impact of one on the other, the resistance of one *vis-à-vis* the other, and the invasion of one by the other. In this flawed frame of reference, they are seen as separated poles and not as circuits or processes, and thus one confuses physical sites with processes. The global–local continuum presented above precludes us from falling into this conventional trap.

Furthermore, these enclaves are not simply transnational communities, but global ethnopoles. They must be seen within the logic of globalization and not simply that of transnationality. The early emphasis on transnationality is misplaced because it looks at the process and not the outcome. Transnationality is the means by which, or the conduit through which, the global ethnopole is produced. The focus here is on the various processes of border-crossing practices, connections, and flows in order to examine the globalized locality and the localized globality. Any theory of transnationality presupposes a theory of globalization. In other words, transnationality is the process by which globality is effected.

Differences between ethnopoles can be better explained in terms of global connections and not simply in terms of local strategies developed by residents in response to, or their local reactions to, Anglo resentment. The strength of their global connections affects these ethnopoles differently. For example, the friendly or inimical relations that the United States maintains with the homeland directly or indirectly affects the ethnopole. For example, the Chinese were at first persecuted by US residents, which led to the Chinese Exclusion Act. As a result, the US government brought in Japanese workers as a labor replacement force; yet once Americans began to consider the Japanese as enemies during World War II, they rediscovered the Chinese as friends. This helped Chinese Americans to strengthen their Chinatowns, while the Japanese lost ground in Japantown.

This new approach of studying ethnic enclaves within the framework of globalization theory forces us to connect local activities and processes to a much larger universe. However, the view that diasporic communities maintain transnational relations with their homelands is not new, though only recently have social scientists begun to unravel their various layers of interconnectedness.[31] What is needed at this juncture of theorizing is not simply a description of the enclave–homeland relationship, but also an analysis and comparison of the transnational modalities of incorporation, operation, and reproduction of these ethnopoles, and the global city status that is the hallmark of the ethnopole's identity.

2
Chinatown: The Ethnopole as an Informal Capital City

The development of Japantown and Manilatown in San Francisco was in one form or another influenced by the existence of Chinatown, the first Asian-American ethnopole in the city. Anglo-Californians developed their prejudices against Asian Americans based on the early model of their interaction with nineteenth-century Chinese immigrants.[32] Various debilitating forms of racism – the manipulation of the legal system to create and maintain a space of difference, racial discrimination, housing segregation, covenant clauses to prevent integration, and spatial ghettoization – that the constructed mainstream system used to marginalize the Chinese newcomers were time and again applied to subalternize both Filipino Americans and Japanese Americans. The fates of these three minoritized groups seemed tied to one another as each followed a different path of development and each exhibited variations in the ways in which it dealt with the mainstream. Since its birth as an ethnopole, however, Chinatown has emerged as the preeminent *informal capital city* for the larger Chinese population in Northern California in particular and a symbolic capital city for Chinese Americans in general.

I conceptualize Chinatown as an informal capital city to suggest its subalternization *vis-à-vis* the city it is enclosed in, its minoritization by the mainstream, its racialization by way of its forced marginal spatialization, and its global status in a network of transnational sites. "Informality" here means that the enclave is seen as a pole of a continuum precisely because it is part of a subjugated network of sites that intersects and crisscrosses the formal network of sites, but does not coincide with it. Informality is symbolic of the racial displacement and reinsertion of the ethnopole in a different spatial order. It shows how racism – in its local, transnational, and global forms – disorders the natural order of things and respatializes it by way of renaturalizing it in a new constructed order. Chinatown is a capital city in a peculiar way, not because every Chinese American considers it as a capital, but because city hall and local entrepreneurs project it as such. However, this social construction of Chinatown as an informal city is not simply or solely a project of outsiders; it has also an internal basis of support. After all, it is the first and best-known Chinese site in the United States, the center of an array of formal and informal social institutions, a world-renowned business district, the headquarters of transnational family associations, the place of residence of a significant number of Chinese Americans – both old-timers and newcomers – and a meeting-place for Chinese Americans in the greater San Francisco Bay Area. It is recognized by every measure imaginable to be the densest Chinese enclave in the United States.[33] I use the informal capital-city concept to refer to its unequal cultural, economic, and political importance for the Chinese population in relation to other sites in Northern California, and to refer to its role as the principal symbol commoditized and used by city administrators, local businesspeople, and Chinese entrepreneurs to entice non-residential shoppers and national and foreign tourists to the ethnopole.[34]

It is a truism to argue that global racism is *global* to the extent that it is locally contextualized, situated, historicized, and experienced. Contemporary San Francisco's Chinatown presents an ideal site to study the *translocalization* of global racism. Three questions are addressed here: (1) how the globalization process has been an important factor in the reproduction of Chinatown as an informal capital city; (2) how the selling of Chinatown on a global scale as a tourist site has reinforced its status as a *racialized ethnopole;* and (3) how global events – President Nixon's 1972 visit to China, the 1975 fall of Saigon, and the 1997 annexation or return of Hong Kong to China – have further transformed it into a *symbolic site* of US global racist practices.

Since this introduces a new concept, it is appropriate to define and conceptualize it so as to identify and explain the parameters within which its meanings are constructed:

> *Global racism is the behavioral and ideological practice that is prejudicial to the phenotypically different other and that has multilocal or transnational ramifications. Its translocality is the cornerstone of its manifestation.*

In the history of the ethnopole, global racism presents itself as a translocal mechanism that implodes in the initial phase of the birth of the enclave. This global content is intrinsic to the genealogy of the local process because it helps keep alive the relations between the residents and the homeland. Globality is inscribed in the birthing process and establishes the ethnopole as a pole of a continuum.

Global racism is located at the beginning of the process, all during the history of its development, and at specific periods – junctural times – that significantly reshape or influence local conditions. It has an overt and covert form, is dormant or active, and has passing or lasting impact. Its local manifestation endures as a sign of its consequences.

Informal capital city

The metaphor of an ethnopole serving as a capital city is worth investigating to understand the order of things in the city.[35] We conceive of ethnic communities, because they have been racialized, as participating both in the formal order of the mainstream system and in the ethnic order of city life. Since these two processes are intertwined, the ethnic order of things cannot be seen simply as a parallel system, but rather as a pole of a continuum. However, while one is right in seeing Chinatown as an enclave inside San Francisco, one is also correct to view it – the birthplace of Chinese America – as a node in a network of connecting ethnic sites. The informal reality of which it is a part must be deconstructed to unveil the informal order of things.

A local analyst provides the reasons why Chinatown maintains its central position *vis-à-vis* other Chinatowns in Northern California. This Chinese American observer invokes the history of the enclave, the tourist factor, and the enclave's concentration of institutions to make her point. As she puts it,

> We are number one because of our history, because of the constant infusion of new immigrants, new businesses, new groups who would live and work in Chinatown. It is not just a tourist spot. When you walk down Stockton Street, [you see that] it is a community where people shop. If you walk on Grant Avenue then, yes, [you see that] it becomes a tourist attraction. But on the side streets, you see businesses and professional offices. Within Chinatown, we have 187 Chinese-speaking physicians practicing here, twenty financial institutions, too. So the community is successful because of all these factors.

To understand the informal character of the ethnopole, one must recognize the influence it wields beyond its boundaries. For example, the Chinese American Citizens' Alliance, headquartered in Chinatown, is a national association that promotes the interests of its membership at the national level.

The informal capital city concept implies the existence of a location that is central not only because of the concentration of informal institutions in its midst, but also because it is connected to satellite clusters inside or outside the formal city proper for which it serves as a center. Furthermore, the role of the informal capital city may be directly reinforced by its global relations or indirectly reinforced by the global connections of the formal city in which it is an enclave. This informal urban system also implies a hierarchy of sites with the ethnopole at its apex or center. The dynamic of this *informal urban system* is unveiled not in the structuralist discourse of system analysis, but rather in the poststructuralist view of subjects serving as actors in their everyday transactional lives.

There are no formal mechanisms that link the satellite clusters to their informal capital city. Linking is accomplished in informal ways via the circulation of people, capital, goods, and communications between these sites. By "people," I am referring to the individual Chinese who live outside the city and visit the ethnopole on a regular or irregular basis, to the farmers who sell their produce in the vegetable stores or restaurants in Chinatown, to the entrepreneurs who invest in the banks there, and to the individuals in the ethnopole (family members, church leaders, grassroots activists, and businesspeople) who engage in multiple telephone conversations with outsiders. These processes daily contribute to the reproduction of the ethnopole as an informal capital city as they reinforce its central position and elevated status in the informal urban system.

Despite the rise of Chinese neighborhood retail stores and suburban Ranch 99 megastores, which stock Chinese groceries and goods, in diverse areas throughout the Bay Area, shoppers continue to use Chinatown as a marketplace.[36] This includes not only those who live in the ethnopole and for whom distance and transportation are not an issue but also others living across the Bay. Chinatown continues to be for them a site where one can find both a wider selection and large quantity of ethnic products and fresh green Chinese vegetables, and where prices are cheaper because of the sheer size of daily competition. As one old-timer puts it,

> Chinatown has been the center of the Chinese community in the Bay Area. The shops sell a large diversity of goods. every kind of

food a Chinese needs, he can find here. In some other areas in the Bay...they cannot get a lot of things they need to buy. So that's why most of the people, when they are shopping for things, come over here to Chinatown to get what they want.

This perception by a senior citizen who has lived in Chinatown his entire life was shared by several Chinese Americans in the Bay Area I spoke to.

Others come to Chinatown to attend social functions, which it is well equipped to supply. One can think for example of New Year banquets, weddings, and family reunions that require facilities that can accommodate large groups of people – family and friends from various parts of the Bay Area. Until recently, the necessary large facilities could seldom be found elsewhere.

Even former residents who have resettled elsewhere in the city or Bay continue to visit Chinatown to attend Sunday church services, to use the Chinese hospital, to visit older family members, to meet friends, to have lunch or dinner, or for other recreational purposes. However, there are Chinese restaurants all over the Bay Area, why would these people find it necessary to go to Chinatown for meals out? When I put that question to a weekly commuter to Chinatown, she replied that it was "mostly because it is less expensive, the atmosphere is better, the cooking is better here, and there is more variety." The rationale for this explanation seems to be that restaurants located elsewhere cater to foreign tastes while those in Chinatown cook authentic Chinese cuisine ("Chinese specialties"). The food preparation for each type is different, as is the taste, according to this Chinese connoisseur.

Ethnic entrepreneurs themselves must also commute to Chinatown, a circumstance made unavoidable by the distance between stores and the entrepreneurs' places of residence. Owners of most of the bigger stores and restaurants do not live in Chinatown, but rather in the Richmond District, Sunset District, Daly City, or somewhere else in San Francisco, and so must commute every day to the ethnopole to take care of business. That's also the case for employees who staff these institutions because they must know enough English to interact with potential English-speaking buyers and the general tourist crowd.[37]

Chinese farmers come to Chinatown to sell their produce, supplying both grocery stores and restaurants with fresh vegetables, herbs, grains, and flowers. Warehouses of dry goods located outside the ethnopole fulfill a similar function as they feed the stores with new merchandise, linking this central site to a network of satellite sites and thus enhancing the capital-city status of Chinatown. What distinguishes Chinatown from the other enclaves is size, volume, and variety of many sorts: Chinatown features a diverse group of churches; different culinary traditions from mainland China, Taiwan, Hong Kong, and the ethnic Chinese from Singapore, the Philippines, Thailand, Vietnam, and Korea; different languages; and procommunist and nationalist political organizations. It is *ethnic multiculturalism* in its dynamic complexity.

One finds here a concentration of social services provided by both grassroots organizations and government agencies staffed by ethnics. It is the place where services are provided in one's language, and where lawyers and physicians are available. Chinatown boasts the first and only Chinese hospital in the nation. Chinese throughout the Bay use its facilities, especially the aged who are not fluent in English.

Like so many cities in the United States where the rich have fled to the suburbs, Chinatown has experienced middle-class flight. The "new" Chinatown in San Francisco's Richmond District well symbolizes this phenomenon. What the Chinese Americans who fled left behind is a business district where "the rents are high, the facilities are poor, and the majority of the residents do not know English," observes a longtime Chinatown resident.

But one also remarks the return migration of some elderly to Chinatown after they have lived elsewhere. I was told by a social services provider who has labored for many years in Chinatown that,

> by and large, the elderly population is mostly foreign born with low to moderate income. We do have wealthy Chinese, who, when they made it, moved to Walnut Creek, taking their elderly with them. But the seniors are devastated in these environments since they have no one to speak to, and then they deteriorate both physically and mentally. So lots of those elderly parents have moved back to Chinatown. They would rather rent a small apartment than live in a five-bedroom home with their children. In Chinatown, they can walk out and have tea and fresh vegetables. Chinatown really supports the elderly.

The autonomy of the ethnopole as an informal city has been achieved to the extent that dwellers have developed a genuine informal political system that allows them to both interface with the outside power structure of city governance and maintain internal, or self-regulation.[38] In this sense, Chinatown is the central site of location of informal and formal organizations that focus their attention on issues affecting the lives of the Chinese population in San Francisco, as well as on political issues that connect them to or heighten their interests in mainland China, Hong Kong, or Taiwan.

Among Chinatown residents, there are various and diverse opinions on the exact architecture of this ethnic political system, its nature, and its effectiveness, but no one seems to doubt its existence.[39] Some see this system as more effective when dealing with issues pertaining to China than with city hall; others see it as a mechanism that strengthens the position of Chinatown *vis-à-vis* the rest of the city; still others believe that its effectiveness is purely internal in its self-regulation capacity. One old-timer offered the opinion that this informal system is not a single piece, but rather is made of disparate pieces. For him,

> all the political organizations that are connected to China are here, like the Nationalist Party. That's really the main political one. From Chinatown they can control the larger organizations. And of course, you do have a lot of the other organizations that are normally not political but are politicized since they are staffed by Taiwanese. Because there are different layers, there is no one group that can say "I am speaking for the Chinese." You have different ones: for elders, etc. They each have a little base.

The Chinese Consolidated Benevolent Association known as the "Six Companies" was once the major force in the community.[40] It is now only one of the players. According to a Chinatown analyst,

> They are kind of an anomaly in San Francisco. They are ultraconservative. But, they are not good in local politics... At the present time, as far as effectiveness is concerned, I would say that the Chamber of Commerce is more effective. You see, the "Six Companies" is just too closely tied to Taiwan; that is why it cannot move... The majority of Chinatown residents are prounification of Taiwan with China.

As noted earlier, the informal city has its own informal mayor, who provides leadership and harmonizes the interactions among diverse interests. The mayor is not elected or selected, but is labeled as such by outsiders more than by insiders. The title is, nevertheless, one of endearment that acknowledges the person's lifelong dedication to the affairs of the community and role as point man for outsiders. Because of the mayor's knowledge of the ethnopole, an outsider, regardless of the angle of his or her approach to the community, would sooner or later be referred to him. Harvey Wong is currently considered mayor of Chinatown. Writing for the *San Francisco Examiner* Marsha Ginsburg earlier referred to him as "Chinatown's unofficial mayor," whom she interviewed at "Victory Hall, Chinatown's unofficial City Hall."

This opinion is not shared by some members of the community who, because of their different ideologies, agendas, and tactics, tend to see factionalization, polarization, and dispersion of power centers in Chinatown. As one local observer puts it,

> I think prior to the late 1960s, you could probably identify two people who were prominent enough to deserve some title or tribal chiefdom or [to be called] mayor of Chinatown. I think that with the Civil Rights movement and the quest for ethnic identity, a lot of things have changed. Many young people brought these ideas back to the community and said that they could no longer trust traditional leadership. And traditional leadership included the Six Companies. And so from that point on, room had to be made for the younger generation.

If Chinatown can be characterized as an informal capital city, the Richmond and Sunset Districts are definitely its suburbs. Another way to put it is that Chinatown is the downtown for the Richmond and Sunset residents. Moreover, some residents of these districts either own stores, work as staff personnel, or are leaders in civic organizations in Chinatown.

The informal capital-city status presupposes an informal hierarchy of scale in which satellite communities like Oakland, San José, and Walnut Creek have lower status compared to Chinatown. This hierarchy is found not only in terms of enclaves or clusters but also in terms of institutions. For example, Self-Help for the Elderly, headquartered in Chinatown, has a satellite branch in San José. Similarly, there are family restaurants, medical clinics, law offices, flower shops, and stores that maintain headquarters in Chinatown and satellite subsidiaries elsewhere.

This hierarchy of scale is further complicated by economic factors. It is one thing to establish a scale based on population density, but another to do so using marketplace dynamics that serve as a magnet to the local population. A local analyst observes that

> there are a lot of places that are so-called imitations of Chinatown that I would define as coalescing to provide a draw because of scale. You find them all over the place. Chinatown no longer has that exclusive monopoly – that you either have to go to Chinatown or you cannot get that kind of whatever it is. So your largest supermarkets are not in Chinatown. I do not know of any supermarket in Chinatown. And yet there are supermarkets owned by Chinese that would rival any supermarkets normally located outside in the suburbs.

The earthquake of 1989 was a major event in the history of Chinatown because of the collapse of the Embarcadero Freeway that had until then provided easy access to Chinatown. As one local observer puts it,

> After the earthquake, San Francisco's Chinatown feeds the growth of other Chinatowns. In Milpitas there is a very big shopping center catering to Asians. So in our mind, hierarchy means "San Francisco's Chinatown is the best," but I cannot underestimate the growth of Oakland Chinatown or San Jose or even San Mateo or Santa Clara. But when you talk about California, we're number one. People still want to come to San Francisco's Chinatown.

The global dimension of the capital city is evident in the newspapers available to the local community. Two of these papers that compete for the ideological soul of the community are owned by foreign interests: one by a Chinese Company in Hong Kong and the other by a Taiwanese company. While the foreign-owned newspapers are satellites of overseas operations and are well equipped with computers, a third, local, paper has meager means. As a result, the latter is published strictly for the Chinese-speaking population and has no English columns.

As noted earlier, many of the items sold in Chinatown are foreign made. Tourist gifts, for example, are usually imported from China, Hong Kong, or Taiwan. The global connection is sustained as merchants purchase these items from family shops or producers elsewhere, or from import–export companies. This family business connection between Chinatown and China, Hong Kong, and Taiwan has been uninterrupted over the years – legally when allowed by both governments and illegally when forbidden.[41] This applies as well to dried and canned foods,

Chinese shellfishes, Chinese sausage, and medicines. Residents think that the better ones come from China, Taiwan, and Hong Kong. The globality of these connections takes various forms and does not evolve in a linear fashion; rather it follows the vicissitudes of family ties and the law of the market. In an informal conversation, one oldtimer provided the following insights as he attempted to delineate a limited genealogy of the globalization process in the ethnopole:

> Chinatown has its global relations. The global ties have been established for many years. People come over here and, well, if people who come over here have family ties back in their home country, back in their hometown, they, of course, sometimes travel to and from here. If they have friends coming over here to visit them, they go back to visit their friends. Businesswise, it all depends on what businesses they are in. If they can get their products cheaper in their home country, of course, they would do business there. But if they can get a product in the Bay Area, if they can get it from the large import companies, import warehouses, they would get it there. It is money-wise. Anywhere they can make the most profit margin they would go there.

The globality of Chinatown is not something new; it has existed all along and was shaped according to the vicissitudes of US relations with China. Little can be understood outside the framework of this foreign policy and global geopolitical arena. A longtime resident of Chinatown recalls when

> my father was sending money back to China. We did not have much, but we sent as much we could. We had fund raising meetings to support Chiang Kai Shek. And there was all this patriotism that could not go away. One of the common things we used to hear when I was growing up was, when I die, I want my body sent back to China for burial.

This man sees this familial and political form of globality as enduring and endemic to the local community.

Chinatown and President Richard Nixon's trip to China

Impact studies assume that the "global" and "local" are two distinct and separate realities while, in contrast, I see the two as poles of a continuum, which is a different way of positioning a problem and approaching it. Consequently, I will not examine the relationship of Chinatown to President Nixon's China trip in the tradition of impact studies; in other words, I will not examine the impact of the trip on Chinatown. The push for relaxation of US policies toward China had been advocated long before the trip, notably by diverse activist groups in Chinatown who had participated in the Civil Rights movements a few years earlier. These activists had called for a more rational foreign policy ever since the United States had begun engaging in productive dialogue with the Soviet Union. For many residents, the matter was not simply one of foreign policy but also of race.

Beginning in 1967, Chinatown leftists were not the only advocates asking for a sea change in US foreign policy toward China. Up until that time, Taiwanese leaders and organizations had had the upper hand over Chinatown, which was constructed as one of Taiwan's overseas allies and as a satellite center on which they depended for ideological support. A resident observer remembers that well before the Nixon trip, support for the People's Republic was on the upswing in Chinatown. As he points out, the relaxation started before the trip:

> So about 1967, a liberal newspaper, advocated more rational policy. Then, The *Chinese Voice* and the *East–West,* which is a kind of neutral newspaper, [followed suit]. And then, you have bookstores over in the next block. So, before, it was just a single column. Nobody really said anything in public. It was really more McCarthy than McCarthy.

The Nixon visit crystallized a new awareness among the residents of Chinatown as their identification with the People's Republic gained momentum and widespread recognition. Support for the People's Republic was no longer seen as the cry of some leftist groups. The left was divided. With the death of Mao Tse-Tung in 1976 and the ensuing battle over China's leadership, the left only became more divided. However, the opening of the United States to China in 1979 ushered in a new migratory movement initiated by Chinese Americans who took the opportunity to visit the homeland, and Chinese immigrants who came to the United States to be reunited with family members or to pursue economic interests. The normalization of relations between the two countries finalized the negotiations begun by Nixon.

Prior to the visit, Chinatown residents were afraid to travel to China to visit relatives or engage in business transactions. Many residents had family members in China, and older Chinese wanted to reconnect with their roots. One old-timer sees the normalization of relations as a breakthrough that both provided legitimacy and ended the fear that one's sympathy toward China could have devastating consequences for one's life in the United States. He reports that

> Nixon's recognition made it possible for people to express themselves legitimately. So any hidden alliances no longer needed to be suppressed. In one way, the recognition permitted the expression: they no longer had to hold back or hide their feelings. Though there had always been a group that had aligned themselves with the PRC, a stronger group had aligned themselves with KMT. The vast majority of people did not express themselves one way or the other. Now, getting back to removing the fear, I would say a lot of people no longer had fear. And secondly, among the businesspeople, a lot of them who had aligned themselves with KMT did so for purely economic reasons. But now, they are able to take their trade to mainland China. And they can express themselves at will.

In terms of a time frame, it was not simply the visit but the consequences of the visit that led to the United States' recognition of the People's Republic of China. Official recognition, however, did not take place at the time of the visit but a few years later.

The post-1965 immigration of Chinese to the United States was a major factor in the reshaping of the Chinese population in Chinatown. It brought a diverse group of Chinese not simply from the mainland but also from Taiwan, Hong Kong, and Vietnam. These newcomers who resettled in Chinatown were not the rich, but rather immigrants of meager means.

Another old-timer who now lives in the East Bay recalls that "Nixon's visit elevated the status of Chinatown. In a way, now it was okay to be Chinese. We could be proud to be Chinese. And China, instead of being an enemy, became a friend." She refers to the uneasiness prevalent as a result of knowing that China was not until then on good terms with the United States, and to the unpredictability of the future. Her statement also alludes to a similar situation the Japanese found themselves in during World War II. Until Nixon's visit, Chinese Americans had lived with the tension that resulted from the ambiguous relations between the two countries.

An activist leader engaged in the reshaping of the face of Chinatown during that period provides his own assessment of the situation:

> Prior to Richard Nixon's visit to China, the politics in this community amongst first generation residents, those who are immigrants, were weighted heavily towards the Chinese Nationalists. Before Nixon went to China, there was heavy lobbying by this Nationalist group to discourage Nixon from going. But once Nixon went, it shifted the balance away from the Nationalists. Prior to that, there was zero tolerance for communists or communist sympathizers. But there were other dynamics that were unique to this community. One was the creation of the Red Guards. They have little to do with the Red Guards in China, but [the organization] fulfilled the need by adolescent youth in this community to find something they could hold up. So they organized themselves as the Red Guards and created their own version of a People's Movement. The Red Guards were American-born Chinese kids mimicking the Red Guards in China. But there was also a steady group of sympathizers who were also probably from China and who published a newsletter, and who were considered outcasts in the community. I don't know if anybody has written on it. But it was a unique time in the history of Chinatown. It was so chaotic. You had people running around making demands of everyone whom they considered "the establishment." Then there was another group that was more in line with the socialism of China; this second one was more of a pure group of revolutionaries. And these people were both the ideological and physical targets of the existing Nationalist Party here. If you just walk down the street, you can see the headquarters of the Chinese Nationalist Party. And the buildings that they own are just half a block from us. And they have had these ever since I was a little kid. In recent decades, Taiwan's government has floated a lot of money into these organizations, and you can see some capital improvement. So when Nixon went, it shifted the balance of politics in Chinatown. Not right away, but it was the beginning of the normalization between the US and China. There were a number of demonstrations, prior to Nixon's leaving, and also there were parades. You can identify the establishment in Chinatown, since they were pressured to demonstrate. I have films on that. So that's all I can tell you. But I think that the merchants were ambivalent: on the one hand, they did not want to be identified as communists, yet on the other they knew that the things they had to sell that were popular

to consumers came from China – you take the herbs and even things like mushrooms. Once trade was restored with China, many stores opened up again. We had no mushrooms, we had virtually no herbs stores, prior to Nixon's visit. Then they all opened up again with free trade. Prior to that, we were still getting some goods, but they had to be shipped in illegally from Canada. Once Nixon went to China, it opened up trade and a lot more tourism picked up from here to China.

A Chinese medical doctor who had been in China during the Nixon visit, and who came to Chinatown in 1980, argues that one of the consequences of the visit is the diversity of Chinese languages now spoken in Chinatown. She recalls that

in the 1980s, if you spoke either Mandarin or Shanghai dialect at the store, they just stared at you and made you feel an outsider. They didn't understand what you spoke. Only when I changed my tongue to Cantonese, or may be a village dialect, then they felt very comfortable. But right now, in Chinatown, every word you can hear is either Mandarin, Shanghai, or dialects other than Cantonese. This is a big difference.

A high-profile third-generation Chinese American professional who grew up in Chinatown and who continues to help the people there through an agency she heads had the following to say about Nixon's visit:

President Nixon's visit was like a watershed year. Everything else happened from then on, that means postnormalization with China. China really opened their doors. So I think up till that time, China had neither trade nor immigration into the United States. But since then, however, the US has allowed a quota of 20 000 a year for Chinese from mainland China to immigrate to the United States. That started an influx of mainland Chinese and refugees into Chinatown. And Chinatown really prospered from the early 1970s all the way to the 1990s.

I think that the earthquake of 1989 is another benchmark, since it caused serious damage to the Embarcadero Freeway, a lifeline leading all the out-of-town traffic through Chinatown. The successful Chinese who had moved out to suburbs like San José and the San Mateo had always come back to Chinatown to do grocery shopping and a lot of other things. Since 1989, the freeway was demolished, and the closest freeway located as far away as Third Street does not directly lead people into Chinatown; we were literally cut off from all that traffic. As a result, tourism and businesses in Chinatown decreased quite a bit, as much as 40 percent. This lack of access into Chinatown also indirectly led to the construction of small shopping centers specializing in Chinese groceries and medicines in suburban areas. If you go to Milpitas, Foster City, San Mateo, and even Daly City and Pacifica, each has a huge supermarket that sells literally everything that people usually have to come to Chinatown to get. So although 1989 was the beginning of the demise of businesses in San Francisco, it was also the birth of many successful Chinese and Asian businesses elsewhere. For they don't only cater exclusively to the Chinese, but to the Vietnamese, Korean, and Japanese as well. As all of these markets have all the Asian ingredients, they are very successful. One of these stores, called Ranch 99, is a phenomenon. They started in Southern California, and in the last three to four years they have expanded since to nine to twelve Ranches. Once a Ranch has anchored down an area, a lot of jewelry stores, bookstores, shoe stores, and other businesses quickly locate around it. So it's kind of a dichotomy. But I think that the Nixon visit has had an important impact. In the past, many of the people who had originated from China needed to first go to Hong Kong or some other Southeast Asian country before successfully immigrating to San Francisco. Many left while still having lots of relatives in China knowing that there would be no way to communicate in the future. However, since the Nixon years, much has opened up. In the beginning, one would see a lot of people traveling back to China. Following Nixon's visit, tourism in the 1970s provided a real economic boom for China. But at the same time, the Chinese are family oriented and traditional, so a lot of old-timers who had left the mother country for forty to fifty years, now can actually take the money they raised here and go back to China to rebuild their homes and schools and hospitals for the villages. So, there have been tremendous implications in reopening communication with China. It also continues the growth in Chinatown's fame, contributing to its success and longevity while other ethnic enclaves collapse or disappear. So the Nixon visit is a major benchmark, contributing to San Francisco's Chinatown's ability to succeed as a business extension of Asia while fostering local businesses through the support of its local residents.

She further adds that

> unlike Japantown where a lot of the buildings are owned by Japanese corporations, one-third of the assets in Chinatown are owned by American-chartered non-profit family associations such as the Chen, Wong, and Chu. These are family associations that have been built up since the mid-1800s with the arrival of the first Chinese immigrants. These family associations are very wealthy, powerful, and are all local. In a way, they are tied to local politics. If the United States continues to trade with China, San Francisco's Chinatown and other Chinatowns would be able to benefit, since there would be an increase in import–export trade. Many bilingual Chinese are acting as bridges between local companies who want to do business in China on a smaller scale. Found in the import–export businesses, they are the financial real estate brokerages helping to open companies in Chinatown which sell more health products, like mushrooms and Ginseng. So China is actually investing in and opening up businesses right here in San Francisco's Chinatown...I anticipate that economic growth in China will foster a lot of interchange between China and San Francisco's Chinatown.

The fall of Saigon

The fall of Saigon ushered a number of Chinese Vietnamese into Chinatown.[42] This migration was felt in a peculiar way in Chinatown, dissimilar to other recent migrations. Its specificity stems from the fact that, upon arriving suddenly in the mid-1970s, the migrants made an impression on the community because they were refugees and, unlike others, were eligible for financial aid. Their presence in the ethnopole was felt mostly in three major areas: in housing, where they competed with the local Chinese; in the produce stores they operated, which competed with those of old-timer merchants; and as a non-residential clientele who shopped in Chinatown. This last category also included those who lived in the Tenderloin District and commuted daily to use the public facilities of the ethnopole. For example, Chinese Vietnamese would go to Chinatown to eat in the restaurants, buy groceries or shop in general, and attend church services.

The Vietnamese could not move into Chinatown in large numbers because of the dynamics of local housing politics. A local observer remarks that

> in the first place, housing is very tight and expensive. There is also the phenomenon that many of these buildings are owned by the family associations, who are very selective of who lives in these apartments. You also have many SROs [single room occupancy] buildings where bathrooms and kitchens are shared by all the tenants on a particular floor. So, this housing does not lend itself to families, but more to singles and elderly. Thus, once you go a few blocks into the Tenderloin, a place better suited for families, you will find Vietnamese families.

The ways in which the fall of Saigon imploded in Chinatown took many forms. Sometimes the effect was direct, as it was when Chinese Vietnamese immigrated into the community, while at other times the effect was indirect, because of their very presence in the Tenderloin District and their use of facilities in Chinatown.[43]

According to a local leader,

> The 1975–6 migration was composed of people associated with the government on the losing side of the war; they are called the "Ethnic Vietnamese." The impact on Chinatown did not occur until 1979–81, with the boat people, where you see the integration of Chinese Vietnamese into Chinatown. Now, the initial impact as far as San Francisco was concerned occurred in the Tenderloin, whereas the ethnic Vietnamese impact took place in the South Bay. The people around the Tenderloin were largely Chinese Vietnamese, with a smaller percentage of ethnic Vietnamese. So, the impact of the fall was more psychological than physical. Now, how much of Chinatown has been impacted by the Vietnamese? Not much. If I had to guess, I would say 10–15 percent in terms of business ownership; even less in terms of capital assets. The integration of the Chinese Vietnamese into the Chinese community has been simple. I mean, they are Chinese.

A social worker who heads a social services agency in Chinatown looks at the issue from the angle of the resident Chinese community which was called upon to make room for the incoming immigrants:

There was definitely a flood of Vietnamese refugees. Because of the Vietnam War implication, the refugees enjoyed instant public assistance when they got here. It actually created some tension and conflicts with the local immigrant community. A lot of the old-timers were upset, for when they had first arrived, they had worked very hard but had never been given a penny in public assistance. As a matter of fact, the welfare reform that had been passed limited federal benefits to US citizens only. However, if you are a refugee, you are automatically listed onto the welfare roll. So it actually created tension against Vietnamese refugees. This, I believe, other community groups, like ourselves and the Southeast Asian community center, need to work hard to overcome. But the positive effect of the Chinese Vietnamese is that they are very hardworking. So gradually you see the Chinese Vietnamese becoming a part of the Chinatown infrastructure. If you walk around, most of the produce markets are now owned and operated by the Chinese Vietnamese. They might be ethnic Chinese, but they are still Vietnamese. Also, many doughnut shops around much of San Francisco are now owned by Cambodians. And they just spread. When you open one, you have started a network. So, when the next one is open, your aunt or your uncle or sister or brother will operate it; it becomes a family business. Now the produce markets are owned and operated by Chinese Vietnamese families, and doughnut shops by Cambodians: those are very specific roles for those communities. They also moved into the Tenderloin. They have taken over a very poor and scary part of San Francisco. However, family orientation literally improved the Tenderloin from a red light, shady community to a family community for them. As Vietnamese or Southeast Asian refugees escaped war and many pirates to make it here, they are very tough. They don't mind living in a neighborhood like that since the rent is cheap and it's close to Chinatown. In a way, because they live and survive there, the whole community rallies behind them; now the Tenderloin is a different neighborhood than, let's say twenty years ago.

Chinese Vietnamese immigration also caused an expansion and diversity of population and businesses in Chinatown. A few types of stores there are now owned primarily by the Chinese Vietnamese–mostly restaurants, grocery stores, video shops, beauty salons, and delicatessens.

The reunification of Hong Kong with China

This event was a proud moment in the history of Chinatown. Residents had advocated it and had been preparing for it for years. After the impending reunification had been announced two decades earlier, there was much interaction between the two communities because of immigration caused by the announcement and because of investment in the banking institutions in the outlying areas of Chinatown.[44] Because the immigration was spread over several years, and because the Hong Kong rich were moving to Vancouver, Canada, and parts of the United States, Chinatown did, in fairness, receive its share of a small number of immigrants.

According to one long-time resident, the Hong Kong episode influenced Chinatown in two ways:

> Psychologically it was a boom, but not materially. What investments went to Hong Kong and China were hardly from residents in Chinatown. There may be Hong Kong people who do business in Chinatown, but not many of them live in Chinatown; it's close to zero. A few had retail outlet business here; however that's not where the headquarters are located nor where the decisions are made.

The implosion of Hong Kong occurred in Chinatown not at the time when reunification became a reality, but earlier after the Nixon visit – during a twenty-five-year period. Recognition that Hong Kong would be reunified brought about the triangular trade between China, Hong Kong, and Taiwan that made it much easier for Chinatown storeowners to access Chinese goods through Hong Kong or Taiwan and eventually from China.

A social worker points out an indirect linkage, remarking

> I think in the last three years, even Taiwan and China have opened up for a lot of intertrade. Officially, though, the Chinese and Taiwanese governments will not admit it. Still, everyone knows that they conduct a lot of trade with Hong Kong, which is the so-called neutral ground. So, Chinatown benefits when that happens. Now you are able to deal with a country that has 1.3 billion people; this helps tremendously in economic growth. So, the fact of Hong Kong's going back to China – as long as China does not impose its communism on Hong Kong – would really continue to be beneficial to overseas Chinese as a financial center.

One notable result of immigration from Hong Kong is the fact that the immigrants brought new diversity to the culinary traditions of Chinatown, developed modern restaurants that cater to both locals and tourists, and, in the process, competed with existing restaurants for clientele. However, while locals remark that the Hong Kong people establish beautifully decorated, comfortable restaurants with nicely dressed waitresses, they also complain that the *dim sum* gets smaller and smaller in these places.

City hall and Chinatown

In 1985, the city of San Francisco issued *Chinatown: An Area Plan of the Master Plan of the City and County of San Francisco*. The plan contains and provides sufficient elements for an analysis of the relations between the city government and the ethnopole. The existence of Chinatown as a capital city could not be sustained without the help of city hall. The *Area Plan* does not create a new blueprint for Chinatown, but simply formalizes a practice that has existed since the end of World War II. By formalizing it, the plan spells out the vision and strategies of intervention that are necessary for its implementation if not its enhancement. The plan identifies the three main characteristics of Chinatown: it is a capital city, a tourist site, and a residential neighborhood. Reinforcing these three aspects without neglecting any of them at the expense of the others is the role that city hall will continue to play in the reproduction of the ethnopole.

The *Area Plan* defines these three main characteristics of Chinatown in the following fashion:

> [Chinatown is] A residential neighborhood with 10 000 to 15 000 population, primarily elderly and recent refugee/immigrant households. It has its own language and newspapers, groceries, fish and meat markets and small shops.
>
> Chinatown functions as a capital city and center of civic, religious, political and social service organizations, as well as a specialized shopping center for the larger Chinese population of the Bay Area.
>
> Chinatown is a destination for most visitors to the city and many Chinatown restaurant and gift store enterprises have a strong tourist trade.

To ensure that these three mutually reinforcing functions continue to be protected as such, the city government has developed a regime of intervention. Such techniques of intervention impact not only Chinatown but city government as well, because they entail the allocation of resources, humanpower, money, and the participation of different government agencies that plan and/or implement these programs: agencies that maintain and enhance the infrastructure, regulate neighborhood and tourist economies, and police housing alteration and development to meet the requirements of zoning ordinances.

The role the city plays in each of these sectors is crucial for the reproduction of Chinatown, because these forms of intervention contribute to the micromanagement of the enclave as well. The maintenance of traditional housing forms is a main concern of the city, and one that is materialized in the ways it intervenes in the Chinatown's affairs. For example, intervention in the housing domain consists of preventing construction of buildings more than three stories tall. Such buildings would not match existing structures. Preventing construction of tall buildings is seen as having two major goals: to preserve the enclave's overall architectural style and its wind-free environment. The *Area Plan* for Chinatown also calls for maintaining the old exotic facades, preventing construction of unmatched alterations, and building new structures that harmonize "with the scale of existing buildings and width of Chinatown's streets." The preoccupation with height and facades, then, is concomitant with the existing design of these historic streets.

But the city's preoccupation with height and facades also indicates that the well-being of residents is not the only thing the planners have in mind: they are also concerned about the area's ability to continue to attract the tourist crowd. This local and global concern is stated in the *Area Plan* where it justifies the actions of the formal urban planners of city government: "the sunny and wind-free climate is important to the comfort of residents and visitors because most people walk rather than drive in Chinatown." Thus the *global concern* of the city is inscribed in the techniques of intervention it uses in matters related to housing in the ethnopole.

The city's intervention in the ethnopolitan economy is meant to protect small and family enterprises, to prevent larger corporations from displacing existing businesses, and to provide a climate in which local businesses may continue to prosper by meeting the buying needs of the tourists. The reproduction of the neighborhood is tied to the sustenance of the neighborhood economy. The city's goal is to maintain an equilibrium between these two economies, rather than backing one at the expense of the other. Thus, protecting the neighborhood is seen as beneficial not only for the residents but also as a way of sustaining the tourist industry. The *Area Plan* states that

> the neighborhood economy is vital for the tourist industry itself. Tourists come to Chinatown not only to shop and eat, but to see a thriving Chinese community with small businesses and institutions that cater to residents. These uses should not be crowded out by tourist-oriented uses.

The city has a global preoccupation in its intervention in the economies of Chinatown. It is as if the city wants to help the people in order to lure the tourists in.

Strangely enough, the city's intervention in the regulation of the tourist industry is also seen as a means to help stabilize the neighborhood. The *Area Plan* states that

> the San Francisco Convention and Tourist Bureau reports that of the two to three million visitors to San Francisco each year, at least three out of four visit Chinatown. During peak visitor days, visitors may outnumber local residents. An estimated one-third of the estimated 20 000 jobs in Chinatown are related to visitors and therefore its tourist role is important to the neighborhood.

Not only does city intervention have the tourists in mind, it also reproduces the sectoral makeup of the ethnopole: Grant Avenue as a tourist or specialty retailing street and Stockton Street as the marketplace of the local residents. The physical division of the infrastructure is reflective of the globality of the ethnopole as well.

The local Chinatown neighborhood has for city hall a translocal meaning, since it includes non-local users: the tourists and the Bay Area Chinese for whom it serves as an informal capital city. Planning for the neighborhood is done with that extralocal and global view espoused by city hall. In fact, one may argue that the city government is involved in the construction and sustenance of a translocal and global space. The *Area Plan* calls for protection and expansion of cultural institutions (e.g. family and district associations, social service agencies) and community businesses that fulfill their status as headquarters in the informal capital city.

Transportation is another area of city intervention. Transportation is designed to meet local, tourist, and Bay Area shoppers' needs: it maximizes pedestrian space and short-term parking availability. Even the redirection of traffic and the timing of truck delivery schedules are done with global purposes in mind: to allow the tourists to circulate freely in Chinatown. City hall's planning of Chinatown is not simply a local but also a global issue. The city thinks globally while it acts or operates locally. One sees here how the global disciplines city hall in terms of its alternatives regarding Chinatown. Local decisions about the ethnopole are shaped by this global preoccupation. City hall is caught in a global dilemma: how can it reproduce a racialized local site for the enjoyment of incoming tourists?

The commoditization of local exoticism

Several sectors are involved in the global selling of Chinatown: the municipal government, the travel–tourism industry, the Chamber of Commerce, and Chinatown's business elite. Global publicity is undertaken to bring tourists to San Francisco and to lure them into Chinatown. The money they spend there consolidates in three coffers: that of the business community in general, the Chinatown merchants, and city hall itself by way of the tax system. Despite the global use of Chinatown's exoticism, the money collected by the city is not primarily used for the modernization of the ethnopole, but rather for city hall's other priorities.

The city's global publicity makes use of newspapers, magazines, television ads, and travel guides as an efficient way to reach out-of-town tourists both foreign and national, as well as the Chinese "yellow pages" – special advertising directories aimed at Chinese businesses and Chinese audiences – to attract diasporic and homeland Chinese to Chinatown. And since the city is selling exoticism, the image projected is not that of the struggle of residents to develop their neighborhood, but rather that of an out-of-place-exotic site. In this logic, the policy of the city has not been to de-exoticize Chinatown, but rather to reproduce its exoticism so that it may lure more tourists to town.

The residents are caught in a dilemma. Their ethnopole is being used as a living museum in which their very presence provides a daily spectacle to tourists.[45] Some visit the place not to buy gifts but to see the "exotic natives" on display against their will. One tragic difference – among many others – between this living museum and the frozen ones dispersed throughout the city is that there is no entry fee offered for the maintenance of the infrastructure of Chinatown.

Local racist practices that have confined the Chinese to their ethnopole are now projected on the global scene to accentuate difference, otherness, multiculturality, and exoticism. While global racism has a local dimension, it is located not simply in the domain of behavioral relations but also in the concoction, projection, and selling of the images of the others. This form of racism does not require the direct participation of, or confrontation with, others. It is the depiction of the other without consent, knowledge, or collaboration. This is the one-dimensional side that complements the other side of global racism. Here both dimensions are important in the reproduction of Chinatown as a racialized global site and globalized racial site.

The selling of Chinatown to tourists comprises two intertwined processes. The global image projected of Chinatown does not require the participation of the Chinese or their knowledge for its success, for it is accomplished within the larger context of selling the city to tourists. In this imagery, Chinatown appears only as a site in a multiplicity of other attractions. While its inclusion no doubt enhances the package, Chinatown cannot be singled out as the most important site, because tourists have diverse tastes.

In the second process, the city colludes with the residents because the survival of the site as an exotic place requires the collaboration of home owners. While the city sees Chinatown as a tourist spot and a business district or corridor, the locals see it as their home or spatial turf. Furthermore, the city desires to keep the area as a landmark because it is seen as such by the larger population, which benefits from such a designated status. This entails keeping the buildings as they are or, if they are demolished, replacing them with similar types of housing. Locals have a different view on this issue and justly so. They are not interested in exoticism but in having larger and more comfortable homes.

According to a local resident,

> There has been a lot of discussion as to whether Chinatown should be designated as a historical district or area, [and whether] within those parameters, one cannot tear down the buildings. And most of us object to that because, as I said, Chinatown has a very old housing stock. People viewing it as simply for tourism, is one thing; but people who live there, they want to modernize this place to make it livable. The rooming houses that exist now where our seniors live are not livable. Does this mean that they will use money for extra garbage pickup or put in more transportation or parking? Yes, we do

need that. But does it also mean no new buildings for Chinatown? No, that means the historical-land-marking of every building so you can stop growth. We do not need that.

Chinatown's two types of publicity, one conducted by the mainstream and the other by the locals, do not have the same meanings: the first is racial and contributes to the mechanism of global racism, while the second is ethnic. The first sells a racialized site or exoticism; the second an ethnicized site or cultural roots. The first dichotomizes the process by seeing the tourist and the native as two distinct entities, while the second connects the local to the Chinese visitor in search of cultural roots and similarities in the name of national unity, a circuit of the transnation.

Commoditization favors globalization and sustains the global process by way of maintaining transnational relations between the ethnopole and the homeland and other diasporic sites. For example, the Chinese retail stores display gifts made in China, Hong Kong, and Taiwan. Merchants purchase them overseas to refurbish their stocks. This global market circuit is made possible by the tourists who consume them. Thus, Chinatown has become a first or secondary market for some family firms in China.

Racism in its globality is commoditized. Once used to segregate, inferiorize, and exploit people as a source of cheap labor, racism now makes money by exploiting their site. The cycle is complete, from the exploitation of the people to the exploitation of the site. Thus, global racism has a local economic basis that supports its cultural practice.

3
Japantown: The Deglobalization of an Ethnopole

The opposite of globalization is *deglobalization* or perhaps *unglobalization*. Globalization implies the existence of its opposite, that is, *nonglobalized locality*. In a sense, *preglobalization* is the first step toward globalization because it implies the recognition of locality as a site of social practices. However, preglobalization, which suggests a not-yet-globalized reality, is a different concept. Preglobalization is a passive concept, though not a static one, and deglobalization is an active state of being. The latter process presupposes an active form of *delinking* or *deconnectedness*, suggesting that the community was previously globalized and is being unglobalized.

By "deglobalization," I refer to the process by which a community, in this case an ethnopole, is delinked willingly or unwillingly from its extraterritorial diasporic and non-diasporic ties. In some cases, deglobalization is achieved for the purpose of the group's extinction, as in the case of the Jews in Hitler's concentration camps, or for the purpose of relocation and isolation, as in the case of the Japanese Americans during World War II.

But what does deglobalization entail as a process and an outcome? First of all, I must admit that only rarely does the process encompass an entire community. More commonly it emanates from an individual or an institution who has decided to pull back from extraterritorial connections. In some cases, it is forced upon people by external circumstances. It is rare in the case of an entire community because it presupposes that everyone would want to do this at the same time, and that such a practice would be advantageous to everyone. Because of the rarity of the phenomenon, the deglobalization of Japantown makes an important object of study. This focus will shed light on the process of globalization itself, and in this way both facets of the phenomenon can be unveiled.

Since deglobalization of a community is often a state-led project, it is made up of a series of *subsidiary processes* that entail global delinking, forced isolation, resocialization, and the control of emotions and feelings despite much longing for reconnection with overseas family members, and it has its array of personal and collective consequences as well. Emotions can be domesticated, but they cannot be fully deglobalized, because this requires the full cooperation of human agents who may be unwilling or unable to cooperate. Since in the case of a community, deglobalization cannot be a permanent phenomenon, but rather is transitional, it also entails *reglobalization*. Among the three ethnopoles under study, Japantown is the only one that experienced this generalized form of deglobalization.

The Japanese began to arrive in the city of San Francisco in large numbers only after the enactment of the Chinese Exclusion Act of 1882, and they slowly developed their enclave in the South of Market area with sufficient stores and hotels – some of them located in Chinatown – to meet the daily needs of Japanese American urbanites and incoming Japanese immigrant laborers. On April 18, 1906, an earthquake struck the city of San Francisco and did much damage to the downtown, or financial, district. Most of the structures in this part of the city were demolished, and so were those in the nearby Japanese residential settlement along Stevenson and Jessie Streets. The post-earthquake blaze consumed much of the housing left standing. City officials, with the help of federal troops from the Presidio, were able to contain the fire along Van Ness Avenue to prevent it from spreading itself westward, and thus protected the houses and other buildings in the Western Addition. Van Ness Avenue became the line of separation between the fire burning downtown on the east and the safe residential area in the west. It was in the midst of this human catastrophe that the Japanese residents of South of Market were forced to decide where to establish the post-earthquake Japantown.

One month after the earthquake, the San Francisco-based, Japanese-American newspaper *Shin Sekai (Japanese Daily New World)* – now relocated on Geary Street in the Western Addition after its building in the downtown area burned – published on May 17, 1906, a thoughtful and memorable editorial *"Nihonjin-Machi Mondai"* [The Japanese Town Issue] weighing the community's options in relocating its devastated South of Market enclave. The editorialist, who signed his name with the initials K.K. – perhaps to hide his identity from a few Japanese entrepreneurs engaged in shady business activities in Chinatown, and perhaps to insinuate that his opinion reflected the views of the larger community – gave direction as to what should be done in the near and distant future. In asking a rhetorical question about an appropriate site for the new Japanese town, he proposed two options. Surprisingly, he did not see the South of Market location as a possibility. He states that

> I believe two different kinds [of Japanese Town] will develop. The first of these will develop hand in hand right alongside Chinatown's growth, having connections with so-called 'bad quarters' catering to the Chinese... The second will be similar to the one which formerly existed around Stevenson and Jessie Streets. It is difficult to detect just exactly where this *Nihonjin-Machi* will emerge, but considering factors like rentals and means of living, I think it will very likely center itself formally around the neighborhood of Fillmore Street.[46]

The editorialist was right: this is precisely where Japantown is now located.

The editorialist explains that the development of a Japantown next to Chinatown would be a source of perennial problems for the reputation of the community. In this scenario, he foresees the possibility of unscrupulous and disreputable Japanese businessmen engaging in illicit, scandalous trade and shady activities. He does not see this as what the community wants or deserves.

In contrast, he proposes the Western Addition as a more appropriate site, reaching this conclusion based

> on the observation that the Japanese here in San Francisco are not financially able to lease new structures which will be built on fire-wracked sites. They will therefore have little choice but to seek rentals such as those in the Fillmore District that survived the earthquake and fire.[47]

He further sees this new Japanese town as composed of the law abiding citizens of the former South of Market enclave and some reputable businessmen who had legitimate stores in or near Chinatown. He predicts it will be the biggest Japantown in San Francisco and will eventually overshadow Japanese clusters in other parts of the city.

This editorial is a central document that helps us understand the mind-set of the residents, the set of options they confronted, and the vision they held for the new community. In a sense, the new Japantown was created in their minds before it was actually established. While the first Nihonjin-Machi was not planned in advance by the community but was an accident of history, one that developed as a result of the white community's racial discrimination, the second Nihonjin-Machi evolved out of thoughtful planning, and consensus building in the community. In this sense the editorial served as a catalyst that brought the community together in the pursuit of a common goal. Here "subaltern and informal planning" means not the actual planning of buildings, streets, and infrastructure in general, but the imagining of the locale and the relocation of residents. The editorialist projects the new site as "consisting of hotels at first. No doubt, restaurants, grocery stores and other general merchandise stores will also soon make their appearance. This will become the largest Nihonjin-Machi in San Francisco."[48]

In hindsight, it appears that the editorialist also contributed to the growth of other post-earthquake Japanese clusters by recommending that the residents not immediately move *en masse* to the Western Addition, but rather wait for the price of the house and rent to go down and for better stock to be built. He cautioned the people that some owners and real estate agents would raise prices in order to take advantage of those who had lost their houses to the earthquake and ensuing fire. He predicted that

> as new buildings are completed and become available in the city, rents in the Fillmore District will be forced down, and the Japanese will gradually occupy the buildings in that area. And for now, it would be a big mistake to pay high rents in this area, or to rent defective buildings in need of much repair.[49]

In fact, the wait-and-see attitude the editorialist proposed might have contributed to the growth of three significant Japanese enclaves in the immediate post-earthquake era: in South Park, near Chinatown, and in the Western Addition. Over the years, as the *Issei* (first generation Japanese immigrants) were dying off and more *Nisei* (second generation Japanese immigrants) were relocating to the Western Addition, Japantown emerged – after their concentration camp experience during World War II – as the main center of resettlement for the Japanese-American residents of San Francisco.

"Japantowns" and "Little Tokyos" as ethnopoles

After the first Japantown began to appear in San Francisco during the last two decades of the nineteenth century, similar ethnopoles emerged in Seattle, Los Angeles, Stockton, Sacramento, and Fresno. These were not the first Asian "towns" in California. The Chinese who began to arrive in the state in the mid-1800s had already established Chinatowns in several cities of the western states. For example, Chinatown in San Francisco was already flourishing as a Chinese settlement when the Japanese began to establish their own ethnic enclave there.

How does one go about explaining the existence of these ethnic enclaves? Several explanations have stressed either internal or external factors, or both. For example, Millis conceives of these enclaves as the result of both the low rents that attracted these poor immigrants and the fact that Anglos fled the sites either because of prejudice or the flux of rental costs. He notes that

> the rank and file [of the Japanese] have been forced and led into sections of the city where rents were low, but, as a rule, where houses were being vacated for better ones elsewhere. Once a group has been formed, common language, acquaintance, shops and amusement places cause other Japanese to join it. Available buildings then command high rents as far as the colony spreads. These high rents and prejudice, in turn, cause other races to move elsewhere.[50]

McWilliams sees a correlation between the increase of the immigrant population and the creation of service centers in the port cities where they first landed. He explains the existence of these enclaves as the logical consequence of immigration as service centers developed to meet the daily needs of both residents and nonresidents. He notes that

> as immigrants increased, opportunities were created for service centers in the ports of entry such as Seattle and San Francisco... These service centers (which later became Little Tokyos) were usually located near an already existing Chinatown, which, in turn, was located in the "skid-row" section of the particular city.[51]

He sees them as having three locational characteristics, that is, as being established in a port city, developed near a Chinatown, and located in a less desirable part of the city.

Smith sees the federal Gentlemen's Agreement of 1907, which stopped the ongoing migration of Japanese laborers to California, as the principal cause for the establishment of Japantown. As he puts it,

> When the Gentlemen's Agreement put a stop to the entry of laborers, and those who had decided to stay here began to send for wives, communities began to take shape. Then, in Seattle or

Sacramento or Los Angeles, in Walnut Grove or Stockton or Fresno, you would find the Nihonmachi, the Japanese town.[52]

This federal action led the Issei to send back home for wives and therefore stabilized the settlement. Once married, they settled and developed these niches to fulfill their needs. This period, between 1907 and 1924, saw a massive migration of the "picture brides," Japanese women who came to meet and marry their prospective Issei husbands. 'Probably much less than half of the wives who came were "picture brides." Issei men preferred to return to Japan to have a marriage arranged. This was especially true of urban Japanese. In these "arranged marriages", most often the women did get to meet the prospective groom and accept or refuse via a go-between. He identifies prejudice of the larger community and individual longing of the Japanese Americans for community life as two mechanisms that further led to the development and stabilization of Japantown. He writes that

> Shut off from the outside by hostility and from within by their own group cohesiveness, the Japanese built self-sufficient communities, complicated organisms containing within themselves everything but a formally constituted government.[53]

Kitano likewise thinks that both external constraints and internal needs account for the establishment of the Japantowns. He argues that up till World War II, distinct ethnic colonies of Japanese immigrants were established in San Francisco and Berkeley as a result of both outward pressure from the Anglos and the Japanese American's need to be among their own for self-protection.[54]

Okazaki does not give much weight to the idea that the racial structure of housing is the culprit that caused the formation of these enclaves. She sees the enclaves instead as a matter of practicality. The people established themselves in areas where they could have easy access to basic services and facilities. She notes that

> strangely enough, the Japanese chose to settle in an abandoned area around South Park, converting the neglected buildings into hotels, shops, and eventually, into a little community ... Food, clothing and lodging could be found just a few steps from the dock where they landed.[55]

Such an argument attributes choice to the people and ignores the structural constraints within which they selected the location of their settlement.

Nishi, however, provides a more complicated picture of the various forces that account for the location of the enclaves. She sees racial discrimination and housing segregation as the two main culprits, since the ethnics were forced to live outside white areas. She also identifies pull factors that made these niches a natural enclave for the immigrants: their common ethnic background, closeness to jobs and the Japanese language that let them speak to each other and access goods and services in the community. She notes that

> these "Little Tokyos"…were outgrowths of numerous socioeconomic forces and pressures that had long been influential. Discriminatory zoning restrictions segregated the Japanese and excluded them from the better residential districts…Historically, "Little Tokyo" communities developed as a result of the natural affinity of the immigrants for their own people.[56]

Once these enclaves were established, they served as magnets for other Japanese because they provided a vibrant community life where individuals could use their language, access services, and use community cultural institutions and facilities that they could not find elsewhere.

Glenn identifies three variables to explain the formation of the Japanese enclaves: hostility displayed by the dominant group, protection and self-help that attracted individuals to the enclave, and the maintenance "of a sense of identity." She goes on to develop a structural–developmental model to account for the enclave's history. She then distinguishes a "frontier period" (1890–1910) that was characterized by the immigration of the Issei, the predominance of male immigrants, "geographical and occupational mobility," and the rise of hostility against Japanese immigration and immigrants that led to the Gentlemen's Agreement. Next, the "settlement period" (1910–24) was characterized by the immigration of the so-called "picture brides" (all marriages were arranged, but most were not "picture brides"). the establishment of families, newspapers, churches, and language schools; a sizable reduction of male immigrants; the formation of Nihon-Machis and Little Tokyos; and the Immigration Act of 1924, which restricted Asian immigration to the United States. The "stabilization period" (1924–40) followed, characterized by Nisei attendance at high schools and colleges; the development of organizations and associations that catered to their needs; and their departure for the internment camps. Next, the "resettlement period" (1945–60) was characterized by the return of camp residents as well as those who had moved to Chicago or the East Coast. Since the houses in the San Francisco Nihon-Machi were now occupied by Southern blacks, the returnees could not access most of them. Despite this, they began to develop stores and rebuild their community. Finally, the "dispersion period" (1960–present) is characterized by the prominence of the *Sansei* (third-generation Japanese American), the diversity of the group, outmigration, and inter-ethnic marriage.[57]

These studies have shed an enormous amount of light on the local articulation of the enclaves; that is, on the multifaceted relations they maintain with the city and on their internal dynamics. This local approach is limited, however, in the kind of explanation it can provide. A focus on the *transnational and global aspects of the ethnopole* is a necessary corrective in order to explain the *global and local orientations of these enclaves*. Such a focus will explain the global/local articulation in the production, reproduction, and deglobalization of Japantown in San Francisco.

The historical narrative of the evolution of Japantown that I am about to delineate shows that globalization has *multiple temporalities*: denser in some periods (in non-wartime) than in others (wartime), more voluminous in some sectors of society (in families, businesses) than in others (district associations), and more routine for first generation immigrants than their children or grandchildren. Already within the family one witnesses a kind of *generational deglobalization* since Sansei children have become less likely to maintain ties with older relatives left behind in the old country.

Biography of Japantown

Before engaging in an analysis of the deglobalization process, I will provide a descriptive biographical account of Japantown based mostly on oral history in order to offer a historical and sociological context to my interpretation of the phenomenon.[58] When I began this research project, I was totally unaware that Japantown had begun at another location in the city, far from where it stands today. It was during an informal conversation with a *Nisei-Kibei* (second-generation Japanese American born in the United States, but educated in Japan), who was formerly a CEO in a major bank in Japantown, that the issue came to the fore. I had expressed interest in the genesis of the enclave, and this octogenarian, who had spent many years combing Japantown's archives, went on to locate the site of the first Japantown for me on one of several maps he had drawn of Japanese clusters in the city since the beginning of the century. He identified South of Market, mainly between Jessie and Stevenson Streets and from around Fourth to Seventh Streets, as the location of the main Japanese town before the earthquake. However, he also indicated Chinatown as a second site where a cluster of Japanese merchants had carried on their business activities.

In 1900, a sizable number of Japanese had immigrated to the city; their presence contributed to the demographic expansion of Japantown. Nishi informs us that the Japanese Government Act of 1885, which allowed laborers to emigrate to the United States, accounts for that infusion. Thereafter, as a consequence of this Act, the population movement

> increased steadily, the unusual number in 1900 (12 635) being due to an outbreak of bubonic plague in Hawaii which caused ships loaded with Japanese immigrants to be diverted from Honolulu to San Francisco. Subsequent to Annexation by the United States in 1898, there was a secondary migration of Japanese from Hawaii, 1901 to 1908.[59]

The global factor cannot be ignored here, because these two international events reoriented and temporized the flow of Japanese immigrants into San Francisco. The formation and sustenance of the ethnopole heavily depended on that foreign factor. By relocating itself inside the American national space, this foreign factor became a localized reality without delinking itself from its site of origin. So the birth or formation of this ethnopole was itself a global event.

Thus, this early Japantown formed as a result of the recruitment of Japanese immigrants to toil in the fields of California and to construct railroads, their inability to relocate in white residential areas because of racial discrimination and housing segregation, and the sojourner orientation of some who had no intention of living indefinitely in the United States, but wished to amass some money quickly and return home. The latter were transnational migrants living in transition and preparing for their return to the homeland. On the transnational posture of these immigrants, Smith notes that until 1908

> Japanese immigrants in California were young men – students, laborers, merchants, seeking the wealth or the knowledge which would establish them at home. Not one in a thousand expected to stay. Many did go home; many one-time "schoolboys" became leaders in government and industry.[60]

These young men's transnational orientation toward the homeland was sustained and enhanced by their inability to find Japanese women of marriageable age in San Francisco. Around 1900, proprietors of Japanese inns and boardinghouses in the South of Market community were a key factor in the transnational network linking railroad labor contractors and Japanese laborers, since they served as middlemen in these transactions. For an agreed-upon commission, the owner of such an establishment supplied workers to would-be contractors. According to Ichioka, "One of the largest proprietors was Tamura Tokunosuke, a native of Hiroshima Prefecture, who owned and operated three boardinghouses and the Tamura Hotel."[61]

As noted earlier, post-earthquake Japanese clusters emerged in three different sites in the city: South Park, Chinatown, and the Western Addition. By and large, the majority of the businesses in South of Market moved to South Park in the aftermath of the earthquake when it emerged as a bustling Japanese commercial district in the city. The cluster in Chinatown was still seen as a business district, and it did not establish an identity separate from that of Chinatown. The Western Addition cluster, which became both residential and commercial, was known up to the evacuation period as "Little Osaka," perhaps because of the regional origin of the residents or simply in reference to the prominence of Little Tokyo in Los Angeles.

The importance of the South Park Japanese-American community should not be underestimated. It was a strategic location for commerce and a place where rents were low; besides, it was close to the earlier settlement. It presented advantages that could not be found elsewhere. As Oka, the director of the Japantown archives, states, "It was a very convenient location for Japanese going back to Japan or coming in from Japan, or even for those Japanese working in the country outside of San Francisco, coming into the city."[62] For many immigrants newly arrived from Japan and some who worked in the agricultural fields or railroad sector in California, it was the site where they were socialized to the ways of urban America.

The Japanese cluster located at South Park presents a number of singular characteristics. South Park is near the port of disembarkment where most of the Issei landed, and it was the site of the Oriental Warehouse that handled silk, rice, and tea imported from Japan and China. South Park developed as a Nihonjin-Machi because some very popular Japanese hotels, such as Omiya Hotel, Iki Hotel, Bo-Chow Hotel, Kinokuniya Hotel, and stores such as Omiya Company were located there and catered to the incoming Japanese who landed at the nearby

Pacific Mail Dock. "Japan Street" in South Park, now Colin P. Kelly Jr. Street, was once a busy street where Japanese workers performed their daily activities. Since no Japanese were in a municipal administrative position in which they might name a street after their country, it is proper to assume that the name was conferred by the dominant sector in reference to the working-class Japanese presence in the area.

Incoming immigrants and residents were able to access these facilities because they were in the neighborhood, because they could converse in Japanese with the managers, and because of the availability of cheap housing. The community was also characterized by the large number of single men who, as noted, did not expect to stay. Another important characteristic of the community is that because they were bachelors, these men were very mobile. They were ready to go wherever they could find employment, and this contributed to their sense of Nihonjin-Machi as their informal capital city, a center where they acquired their socialization to the American ways of life, and where they came to for business and pleasure.

Above all, this neighborhood was established as a result of segregation practices that prevented its residents from establishing themselves in white neighborhoods, and because some were able to buy land prior to the Alien Land Act of 1913 and develop businesses there that gave more stability to their community, and because of white flight. As incoming Japanese occupied abandoned houses and warehouses in the area, white families – mostly Irish and Italian – moved out to other white neighborhoods. South Park thrived for the next two decades, until the construction of the Bay Bridge, which caused intra-urban migration of most of the population to the Western Addition.

There was also during this period a Japanese cluster centered on Grant Avenue (formerly Dupont Street) in Chinatown. Some of its residents had migrated there directly from Japan or indirectly from South Park. One old-timer recalls that

> in those days Chinatown was pretty notorious for gambling and prostitution... and so forth... Before the war, before Japanese evacuation, well in Chinatown, many of those nicer stores were Japanese art goods and the import–export stores, and there were about 50 of them... [There were also] restaurants, hotels, not necessarily on Grant Avenue but around there.

The Western Addition, unaffected by the earthquake, attracted many Japanese as a place of residence. Victorian houses built in the late nineteenth century presented comfortable residences because they were in relatively good shape. Although racial discrimination was still prevalent, many white home-owners were willing to lease part of their houses to those who could afford them. Some whites who could not afford such dwellings cried foul at the integration experiment led by economic profits. Thus, the Western Addition offers a good example of how economic forces can overshadow race animosity in housing transactions.

One year after the earthquake, the *San Francisco Chronicle* in its Sunday edition of March 24, 1907, published an alarming article on the invading Japanese, flamboyantly titled *"A Greater San Francisco or a Lesser Nagasaki – Which?"* The article gave a glimpse of the Japanese residents in their newly found place in the Western Addition:

> Geary Street, which, between Van Ness Avenue and Fillmore Street, is almost entirely Japanese. Especially is this the case on the block from Laguna to Buchanan, where there are but two whites... Bush and Pine streets are Jap infested, and Gough Street between these two streets, is solidly Japanese.

That alarmist article had no other reason than to alert the Anglo population to the sea change in the ethnic composition of the neighborhood brought about by the earthquake. As if to show the contrast before and after that onslaught of intra-urban migration, the journalist informed readers that

> this is the district formerly devoted exclusively to high-class family hotels, adjoining the St. Hilaire apartments, among the finest in San Francisco. Almost within a stone's throw are the Majestic, Dorchester, Atherton and other big hotels, where the city's transient elite lodge.

The demographic shift in the Western Addition – the site of the new Japantown – had been massive and almost instantaneous. More than 10 000 Japanese were living there in 1907, according to a census undertaken by the police (This was a wild exaggeration used as scare tactic. US Census for 1910 showed 4518 Japanese residents in the entire city of San Francisco.) The police census also provided a list of Japanese businesses in the area, which amounted to more than 300 and included the Japanese *Daily New World,* relocated on Geary Street, and the *Japanese Daily News* on Laguna Street.

Despite the prejudice of local whites, the Japanese were able to establish themselves as a consequence of the laws of the market. We are told that some families built extra apartments or sublet rooms in their houses to Japanese; some did it in order to help pay their mortgage or high rents; others owned hotels and took Japanese in. Rents were being raised at a rapid rate, and realtors did not mind renting apartments to Japanese if the latter were willing to pay more than the white families would; likewise, many Anglo families rented their basements to Japanese as a way to earn extra income.

In a sense the earthquake fuzzied the racial game and gave the Japanese an opportunity for upward residential mobility that would not have occurred in a more stable period. The earthquake changed the grammar of the residential area of the landscape, allowed the Japanese to make inroads into white neighborhoods, and, once there, to strengthen their position of control. Indeed, the earthquake brought paradoxical results for both whites and Japanese.

With the implementation of the Gentlemen's Agreement of 1907, Japanese laborers were no longer allowed to come to the United States. Paradoxically, this led to the great wave of female immigration, as male Japanese residents were allowed under the Agreement to send for their wives or wives-to-be. As Okazaki notes,

> The custom was to have the Japanese man living in America who wish[ed] to marry, write home and ask for a suitable woman to be his bride...The family would then seek out an eligible woman and make arrangements to have her become his bride...Once the arrangement was made, the man would then send passage money to Japan for his bride to come to America.[63]

Issei men borrowed money or used savings to return to Japan to pick a bride. Those who were poor or perhaps "old" were more likely to resort to picture bride marriage. This process led to the development of a more stable family life for the Issei, and this stability contributed to the prosperity of the ethnic enclave economy, as more established families were now involved in the education of their children. This new development also intensified the transnational outlook of the community as Japanese American men either traveled to Japan or sent for wives. In consequence of the Agreement, "female immigrants began to predominate. As a result, the sex ratio among Japanese in America began to change from one that was overwhelmingly male to one that by 1924 was beginning to approach a balance."[64]

While the enclave was very much articulated with the rest of the city in terms of employment and services provided to rural and city dwellers, it had also the characteristic of a globalized local community. By "globalized local community," I mean a neighborhood or enclave that maintains *sustained transnational relations with the homeland and extraterritorial entities that are a key factor to its everyday life*. In this instance, three types of transnational relations were prevalent: correspondence with family members left behind in Japan, sometimes in preparation for one's return to the homeland; business relations with the homeland that became a source of profit for merchants; the Japanese government considered the Issei Japanese citizens and monitored their situation through the Consulate, and the Issei themselves went to the Consulate for assistance; and group transnational relations as materialized in the existence of prefectural associations based on the *ken* system, a Japanese administrative unit. In scholarly literature, local aspects of the operation of this institution are usually emphasized at the expense of transnational relations, though without ignoring the existence of the latter. For example, Smith points out that "the kenjinkai...served as a means of self-aggrandizement for those whose qualities of leadership could find no scope or acceptance in the larger community surrounding the Japanese."[65] Likewise, Light notices that "the hotel and boarding house attracted a clientele from the ken of the owner-proprietor, and naturally the owner-proprietor became the employment agent of kenjin residing with him."[66] These associations sustained the relations of the group with a specific town or province in Japan. These prefectural associations fulfilled two major purposes: they helped incoming migrants in various ways in their resettlement and adaptation process (welfare, employment, information), but were also crucial in maintaining the links between Japantown and the sending community. In addition to these traditional organizations, there were also church-based or secular ones with a more ecumenical membership, such as the Nihonmachi Improvement Association, which provided relief aid whenever a natural disaster occurred in Japan.[67]

In a feature essay entitled "The Japanese: Two Generations of Japanese in San Francisco," published on Sunday, December 23, 1923, the *San Francisco Examiner* revealed the importance of the two main Japanese clusters – the Western Addition and Chinatown – as they overshadowed South Park. By then, the bulk of Japanese business activities flourished more particularly in these two principal niches, each catering to different groups of people. Stores in the Western Addition attracted mainly a Japanese clientele, while those handling both

Japanese and Chinese wares and that dealt with mainstream American buyers and tourists were in Chinatown. The newspaper also identified a number of businesses engaged in transnational transactions, among them "two Japanese banks, a steamship company, sixteen general exporting and importing firms, some fifty or more wholesale dealers in art goods and...a stock and bond house." The existence of these businesses suggests that overseas ties implied constant transnational interactions between the commercial establishments here and their suppliers or headquarters in Japan.

The *San Francisco Chronicle*, in an article published on March 20, 1932, confirmed the continuing existence of South Park as a Japanese cluster – shortly before construction of the Bay Bridge. It also gave a brief description of the enclave's location:

> the...largest is what the Japanese call 'upper town'...the area between Pine and O'Farrell, from Octavia to Buchanan. Another is South Park, below Market. The third is, paradox though it may sound, Chinatown...On Grant Avenue, between Bush and Sacramento Streets, there are seventeen Chinese shops and thirty-six Japanese shops.

Austin provides a description of the Japanese merchant cluster in Chinatown in 1940 and the concentrated residential area in the Western Addition – just prior to the evacuation of the Japanese.

> As for the American trade they cater to it with over a hundred cleaning and dyeing establishments, as well as laundries, curio shops and photograph galleries. The merchant quarter adjoins Chinatown where one-third of the shops are Japanese...the center of the Japanese colony or 'Little Osaka' as it is called...is the corner of Post and Buchanan streets. The shops, restaurants, hotels are here, and all the needs of a self-contained immigrant community are located within a few blocks.[68]

Japanese contribution to the construction of the community antedates World War II. For example, we learn that Japanese money had been injected in the construction of the YWCA. *Hokubei Mainichi* reports,

> It has been established through historical records that a group of Issei Christian women received contributions from Japan and the local community to help build the Japanese YWCA in 1921.[69]

Japan contributed to the well-being of the community not only politically through the ken institution but also by helping financially at certain times when external aid was required. Similarly, Japantown helped out Japanese communities financially in times of national disasters. According to Okazaki, "Whenever a major disaster, such as an earthquake or fire occurred in Japan, many Issei here in America responded swiftly by raising funds, gathering clothes items and survival goods and shipped them to their homeland."[70]

Transnationality affected differentially these three sites of Japanese settlement. South Park depended on transpacific passengers and international commerce. Its boardinghouses and hotels attracted the newly arrived and became a recruiting ground for railroad contractors. Chinatown depended on import and export, traded prostitutes, and provided entertainment to lonely laborers, while Japantown, because it was a heavily residential area with mom-and-pop shops, concentrated transnational family interactions, materialized through correspondence, remittances, the return of children to Japan for schooling, culture and language learning, and family relocation. These forms of transnationality had different tempos: *cyclical,* as in the case of the labor contractors; *routinized,* as in the case of the import–export business houses; *occasional,* as in the case of residents with family members left behind; *transitional,* as in the case of the "picture brides" and later the "war brides"; and *incidental,* whenever a disaster struck the homeland.

Genealogy of a globalized locality

The preceding brief biography of Japantown reveals that local ethnic niches have a global history, and that one cannot grasp the history of their insertion in the city without an archeology of their globality. They are inserted or incorporated in the global city not as isolated local entities, but as *global ethnopoles*. The process of their incorporation, their everyday operation, and their chance of survival as viable communities all hinge on their global connections. The global aspect, then, is not peripheral, but central to their reproduction in the city.

The birth of the Japantown at the South of Market site was an *international event* that required the collaboration of Japanese willing to temporarily leave their country; of the Japanese government, which reversed its anti-emigration policy practice to let them go; of the US government, which facilitated recruitment of Japanese for California's fields and railroads; and of US entrepreneurs who were actively engaged in contracting them as laborers. Without these transnational actors, there would have been no Japantown in San Francisco in the first decade of the twentieth century.

But once that global community was formed, one could not expect it to remain an isolated entity, since many of its residents adopted a sojourner mentality with the intent of returning to Japan once their capitalist goals had been met. Thus, connection with the mainland because of family ties became a permanent feature of the ethnopole, as it is of most diasporic communities.

The history of Japantown is traversed by these transnational family relations as they influence the shape of the enclave. One's household budget could not be used exclusively for the well-being of the household's members, but rather was calculated to take into consideration remittances sent back home. The formation and stability of households depended a great deal on male immigrants' ability to bring brides from the homeland. The transmission of language and culture for the reproduction of Japanese identity was also carried out by way of sending children back to Japan for formal education. In all these arenas, the connection to Japan was necessary to achieve the community's collective goals.

On some occasions, the Japanese invoked that global aspect to resolve their disputes with the city government over what would appear to be purely local issues. As noted earlier, in 1907 the San Francisco School Board ordered Japanese students to attend the Chinese school, thereby preventing them from attending schools with Caucasian students. The anticipated outcome of the ordinance was that it would maintain ghettoization of the Japanese even in the educational arena. As long as they attended second-class schools and remained solely among the Asian population, Japanese American students would not have the advantage of a first-class education and camaraderie with white youngsters, considered a major step toward acceptance by whites, and a stepping stone to fair competition with whites. In this project of minoritizing the others, the Anglo community attempted to manage a double mechanism of exclusion: segregation of Japanese school children from Anglo children and the consequent perpetuation of their marginal status through inferior schools; and the pan-Asianization of Japanese students by forcing them to attend the so-called "oriental school," which would tie their fate to that of other Asian groups in the process of their subalternization.

However, afraid of a surprise attack by the Japanese after their victory on the world scene in the Russo-Japanese war from February 1904 to

September 1905, President Theodore Roosevelt involved himself in the issue, resolving it in favor of the Japanese residents. This was clearly a local issue in which the Japanese used their international connections for its resolution. The Japanese community won not because of its local strength, but because of the military strength of its homeland government called upon to intercede on its behalf.

The collapse of the South Park ethnopole and the intra-urban migration of its residents to the Western Addition were also globally produced. The globalization of the Bay Area economy led to the construction of the Bridge, which itself led to the collapse of South Park as a Japanese enclave.

Japantown had reached its highest level of stability during the period between the two world wars. The Immigration Act of 1924 had dried up Japanese immigration to California and caused a stabilization of the community. Although the Alien Land Act of 1913 prevented noncitizens from buying land, the second generation was coming of age and could buy on behalf of their parents. The presence of a number of Kibei meant that transnational relations with the homeland were being maintained, if not strengthened. The more relaxed Issei – with grown children, sometimes a family business and a little of money after many years of saving – were approaching retirement age and could perhaps use it to visit the homeland. A routine kind of family, commercial, and associational transnational relations with Japan had settled in. It was at this specific juncture, when the globalization of the ethnopole had become wholly operational, that it was forced to deglobalize itself as a result of evacuation, dispersion, and incarceration.

What this brief genealogical analysis suggests is that *local history is global history*: that is, the history of the spatial insertion of the local in the global and the history of the site where the global becomes localized.

Deglobalization

Deglobalization refers to the *delinking* of the local from the global or the global from the local. More often than not it comprises a series of processes in terms of units being delinked and in terms of time period. It may be done gradually or abruptly. My discussion concerns these two modalities of delinking, the ways in which delinking takes place, and what one may call its success or failure. Delinking succeeds when it is able to separate the global from the local, if that is possible. Absolute success must be distinguished from relative success. Delinking fails when, despite the effort and intention to delink, some units manage to maintain their transnational linkages. In other words, the delinking may be a success at the level of government or business, but not so at the level of the family. Hence, the deglobalization process presents itself as a hybrid phenomenon: that is, it succeeds in some arenas and fails in others. In other words, in the same ethnopole *deglobalized units may cohabit with globalized units.*

Deglobalization occurs in various shapes and forms. It is partial when only a sector is affected, and it is total when an entire community is globally delinked. It is cyclical when it occurs routinely at a specific time of the year, and it is transitional when the delinking is provisional – that is, not intended to be permanent. It is active when it is a planned action, and it is passive or dormant when no effort is expended to maintain transnational ties. It can be effected by the state, a group, an individual, or an institution.

Deglobalization can also be the result of an *antiglobalization* posture. This can be initiated by either side of the relationship, because simple interconnectedness may not be seen as desirable. In this sense, the process is by no means linear, evolutionary, or "irreversible." Hannerz notes that "globalization ... can move back and forth, it comes in many kinds, it is segmented, and it is notoriously uneven; different worlds, different globalizations."[71] The same can be said about deglobalization in its peculiarity, unevenness, and temporal segmentation.

Deglobalization of the ethnopole is often a slow process. It happens, for example, when a unit fails to activate or reproduce its transnational ties because of a lack of interest in the affairs of the homeland or because emotional ties are simply absent, as sometimes occurs with third or fourth generation immigrant children.

Deglobalization can also occur as an instantaneous rupture that delinks the local from the global. This rupture may be brought about by war, which makes travel and transnational communication dangerous if not impossible. Deglobalization can also effect a violent rupture, especially when undertaken by the state against the will of the community, as occurred in the evacuation of Japantown's residents during World War II.

Sectoral deglobalization does not affect the totality of the community, since it is not generalized but rather individualized. For example, sectoral globalization was effected by the state in the case of the Gentlemen's Agreement to deglobalize a sector of the economy, that of the transnational labor system that contracted with Japanese workers. In the case of Japantown, deglobalization was a slow process that finally led to a violent rupture. The Gentlemen's Agreement that prevented male Japanese workers from coming to the United States was a first strike. It was intended to slow the immigration of Japanese workers and stop non-residents from engaging in back-and-forth migration. In fact, some returned permanently to the homeland or temporarily in search of spouses. This deglobalization effort also led to an intensive form of gendered transnational relations: the "picture brides" phenomenon, which brought additional Japanese into San Francisco. And while the Immigration Act of 1924 was intended to stop the movement of people from Japan to the United States, that sectoral deglobalization prospect was undermined by the ability of some to send their children back to Japan for formal Japanese education.

The state-led deglobalization process continued as the state forced on evacuation that resulted in the Japanese-American internment away from their locality of residence. This deglobalization by force included the process of *evacuation,* whereby individuals were taken against their will to another location with few, if any, belongings; the process of *internment,* whereby they were incarcerated for a crime they did not commit; the process of *transnational delinking* with the homeland and other diasporic sites such as Peru, Brazil, and Canada where there were sizable groups of Japanese; the process of *dishonorization,* whereby they had to internalize and embody their state-inflicted humiliation and shame; and the process of *disincarceration,* whereby they had to externalize their *ex-con* status, internal convulsion, and external public shame associated with such an experience.

Among all the types of deglobalization mentioned above, the state-led one is the most devastating for the individual and community undergoing this public act of humiliation. It is a form of humiliation that left its mark on the life of the ethnopole for many years. This type of deglobalization stopped the transnational relations of the community at once, destroyed the ethnopole, and relocalized the people in a way that followed the logic and agenda of the state in a state of war.

The violence of the process materializes itself in its abruptness as it disorders the naturalized order of things and reorders it according to a logic that is favorable neither to the ethnopolitans nor to the other polar side of their transnational relations: the ethnopolitans' transnationality evaporates with the state-constructed locality they are called to occupy as detainees under constant surveillance by the state security system.

Local–global consequences of deglobalization

Deglobalization does not occur without leaving its mark on the community at a personal, institutional, or group level, depending on the form it takes. State-sponsored deglobalization led to major disruptions in Japanese family life, and, ultimately, to the collapse of the ethnopole. Each individual and institution in the community was affected by this state of affairs. Statements by two Nisei who witnessed the collapse of Japantown, and who were themselves evacuees, give a taste of what the evacuation was like. An octogenarian Nisei-Kibei recalls his experience:

> When the war broke out, we were ordered to be evacuated and then relocated into detention camps. Two were in California; one in Tule Lake up north, on the border of Oregon; another one at Manzanar, down near Los Angeles. Other than that there were altogether ten of them, ten relocation centers. But prior to these relocation centers – while they were being built – well, we were put into the assembly centers. The one closest here would be... racetracks. These were converted into assembly centers. Those horse stalls were turned into places for Japanese to live in; they were stinky and so forth. We lived in these temporary shelters from around May until early summer and then we were sent to relocation centers.

A ninety-two-year-old Nisei speaks of her experience during the ordeal of evacuation:

> Executive Order 9066, issued by President Roosevelt on February 19, 1942, meant that all Japanese, anyone with at least one-quarter Japanese blood, would be evacuated, and so they started with people living close to the ocean and the bay, and then gradually worked down. My family was living on Post Street. And so, by the time they got to the south side of Post Street, the San Francisco people were being sent to Assembly Center. By the time they got to Post Street, when we were evacuated, we assumed we were going to Assembly Center, but evidently they did not have enough space or did not have it ready, so we were sent to Pomona... All the people who were sent there... were almost sent to Wyoming – High Mountain, Wyoming. To the High Mountain Relocation Center with people from Washington, Oregon, San Jose, and some from Los Angeles. And I don't know about the people who were living in the north out of Geary or beyond Post Street; I think they went to Assembly Center, because most from San Francisco were sent there. And so, when all the Japanese people were sent to the Assembly Center, there were many houses that became vacant.

What transpires through this deglobalization process was the loss of property, including import–export businesses. Since many of the people were renting, after internment they could not always return to their previous places of residence or business. The neighborhood had been transformed almost overnight from a concentration of Japanese Americans to a concentration of Southern African Americans, who were recruited to work in the shipyards. Maya Angelou describes the dramatic transformation she had witnessed in Japantown as a young girl growing up in the Western Addition:

> In the early months of World War II, San Francisco's Fillmore District, or the Western Addition, experienced a visible revolution... The Yakamoto Sea Food Market quietly became Sammy's Shoe Shine Parlor and Smoke Shop. Yashigira's Hardware metamorphosed into Le Salon de Beauté owned by Miss Clorinda Jackson. The Japanese shops which sold products to nisei customers were taken over by enterprising Negro businessmen, and in less than a year became permanent homes away from home for the newly arrived Southern Blacks. Where the odors of tempura, raw fish and cha had dominated, the aroma of chitlings, greens and ham hocks now prevailed... The Japanese area became San Francisco's Harlem in a matter of months.[72]

The availability of housing and the new racial composition of the neighborhood had led several families to move to areas where they could either rent or buy property. This was the beginning of the dispersion of the population; the community would never regain its prewar strength, since, unfortunately, in the 1960s, the San Francisco Redevelopment Agency evicted several Japanese-owned businesses from Japantown to make room for construction of the Japanese Center and the city-led *reglobalization* of the area.

Deglobalization affected not only the local community but also the people of Japan who were engaged in business or family relations with partners in San Francisco. It meant that business engagements could not be executed and immigrants were stopped overnight from sending remittances to their families in Japan. Those who depended on these remittances were, of course, affected by the new state of affairs, and some Kibei who were studying in Japan had to wait until after the war to reunite with their parents and loved ones.

Understanding the deglobalization process helps one to understand the connections of the local with the global and the fact that any disruption in the relationship that affects the local is likely to affect the global as well. Since this analysis unravels the global process in its *backward motion*, it allows us to better understand its *forward motion* as the opposite aspect of the circuit.

In summary, the *birth, growth, stability,* and *death* of Japantown were globally produced – that is, caused by global processes and events. The immigration and resettlement of Japanese workers came about as a result of the *transnational contract labor system* that brought Japanese to Hawaii (before its annexation to the United States) and the United States at the turn of the nineteenth century. The rate at which Japantown was formed was shaped by the cadence and rhythms of US labor demands for foreign workers.

In 1907, the Gentlemen's Agreement froze the immigration of male laborers from Japan, but at the same time led to the stability of Japantown by encouraging the arrival of Japanese women. The resulting families contributed to the stability of the Japanese residential neighborhood because family obligations forced men to look for jobs in the city, and, as a result, become less mobile. In this case, an international treaty impacted the community in terms of its survival – that is, its ability to stabilize and reproduce itself over time – by initiating the official and formal beginning of Japantown as a family-oriented community. The global connection is evident in the community's dependence on Japan to furnish wives for its bachelors. Although the treaty was successful in formalizing a new transnational *gendered* linkage between Japantown and Japan, it failed to totally deglobalize the male sector of the Japanese immigrant labor force, which makes it a failed attempt at *sectoral deglobalization*.

Another attempt to deglobalize and collapse the ethnopole came about with the Alien Land Act of 1913, designed to prevent non-citizens from buying land, a law that affected the majority of the Issei population at a time when they either had no American children yet or their American children were still young. Since they could not themselves become citizens, this mechanism forced most of them to rent (some managed to buy through third parties, i.e. friends or corporations). As their citizen-children became adults in the late 1920s and 1930s, they were able to acquire property if they had the means to do so. This, however, was just about the time an international event – the Pearl Harbor incident – erupted and led to the *deglobalization* and *total collapse* of the ethnopole, as its residents were incarcerated in detention camps and, in the process, lost their businesses, and, in many cases, homes.

4
Manilatown: Global Exclusion and Global Margins

Like other Asian-American ethnic groups in San Francisco, Filipino immigrants once had their own ethnopolis – Manilatown, a ten-block area located in the vicinity of Chinatown. Filipinos, unlike the Japanese and Chinese, who initially immigrated into the United States in the nineteenth century, began arriving in California in large numbers only in the 1920s. Starting in 1898, the US occupation of the Philippines resulted in the end of Spanish colonization of the islands and the beginning of American hegemonic domination of the territory. This new but imposed partnership between the two countries led to the immigration of Filipino students to the United States during the first quarter of the twentieth century to attend American universities for graduate and postgraduate training. These *pensionados*, mostly children of the elite, were supposed to return to the Philippines to build a new Western-trained professional cadre that would develop their country. In the United States, these young professionals lived in cities and university towns for the most part and were not the contract laborers who later constituted the bulk of the residents of San Francisco's Manilatown.

Several factors contributed to the development of Manilatown as an ethnopolis: the occupation of the Philippines by the United States, the recruitment of Filipinos to work in the agricultural fields of Hawaii and California and the fish canneries of Seattle and Alaska, the enlistment or conscription of Filipinos in the military and their drafting for military services during the two world wars, and the practice of housing discrimination by mainstream American society, which prevented them from living in white neighborhoods. However, the location of Manilatown in San Francisco was influenced by the existence of Chinatown, which served as a magnet because it offered affordable housing and social services. Additionally, Filipino immigrants – some of whom were of Chinese descent – felt more at home and free to mingle with their Chinese neighbors. Thus, three factors were at work in the making of this *global ethnopole*: global (homeland and diasporic sites), local (constraints, resistance, and adaptation or simply diasporic status), and transnational (border-crossing relations) aspects.

In Chapters 2 and 3, I analyzed some aspects of the process by which globality becomes localized, or the implosion of the global into the local, and the deglobalization and collapse of an ethnopole. In this chapter I will reanalyze the globalization process from a different angle, that of *exclusion* and *marginalization*. While Chapter 2 addressed the successful outcome of a localized globality and Chapter 3 addressed the collapse of an ethnopole that brought about the condition of its deglobalization, this chapter focuses on the making of a *marginalized global ethnopole* and how it collapsed without being deglobalized, in contrast to the case of Japantown.

Marginality and exclusion have been so far theorized in the context of locality rather than globality, that is, within the framework of the nation-state. However, to explain the process of *diasporic exclusion* and marginality, one must go beyond the realm of the nation-state to place the phenomenon in a transnational context. One may then speak of a *global mode of production* of exclusion and marginality and seek to explain its modalities.

It was the exclusion and marginalization of the poor Filipinos in the homeland that placed them in a destitute situation and made them willing to seek work elsewhere. However, global capital mediated their migration, displacement, and reinsertion in the margins of US society. The US–Spanish war that led to the US occupation of the Philippines was undertaken as a way of providing direction to global capitalism as a system of accumulation and social control. Thus, global capitalism extracted the workers from their homeland, provided the context for their emigration, and exploited them in the United States as a *racialized reserve force* that, in general, compressed working-class wages.

The American occupation of the Philippines developed the conditions for Filipino immigration to the United States, and influenced its flow, rhythms, and direction. The ideology and practice of the colonizing power racially redefined these colonial subjects, caused their migration via the contract labor system, and inserted them in the marginal social space of the nation. The traveling ideology of the hegemonic colonizing power transformed them into *traveling subjects* and *reracialized* them in a different hierarchical color code, so as to reposition them in the margins of their country of adoption. While in the homeland the dominant ideology defined them according to the hegemonic rules of the colonial context, once they emigrated they were redefined according to the racial code as shaped by local conditions in the United States. In a sense, these marginalized individuals were unable to cross the *racial border* either at home or abroad, since they were excluded from the mainstream in both sites. The data below will allow us to unveil the peculiarities of this form of transnationality undertaken under a *general condition of exclusion and marginality*. This is one way that social class becomes an important factor in the engendering of globalization.

Exclusion and marginality have not only a local content as a result of local interactions, but also a global content. To understand how marginalization and exclusion are globalized, one must deconstruct the content of both processes within the production of Manilatown. I posit that the US occupation of the Philippines marginalized the people by imposing a foreign power and establishing the frame for the direction of their migration. Moreover, once arrived in the United States they were marginalized according to racial rules that overrode all other factors and that immensely contributed to the reproduction of their social position in society. These racial rules incarcerated them both socially and physically in "Manilatowns" and "Little Manilas."

"Manilatowns" and "Little Manilas" as marginalized ethnopoles

Manilatowns emerged in several cities in California in which there was a significant Filipino population, for example Los Angeles, Stockton, and San Francisco.[73] The formation of "Little Manila" in Stockton is in many ways similar to that of San Francisco's "Manilatown." Herminger attributes the development of the former to a constant migration of Filipinos to Stockton during the period between the two world wars, coupled with housing discrimination. She states that "the influx began in 1927 and the population of Filipinos in Stockton kept growing until it came to be known as 'Little Manila.'"[74] Here, as in other California cities, the newcomers were living both inside, and in the vicinity of, Chinatown. One street, Eldorado, functioned as the epicenter of the ethnopole.[75]

McWilliams was the first to provide a systematic explanation of the formation of Manilatowns in the cities of the western states during the first half of the twentieth century. He found that the Manilatowns lacked stability, that they were not permanent settlements. The fact that Filipinos were transient and did not own the houses or apartments they lived in prevented their enclaves from becoming stable neighborhoods. According to Coloma, perhaps another factor that precluded the stability of Filipino settlements was the Repatriation Act of July 10, 1935, which attempted to lure Filipinos into returning home so that the unemployed would not be a burden to the cities where they lived.[76] To this effect, McWilliams notes that

> President Roosevelt signed the 'Repatriation Act' under the terms of which Filipinos were offered free transportation back to their homeland... But Filipinos who took of the offer could not again reenter, so, in effect, the Repatriation Act was a deportation Act, or was intended as such.[77]

Transient living conditions were detrimental to the stability of these immigrant communities and to the development of enduring bonds of friendship among neighbors as well. He further argues that Manilatowns in the western states were "convenient service centers" used by Filipinos "in periods between jobs" and sees these sites as lacking a personality of their own. Rather, such a site would emerge as an "appendage to some long established Chinatown or Little Tokyo."[78]

The instability of the Manilatowns, according to Kirk, is the result of both the inability of Filipinos to develop a family life and their role as a mobile labor force in the US economy. He argues that the 1930 census shows a male-to-female ratio of nearly fifteen to one, with the majority of the Filipino immigrant population less than thirty years old.[79] In the absence of a sizeable proportion of immigrant women of Filipino descent, Caucasian women constituted one possible avenue for prospective mates. However, that avenue was blocked by a California law enacted in 1935, that strictly forbade Filipinos from marrying whites.

Moreover, Melendy attributes the lack of stability of Manilatowns to "California's [longstanding] discrimination against minorities in real estate and housing," implying that these enclaves came into existence as a result of racial discrimination and housing segregation. He cites the seasonal nature of work as another factor.[80] As he puts it, "During the winter Stockton's temporary residents went to Los Angeles or San Francisco to seek other employment or to share with their fellow countrymen the varied experiences of urban living."[81] In so doing, he places

80   *The Global Ethnopolis*

the Manilatowns in a rural–urban continuum that continually fed their existence and for which they constituted a pole.

Influenced by McWilliams, Mangiafico also regards the Manilatowns as ephemeral settlements. However, he considers seasonal employment to be the main cause of Filipinos' mobility and inability to develop permanent settlements equal to those of Japanese and Chinese immigrants. He dismisses the typical Manilatown as no more than "a stopping place in periods of idleness and the place to go for entertainment: gambling, dancing, cockfighting."[82] Pido expresses a similar view, explaining that Manilatowns were places where "Pilipinos congregated between jobs or when they were in town."[83]

In her study of the Filipino experience in California, Crouchett provides another explanation about the formation of these little enclaves:

> The Filipino immigrants sought refuge in Filipino neighborhoods not only because they were not allowed (and could not afford) to live in American residential districts, but also because here among their own people they felt protected from persecution. Thus, little settlements of immigrants...sprang up in California cities and formed little islands of nationalities within the dominant culture.[84]

In a racist climate of insecurity, these ethnopoles provided a shield of protection to the Filipinos and a home away from home as well.

What is missing in this brief history of explications and interpretations of these ethnic communities is the global connection. Much energy is expended in relating their marginalization to the local racial climate and not enough to global linkage that at the same time reinforced their exclusion and prevented their total control by the local state. This paradoxical situation expresses the condition of the diaspora, which deals with both the homeland and the country of adoption. While one cannot ignore the role of racial discrimination and housing segregation in the production of these ethnopoles, it is also necessary to see them the result of a process of reterritorialization that provides an infrastructure to identitary constructions and expressions, a manifest way of expanding and anchoring inside the United States the transnational space of the Philippines transnation.

The social positioning of these ethnopoles was not of the residents' choosing; it follows the logic of their exclusion as non-white immigrants and their marginalization in the hierarchical spatial order of the mainstream. It is precisely inside these marginal locations that they entertained their global connections via the arrival of newcomers, return visits to the homeland, maritime correspondence, and remittances sent home. Because these processes fed and expressed the homeland orientation of immigrants, they contributed to the maintenance of the ethnopoles as global entities and to the reproduction of the marginalized status imposed on them by the mainstream community.

Genealogy of San Francisco's Manilatown

The interplay of the implosion of the local in the global and the global in the local comprises the history of Manilatown; that is, its history is that of an ethnopole where the global intersects with the local. Manilatown was born as a global entity that came into being because of US occupation of the Philippines, which facilitated both the Filipinos' emigration to the United States, and their exploitation by US businesspeople who sought them out for cheap labor.

In an effort to unveil the intricacies of the formation and growth of San Francisco's Manilatown, I engaged a Filipino professional – who had both visited the enclave on countless occasions while growing up in the city and then lived there for several years as an undergraduate student – in a lengthy but informal conversation. I also spoke to other Filipinos who had once resided in Manilatown but later moved out and rented apartments elsewhere in San Francisco or in the South Bay Area. Among them, an older Filipino man who had once served as an intelligence agent during President Ferdinand Marcos's years in office briefly summarized his view of the history of Manilatown:

> When I came, I met many old-timers who told me about the history of Manilatown. There was a shortage of Filipino girls. At that time they could not marry Caucasians. They worked seasonally. They went to Alaska, and when they were through they returned to Manilatown. Since they did not have family here, Manilatown was the closest thing to a family. You know, for the old-timers that was their family. There were a lot of seamen. When they came by, they went to Manilatown. When they came to town, they naturally sought out Manilatown for shelter and entertainment.

The Filipino professional I spoke to was more loquacious; he was an active member of the neighborhood and part of the story he told was:

> One of the main things, if you look at the history of Manilatown, was that it was a disembarkment point. It was the first settlement of

the Filipinos in San Francisco where the *Manongs*, as we call them, lived. The first wave arrived in San Francisco and stayed in an area that was adjacent to Chinatown. That is very common when you go to other Manilatowns, other parts of, let's say, California, like Stockton or L.A. So in San Francisco's Manilatown, there were tenement buildings where they all lived and [were] predominantly men. There were hardly any women. The few women who came over and married lived with their families and children in South of Market. So Manilatown was a bachelors' community.

Manilatown was a place from which they migrated around the West Coast to work in different seasons. Because it was that kind of an unstable neighborhood, they could come in and out... It was not something that would fully grow outward, but it would just remain on that strip. There were quite a few businesses there, but it was not a business district. It was warded by Chinatown and the financial district. The Filipino workers did not build an economic base there. After World War II, the expansion of the financial district, which exploded outward, overran Manilatown but could not overrun Chinatown because the economic base of the Chinese community was already there.

Until the end of World War II, the development of Manilatown was hampered by three internal factors: the immigration pattern of Filipinos, the seasonal work they were called to do in order to maintain themselves in the United States and send money to family members left behind, and their retirement from the military and civilian sectors, which forced them to make do with fixed incomes.

The Filipinos who resided in Manilatown were for the most part individual immigrants who landed in San Francisco in search of labor and who were recruited there for the agricultural fields of the San Joaquin Valley. Among those, some returned to San Francisco during the dead season to spend their idle time there and socialize with other Filipinos working in low-paying, dead-end jobs – as cooks, janitors, bellboys, and the like. In San Francisco, when out of a job, some of these Manilatown residents were recruited to work in the fish canneries of Alaska and Seattle. With the outbreak of World War II, however, more sedentary and better-paying employment became available to them in military installations, including, according to McWilliams, "shipyards and other defense facilities. Those who served in the armed forces were also eligible for citizenship."[85]

Filipino immigrants comprised by and large a mobile and transient population, ready to move wherever they could find jobs. The structural constraints imposed on them by the segregated labor market, their inability to develop a business district that could help stabilize the enclave, and the Repatriation Act that singled them out for *refoulement* to the Philippines had all militated against the strengthening of Manilatown as an enclave. Perhaps the major obstacle was the fact that they lived in hotels and rooming houses because of housing discrimination, poverty, and the fact that most of them were single men. The image that we have of Manilatown residents in journalistic, autobiographical, and scholarly writings is that of an itinerant population constantly in motion.

The seasonal work they did gave a tempo to the ethnopolis. Their recruitment for the agricultural fields or the fish canneries was an elaborate scheme with operators who sometimes recruited them on the ship's deck as they arrived or in the hotels, and who made arrangements for their transportation to their work. Hotel managers sometimes sent Filipino assistants to recruit them as potential guests. Seasonal work allowed them to experience both rural and urban living. They used the money they made in the fields to pay for their everyday expenses in the city, including entertainment, since the majority of them were single men.

Not every Manong lived in a hotel or rooming house during the period between the two world wars. A few were able to rent apartments for their families in segregated areas. As noted by one person interviewed by Cordova,

> By 1930, my son was born so we moved...We got a flat... [with] four bedrooms...We asked our townmates to come and share with us also...We rented a room to them. That's how we get by.[86]

While living in Manilatown, some managed to frequent enclaves inside white areas for entertainment. On January 22, 1936, the *San Francisco Chronicle* ran a front-page article titled "Filipinos' White Girls: Waitress Tells of Mixed Race Parties." The article refers to a party held "in a flat near Turk and Laguna streets attended by Filipino men and white girls." Moreover, Filipinos were not restricted from frequenting some public places, especially if the purpose was to entertain the mainstream public. On such occasions, they performed under the gaze and surveillance of the Anglo-American community. The *San Francisco*

Chronicle of February 13, 1942, reports, for example, that "Miss Grace Fernandez 15, of 45A South Park Street... will be crowned 'Miss Heroic Philippines' by Lieutenant Governor Patterson at the mardi gras which the Filipino colony is giving tomorrow night at the Veterans' Auditorium."[87] This was a public gesture by the mainstream to give a friendly face to the colonial policies of the US government in occupied Philippines. Here the "local" is used to project the "global" in a positive light – a good example of how an excluded group can be *momentarily included for the purpose of performing its exclusionary status*.

By the end of World War II, Manilatown served as a dumping ground or reservoir for older Filipinos with fixed incomes, who had retired either from agricultural labor, the army, or the navy, and especially for those military personnel in the Philippines who were coming to the United States as veterans. Their old age and poverty, along with housing segregation, constrained them to a life in cheap hotels and rooming houses located inside the parameters of Manilatown.

The great exodus after the war brought a slow demographic shift in the location of the majority of the Filipino American population in California. From 1950 to 1960, the Filipino population in San Francisco nearly doubled as a result of the huge migration of workers from agricultural fields to the city. Wallovits reports that "out of a total of 65 459 Filipinos in the state in 1960, 52 091 had moved to urban centers."[88] New urban immigrants who came to San Francisco went mostly to Manilatown, the Mission District, and Bernal Heights.[89] Between the census of 1960 and that of 1970, the Filipino population doubled in San Francisco, going from 12 327 to 24 694.[90] By 1974, it was estimated to be around 35 000.[91]

A middle-aged Filipina whose family came to the city from the Philippines during the post World War II era had the following to say:

> What happened after World War II is that you begin [to notice] the emergence of the second wave. You see people like my mother and other women [who] started coming over in numbers because Filipinos [who] were part of the 1st and 2nd infantry had married. They brought over their wives and offspring, and the change after the war was that Filipinos could become citizens and own property, so they began to quickly move out of the city.

The second wave of Filipino immigration was in many ways different from the first. After the war, new immigrants came as families, and some Filipinos in the United States returned to the homeland to seek spouses, whom they brought back to the United States. Members of this new wave began to establish themselves wherever they could find apartments with suitable rents. Because of the families they were developing, and because they were better off than the first wave in terms of occupational skills, education, and money this wave was not interested in hotel life. In a sense, this new group did not contribute much to the strengthening of the old Manilatown.

With the second wave, fewer came to the International Hotel, for example, the biggest and most popular hotel among Filipinos in Manilatown, because of family members who accompanied them and because housing segregation was waning a little. The International Hotel was more suitable for singles. Some of those who came as single men stayed at the International Hotel until they could find a job and move out, often to rent an apartment or rooms from other compatriots who had bought houses in racially mixed neighborhoods.

Thus, the beginning of the decline of Manilatown coincided with the end of the war, as clusters of Filipino living quarters were established in other parts of town. A Filipino who grew up in San Francisco recalls that

> this is when it began to die, because the Filipino community was no longer concentrated in one strip anymore. It began to grow everywhere, from 16th in the Mission to outer Mission. By the time I was born [in the late 1940s] there were already a lot of Filipinos in the Fillmore area. So, the Filipino community became really fragmented. As the financial district expanded, it became a place where people looked down upon Manilatown's Manongs because they were poor, because they did not have family, and because of the people's fighting. When I was growing up, I was warned never to go there, yet my godfather had his own business there. He was a photographer, and my father would frequently go there. Manilatown began to die out as Filipinos set up businesses in the Mission and Tenderloin Districts and large numbers were moving to Daly City.

The third wave began to arrive in the mid-1960s. With the Civil Rights Act of 1964 and the Immigration Act of 1965, the third wave brought to the United States a large number of professionals, students, and people who had come to join their families. These individuals, unlike their predecessors, were able to locate wherever they wanted to because housing segregation had become illegal. Instead of going to Manilatown, the majority of these middle-class newcomer immigrants settled in Daly City, South of Market, the Richmond District, and various other suburbs of San Francisco.

By the late 1960s, with the closing of some downtown hotels, Manilatown had lost most of its population, including those who had died of old age. It became more and more confined to the 800 block of Kearny Street, where the International Hotel, the last remnant of Manilatown, stood.

The cadence of the ethnopole's development depended on the strategies of the US occupation of the Philippines, which either lured some Filipinos to return or forced them to stay abroad, and the labor needs of the California economy. The Filipino immigrants had no say on these two vital issues that influenced their daily lives. In other words, one cannot grasp the history of Manilatown outside the context of the history of the US occupation of the Philippines. For example, the long waiting time before the United States agreed to the independence of the Philippines in 1946 weakened the position of the ethnopolitans in San Francisco, since they had *no homeland government to speak on their behalf.*

Even during the Marcos administration, as Manilatown became known as a site of protest against the atrocities and dictatorial ways of his government, residents spent much energy worrying about the fate of the homeland and not enough about organizing the neighborhood. Once again, the history of the ethnopole was intertwined with events in the homeland. The ethnopole provided a stage where diasporic dissenters who were not necessarily active in ethnic politics could air their political views about the homeland. In this charged political context, the Manongs neither expected nor received help from the homeland government when they began to experience problems with the International Hotel landlord.

Hotel life

Benito Millano, who had come to San Francisco in 1930, gives a glimpse of hotel life in the early days: "We landed in San Francisco... We took a taxi to the Navarre Hotel on Stockton Street and stayed there about a week... An organization came to the Navarre Hotel and took us to work on the farm in Carmichael, near Sacramento."[92]

The early years of Filipino immigration into the United States were crucial in the formation of Manilatown because life revolved around the rooming houses and hotels. Some hotels were known in the Philippines, and many immigrants, upon landing in San

Francisco, went directly to one of them in order to stay among compatriots. Hotel managers had developed schemes with the help of Filipino operators to recruit incoming Filipinos for the hotels. Many of these hotels in downtown San Francisco could not have stayed in business as long as they did had it not been for these steady Filipino customers.

Because so many Manongs were full- or part-time residents in these hotels, they were able to help each other and develop a group life, the closest approximation to family life. However, hotel life had its limitations. For example, as they could not always cook for themselves in these rooms, they had no alternative but to eat at cheap nearby restaurants owned by Filipinos, Japanese, and Chinese. In particular, Chinatown's proximity made it possible for them to eat conveniently in the cheap restaurants of the enclave.

The cheap residential hotels were processing centers in two important ways. They were the sites where Filipino immigrants learned about US society through their interaction with seasoned compatriots, and where they negotiated their services and were recruited for the fields or the fish canneries. These were also sites where they plotted out their strategies to move to different residential quarters once they were able to do so. As processing centers, these sites became points of juncture to which they returned to meet old friends, and even those who had never resided in these hotels came back to Manilatown from time to time to renew their memories of the homeland.

The presence of Filipinos in these hotels led to the creation of some services (barbershops, restaurants, pool halls) in Manilatown and its vicinity to serve this clientele. A few of these businesses were owned and operated by Filipino managers. However, the seasonal variation in the life of the hotels' residents affected the ability of their owners or managers to project revenues, which made it difficult for them to stay in business. However, the hotels' permanent residents were able to pay their bills because of employment found nearby. For example, Jose Sarmiento recalls,

> I was a waiter in a private boarding house for old men and old ladies on Clay Street in San Francisco...My uncle arrived in San Francisco, and he could not get a job – he was a retired navy man...So, I gave him my job cooking for the family. From that place, in 1928, I took a job in a drugstore.[93]

Julio Orille also found employment near his place of residence: "In 1941 I moved to San Francisco and began working at the Post Cafeteria at Bush and Kearney Streets."[94] Alfonso Yasonia who left the agricultural fields for city life in 1948 recalls: "I found another job as a housemaid on Eddy Street in the Tenderloin area of San Francisco. I worked there for fourteen-and-a-half years straight, and I know the hotel like a book. I took care of the entire building."[95]

As the Manhattanization of San Francisco ensued in the 1960s, hotels in the vicinity of Manilatown were demolished as part of urban renewal. The International Hotel came to be identified as the center of the enclave by both Filipinos and the larger public because it was the last remnant and the most enduring feature of Manilatown.

Hotel life, because it was not supposed to be a permanent way of life, provided the context where transnational and local identities collided and meshed with each other in their fragmentation, hybridity, and multiplicity. The hotel was an ambiguous site of the transnation located inside the ethnopole and not necessarily a part of it, since management belonged to the mainstream. Social identities were performed in a transnational arena that allowed the actors to express their embodied practices in a given site of the transnation where they happened to live at any given moment.

Racial discrimination and housing segregation

In 1943, Captain Guerrero, an FBI agent, and his wife, a newspaper reporter who was then working for the Office of War Information in San Francisco, after months of living in a hotel looked time and again for an apartment. At each step of the way, landlords refused to rent an apartment to this Filipino couple. They decided to inform the *San Francisco Chronicle* about the level of discrimination Filipinos had to endure:

> We are not bitter about this, [said Guerrero,] but we feel that we and other Filipinos who are American citizens should not be discriminated against. Did not the US government feel that I was good enough to be the only [Filipino] FBI agent this government ever has had?...Hasn't the government given me the rank of Captain?...We hunted for apartments all over the city, but none would have us. Some [landlords] tell us point blank that they will not rent to us, but others invent all kinds of stories in order to be subtle in their discrimination.[96]

A senior Filipino American shared with me his recollection of another incident that happened to a friend of his in the 1950s: His friend "wanted to buy a house in the Forest Hill area, and he was told to look for another place. The realtor did not want to show him the house, and he was not given an opportunity to buy. When someone was selling a house, a neighbor would ask them to please sell to Caucasians and not to colored people."

One of the crucial obstacles that prevented Filipinos from mixing freely with whites, confining them instead to specific areas in town, was the racial discrimination that materialized in, among other places, access to housing and public facilities. Until 1946, Filipinos were not eligible to become citizens. They had the ambiguous status of being "nationals" – able to migrate to the United States, enlist in the Armed Forces, and be drafted during wartime, but without the right to citizenship. At the same time, California law forbade aliens from buying real estate. Thus, without citizenship, Filipinos were mandated by law to rent, mostly from whites. California's miscegenation law was repealed in 1948, and so, at least in theory, Filipinos could marry Caucasians, buy land, and become citizens. This set of new laws opened the gate for Filipinos to become full members of American society.

But even then, another set of legal practices prevented Asian Americans from buying houses in white neighborhoods. A mechanism known as the "covenant clause" and widely used in San Francisco prevented white owners of houses in white neighborhoods from selling to non-whites. This ended up being a very effective form of segregation. Since a prospective buyer could not gain access to the covenant clause records, he or she could not challenge in court the decision not to sell. I call this practice a *hidden mechanism of housing discrimination*.

This hidden mechanism of housing discrimination would have failed were it not supported by a *hidden strategy of discrimination* provided by real estate companies and the banks. Agents would not show houses in white neighborhoods to non-whites, but rather would direct them to available houses in non-white neighborhoods. Even if a non-white could afford to buy a house in a white neighborhood, the banks would not provide a loan for the sale. And without a loan the deal could not be closed. Thus, three "white figures" were key to the success of this hidden mechanism: the owner who, because of the covenant clause and personal inclination, would not sell to non-whites; the real estate agent who would not show the house to non-whites; and the banker who would not provide the loan. This practice was ingrained in a *culture of discrimination* and was based on economic calculations and profit considerations. To prevent property devaluation, the white owner would not sell to non-whites; to avoid precipitating white flight and minimizing business returns, the real estate agent would not show the house; and to avoid owner default the banker would not grant a loan, since the non-white owner could be forced out by white neighbors. Should this happen – and there was a good possibility that it could – other houses in the neighborhood, which may have paid mortgages to the same bank, would be negatively affected as well!

Many other facets of racial discrimination helped to forestall housing integration. All served to sustain the separation of non-whites from white neighborhoods. One form that had an immediate impact on housing was the miscegenation law, which prevented minorities from marrying whites. Without this law, inter-racial marriage would have provided an avenue for upward mobility since a white spouse could buy property for the couple. The mixing of Filipinos with white girls was, however, tolerated in places of ill repute, such as bordellos, dime-a-dance halls, and prearranged private parties. While these encounters could alleviate the loneliness of the Filipinos, they did not lead to marriage and a stable family life. These were transactional interactions at the social fringes of a segregated society.

Moreover, discrimination on the bus and in other modes of public transportation brought home the message that Filipinos were not welcome outside of their enclave. But public transportation was frequently the only means for Filipinos to get to and from their places of employment. Valangca recalls:

> One day in the Spring of 1932, my cousin, Seriaco, and I boarded a streetcar on Market Street in San Francisco to get to the Ferry Building to look for a job...I had just paid my fare when suddenly the man behind me shoved and kicked me in the calf for no reason at all. I turned to ask him, "what have I done?" but before I could speak, he growled and said, "come on, you savages – get out of my way."
> A woman sitting in a seat near where I was standing got up to get off. She had been sitting next to a fairly well-dressed, middle-aged man, who was reading his morning paper. I moved to sit in the seat the woman had just vacated, but the man put half of his paper on the seat and said , "I do not want a monkey to sit beside me." I was hurt and embarrassed.[97]

Outside Manilatown Filipinos were not welcome in white-owned restaurants. As patrons, they were ignored or were served last by white waitresses. Valangca tells of his experience:

> Another morning I went to a dinky coffee shop on Geary Street. I sat at the corner near the door. There were two waitresses on duty and the place was not busy. I sat and waited for service for twenty-five minutes or more. But the two waitresses simply ignored me, laughing and joking with the other customers – acting like I was not there. Other customers came and went – some even sat beside me. The waitresses served them but did not bother to even talk to or look at me...I left the shop, feeling low, sad, ashamed; I realized then that I could not go anywhere because I was a Filipino.[98]

During the war years, while walking in the streets of San Francisco, Filipinos were often called "go-go" or "monkey" by white passers-by. At night, some were mistakenly identified as Japanese, and they suffered at the hands of white thugs. It was not enough to endure racial discrimination as Filipinos, now they had to carry the burden of being identified as Japanese enemies as well. Valangca recounts the incident of a Filipino mistaken for a Japanese and the trauma he experienced as three white sailors ran after him. If not for help from a policeman who rescued him, he would not have been around to tell his story. Carlos Bulosan, who witnessed acts of police brutality toward Filipinos, notes, "I came to know afterward that in many ways it was a crime to be a Filipino in California. I came to know that the public streets were not free to my people: we were stopped each time these vigilant patrolmen saw us driving a car. We were suspect each time we were seen with a white woman."[99]

Manilatown would not have remained a segregated ethnopolis had it not been for the police surveillance by the majority, which kept the Filipinos in their place. Valangca recalls that

> without a warning or warrant, the police would come and grab any Filipinos they could find sitting or standing on the side walk...During the period it was not uncommon for the police to periodically harass the *Pinoys* [Filipino Americans], just for being together at a certain location...One Saturday evening in the fall of 1935, while waiting for my turn for a haircut at a Kearny Street barbershop, I heard someone shout, "kap-kap." This was a warning that the police were coming to frisk the Filipino establishment again.[100]

The police routinely invaded Filipino gathering places in Manilatown (pool halls, business places, and street corners). These repeated acts of harassment, discrimination, brutality, and disciplinary control were intended to keep the Filipinos in their place in society – in Manilatown – and to remind them while there to keep order and not disturb the peace of the surrounding white community. Manilatown was an unwelcome enclave that needed to be controlled to prevent it from spreading to the neighboring white residential areas.

Chinatown's proximity

Throughout the western states, each Manilatown was located next to a Chinatown – e.g. in Stockton, Los Angeles, Seattle, and San Francisco. It was as if Manilatown could not maintain a viable existence by itself. There are several reasons that explain their proximity to Chinatown. To begin with, by the time Filipinos started coming to California, the Chinese had already established their Chinatown in San Francisco, a distinct neighborhood that became a home for other Asian immigrants as well. Unable to relocate among whites, the various Asian immigrants found that their best bet was to rent homes in or near Chinatown or another minority neighborhood. Some Filipinos found homes in black, Japanese, and Latino neighborhoods as well. Moreover, since the majority of them were single men, they lived near Chinatown in order to use the services and facilities already established there (e.g. restaurants, barbershops, affordable housing). There were also Filipinos of Chinese descent among the group of immigrants, and these were able to mingle effectively with the old Chinese settlers.

Proximity to Chinatown prevented Manilatown's development as a strictly Filipino neighborhood, since there was constant back-and-forth movement between the two enclaves. The overflow of the Chinese population in Chinatown naturally ended up in Manilatown (and Little Italy as well). And since the Filipinos did not own the land and houses, they could not develop protectionist policies in terms of housing practices in order to give preferential treatment to their compatriots in the selection of renters in Manilatown. In addition, some of the businesses in Manilatown were owned by Chinese, and some residents of cheap hotels inside Manilatown were also Chinese.

Filipinos' dependence on Chinatown was evident also in their dealings with city hall. After President Lyndon Johnson began his War on Poverty, the Chinatown Antipoverty Board of the San Francisco Economic Opportunity Council was established. Their mission was to help the poor in the greater Chinatown area, which included the adjacent Filipino cluster. Two Filipinas – Asuncion Panlibuton and Rose Postorete – were employed as community assistants to make the board aware of urgent problems facing the residents of Manilatown, a circumstance that reinforced Filipino dependence on the Chinatown leadership.[101] Moreover, outsiders tended to see Manilatown not as a distinct neighborhood but rather as part of Chinatown because of Manilatown's Chinese residents, Chinese businesses with distinct Cantonese commercial signs, and the lack of a physical separation between the two communities.

Even when Manilatown was recognized as a separate Filipino entity, it was seen as a little appendage to Chinatown. It could not compare with Chinatown's ethnic visibility, vibrant business sector, and tourist crowd that together made Chinatown shine as an exotic place. Unlike Chinatown, Manilatown did not attract large numbers of tourists, and by the 1970s the Kearny Street ethnopolis did not have much to show to those in search of exoticism. Establishment of Manilatown as a separate enclave could have been accomplished only if the Filipinos had been able to stabilize the population of their enclave, purchase the houses where they lived, and transform the place and perhaps expand it as a residential quarter and a business district. But that spatial expansion could not be achieved because the ethnopole was bounded on the west by Chinatown and the east by the financial district.

A one-street phenomenon

San Francisco's Manilatown as an ethnopolis is identified with part of a street, the 800 block of Kearny Street. The one-street enclave pattern is not peculiar to San Francisco, but is repeated elsewhere in the western states. For example, in Stockton "Little Manila" is identified with Eldorado Street, in Los Angeles with Temple Street, and in Seattle with King Street. Kearny Street took the identity of the enclave because it served as a built place whose facade was worked on to reflect the spirit of Manilatown. Kearny Street's International Hotel, because of the Filipino stores, offices, and residents it housed, was known as the center of Manilatown.

The enclave was where street life best represented the social life in the old country, since it was where people came to mingle with compatriots. And it was often on Kearny Street that an immigrant first became socialized in city ways, where information for almost everything (e.g. housing, the political situation at home) was exchanged, and where the stores that served the community could be found and commercial signs in Filipino languages could be seen.

Kearny Street attracted Filipinos from other parts of town who patronized the Chinese and Filipino businesses in the area. Street corners and certain businesses served as places of gossip and assembly. An old resident of Manilatown recalls the social atmosphere of the area during the 1930s: "Kearny Street between Washington and Jackson in San Francisco was where the Filipino pool halls, restaurants, and barbershops were located. Here Filipinos congregated with their townmates and sweethearts to relax after work."[102] All of this gave an air of the old Manila that no other street could rival. Even when the ethnopolis lost its cachet, the people continued to stick to that street. The collapse of the street as a pole of attraction necessarily meant the collapse of the ethnopolis in its pristine appearance. The fact the Filipinos did not own the buildings on that street meant that the ethnopolis was vulnerable. Their eviction from the International Hotel would eventually lead to the collapse of Manilatown.

Center of attraction

As Manilatown's epicenter, Kearny Street was linked to satellite communities and individual households. In that sense it was a pole of attraction. It is here where the linkage between the old-timers and the new immigrants was daily negotiated.

When an ethnopolis is well entrenched in a city, it becomes a center of attraction for tourists, as is the case with Chinatown, Japantown, and the Mission District. However, most tourists who came to peer at Manilatown had been attracted by Chinatown and only glanced at Manilatown as a side effect. Manilatown was a center of attraction mostly for Filipinos who were living outside the area. Because of its heavy concentration of Filipinos, Manilatown became also a spying arena for the Marcos government. Some of these spies were members of the diplomatic corps (mostly security) attached to the consulate, I was informed by one of them. And, from about 1968 on, the area attracted activists who protested against the unsanitary conditions of the International Hotel, the ill treatment of the Filipino guests, the eviction of these individuals, and, later, the closing of the hotel. The last remnant of Manilatown, the hotel became the focus of activists who picketed the place on several occasions, thereby attracting national and extraterritorial attention to the plight of the residents of this global ethnopole.

Urban renewal and development

The urban renewal movement that would close the International Hotel and other businesses led to a severe and negative impact on the ethnopolis. The small hotels in the area that had provided cheap shelter to older and poorer Filipinos were upgraded and, as a result, became more costly.[103] This caused a massive displacement of the population toward South of Market and other poorer areas where housing was available and affordable. A Filipino politico who fled Manila after persecution from the Marcos government shared with me his view on how the urban renewal program had bifurcated the life trajectory of Manilatown:

> The heart of it was taken away; they lost the place they would come to. Urban development did away with it. It was the same thing with other development efforts in the Western Addition that forced African Americans to move out to other districts.

As a result of a number of factors – such as this increased migration to other parts of the Bay Area, the accelerated rates of inflation resulting from the oil crisis in the early 1970s, and *laissez-faire* competition among developers with Manhattan-like plans to restructure the housing market – rent in particular and the cost of housing in general became much higher than it had been before.[104]

The city was forced to mediate between two interests: the protection of the poor and the expansion of business as a tax base and source of employment. These two interests collided: compassion for the poor, and a decision to allow an expansion of business in the hope that what the poor would lose in terms of shelter, they would gain back in job availability. It was a choice between long-term benefits for the city and presumably short-term losses for the poor. But in fact, urban renewal created a long-term problem for the poor as a result of the tighter low-income housing market.

However, homeowners, in the expectation that business expansion would reduce their property taxes, sided with the city against the poor to capitalize on the short-term advantages of such a strategy. For them, the best choice was to stabilize or reduce their home taxes. If that meant evicting the poor so that business could expand, so be it. The alternative was to let poor people live in this area of high monetary value despite the fact that would be an impediment to business. In such a context, the poor Manongs were vulnerable.

Unwilling to get involved too much in the salvaging of the International Hotel, the city government referred the issue to the taxpaying public for resolution. Necesito informs us that

> in the city elections of November 8, the electorate was asked under Proposition U whether or not the city shall purchase the hotel and use it for low-rent housing...Some 107450 San Franciscans rejected the proposition and only 52859 voted in favor of the proposition.[105]

From the time the Manongs received their eviction notices in 1968 to their actual eviction in 1977, the area around the International Hotel witnessed a boom in the construction industry, with new skyscrapers such as the Bank of America building, Pacific Gas and Electric Company building, Mutual Benefit building, Crocker building, First Savings building, and TransAmerica building, each having more than twenty floors.[106] The rise of the skyscrapers was preceded by the demolition of the cheaper hotels, such as the Palm Hotel at the corner of Washington and Kearny Streets, which had provided shelter to low-income residents.

As these small hotels were evicting their Filipino residents, Kearny Street attracted more attention and became the street with the densest Filipino population. Finally, urban renewal was imminent on Kearny Street as well.[107] The International Hotel was slated for upgrading, since this would bring more profit to the owner. However, this did not happen without a fight.

The demise of the International Hotel

Built in 1854, the International Hotel attracted visitors from all walks of life during the second half of the nineteenth century. The earthquake that did so much damage to the infrastructure of the city did not spare the hotel, and it was rebuilt in 1907.

Wong points out that the existence of the hotel was well known to Filipinos prior to their arrival in the city:

> Aniano Ruivavar, a 66-year-old Army veteran who served from 1919 to 1939, said the International Hotel is known throughout the Philippine islands. Any Filipino arriving the first time heads here. "This is our home," he said.[108]

Alfonso Yasonia, who came to San Francisco on May 3, 1928, tells a similar tale:

> I met somebody on the boat and we got a taxi together and went to the International Hotel...I stayed one week in the International Hotel and then I heard there was work in Stockton. So my friend took me to the Ferry building and told me to take the ferry.[109]

In the mid-1960s, the *United Filipino Association*, a multiservice corporation, began to organize the Filipinos at the International Hotel because most of them were old, had no family in the city, had no place to move to, and were on welfare. As management was about to sell the hotel, ostensibly because it was not up to standard, but also as a way to evict the Filipinos from the premises, the United Filipino Association was able to renew the lease on behalf of the Manongs. This was the beginning of a long fight that lasted until the closing and later demolition of the hotel.

The demise of the International Hotel after more than fifty years of continuing Filipino residence brought an end to this ethnopolis as a thriving community. The problems of the Filipino guests at the hotel began in 1968 when they were told that they would have to leave soon because the building was going to be demolished. The hotel became the center of activities in the 1970s not only because it housed the largest number of Filipinos in San Francisco, but also because it served as a business center, the main site of police clashes with the Asians, the principal site where the Asian population staged public protests, the meeting place for Filipinos clustered around the city, the site where big business, or the Manhattanization of the city, was contested, and the site where the interests of city hall and the Filipinos intersected.

Communities are spatial entities that thrive in spaces of place. The attachment of ethnics to a place turns an enclave into a marker of identity because it provides the infrastructure for social interaction, for enduring social relations, for coping with daily life, and for locating oneself on the social landscape of the city: the space provides a sense of community. The impact of space on the shaping of community life, and vice versa, was ongoing. For this reason, Filipino old-timers did not want to give up the International Hotel, a place that had constituted the site of their ethnopolis for more than fifty years. For them, it was a landmark that deserved preservation, not simply because the eviction of the Manongs would cause them much suffering, but because it would destroy the spatial basis of the community.

The voices of the old Filipino residents were not enough to turn the place into a *cause célèbre*, because elsewhere in the city other poor people were being evicted in other tenement hotels. What started as a local problem involving a landlord and tenants escalated into a city problem that attracted national coverage. This visibility of the enclave must be explained by the interplay of a combination of factors, such as, for example, what Nagai describes as "the key role played by the many political groups and small business renting space in the International Hotel."[110]

As noted earlier, the International Hotel had been the residence of Filipino immigrants since the early 1920s: some who resided there were recent arrivals who came to look for employment and who hoped to work in the fields or the canneries;[111] others were full-time residents who had jobs in the city; and still others were transitional residents who came to the hotel to spend their time between crop seasons, when they were resting or looking for temporary jobs before returning to the fields. After World War II, Filipinos who retired from the canneries, the agricultural fields, and the US armed forces came to settle in San Francisco, and many of them at one time or another resided at the International Hotel. Later, many of the retired servicemen who came here had been denied pension funds for their services in the military. In a law enacted by Congress on September 2, 1958, Filipino servicemen were denied full credit for services rendered in the US army prior to July 1, 1946. The law allowed those who served during this period to collect only half the benefits due them, which meant that they were unable to get essential benefits that would ensure them a decent retirement life.[112] To add insult to injury, a three-judge federal court ruled in 1974 that "most Filipino soldiers who served with the US army in World War II were not entitled to GI veteran's benefits."[113] These former soldiers were left to live in cheap hotels like the International Hotel.

Some blamed the demolition of the hotel on city hall, which sided with big business instead of protecting the poor. Thus Vince Reyes reports in the Stockton-based Filipino newspaper *Ang Katipunan* that "San Francisco's policy of coddling real estate developers and their expansive 'Manhattanization' plans at the expense of the low-cost housing needs of working class minorities"[114] was a major factor in the eviction of the Filipinos from the International Hotel.

In the late 1960s, the hotel was a busy place because its facilities and the services it provided were open not only to residents but also to a large number of non-residents. Emil DeGuzman, then an activist in the movement to save the hotel, provides an informative description of these facilities and services:

> Directly below the International Hotel are some commercial spaces (store fronts) which many community groups have utilized in trying to serve the needs of the community. The EastWind is a drop-in center for newly arrived young people from Hong Kong. There is a Legal Defense Center for those needing draft consultation as well as legal matters relevant to Asians. Lee-Way is a place where brothers and sisters can come to learn self-defense and photography as well as shoot pool. Everybody's Bookstore is a "right on" store concerning itself with movement literature, particularly with material from the People's Republic of China and Asia. Directly below the bookstore is the Asian Community Center which serv[es]the needs of the people in Chinatown...There is also a Chinatown Youth Council which attempts to meet the needs of our young people in the community.[115]

By 1969, the majority of the hotel residents were retirees on a fixed income. Unlike those who resided there in the period between the two world wars, these residents were sedentary – they had no place to go and did not expect to move elsewhere. The number of Chinese and Filipino residents at the hotel at this time decreased to 196, 125 of whom were over 65 years old, 90 per cent of them veterans.[116] An April 1969 survey on length of tenancy at the International Hotel showed that 17 members (12.2 per cent) had lived there for more than ten years, 20 for more than five years; 55 for more than one year and 47 for less than a year.[117]

The same survey shows that 77 were employed and 82 were receiving some combination of welfare benefits, Social Security, and veteran's pension. There were also three minor children and nine students. The economic status of fifteen others could not be verified.[118]

Another survey conducted by the Chinatown–North Beach Economic Opportunity Council in December 1969 indicates that eighteen of them were 65 years old or older, and 90 were between the ages of 40 and 64; 60 were men between 26 and 39 years of age, and fourteen were men between 18 and 25 years of age.[119] These studies indicate that the residents of the International Hotel were not all old and unemployed.

The collapse of the hotel affected not only the residents, businesses, and facilities located within the building but also services in the neighborhood that catered to the International Hotel clientele. In that sense, the fall of the hotel had a snowballing effect on the community. Local businesses lost their clientele and consequently shut down shortly thereafter.

By and large, the Chinese of Chinatown were strong supporters of the Filipino community's attempt to safeguard the hotel, because there were also Chinese living there. Emil DeGuzman, who lived at the hotel, reports that in 1971 there were "around 130 Chinese and Filipino elderly" there.[120] These elderly residents were a built-in clientele for Chinatown businesses. They shopped at the markets and ate at the cheap restaurants in Chinatown. In one of the protests aimed at Milton Meyer Inc., the owner of the hotel, one picket sign read, "Chinatown supports Filipino Community."

The International Hotel crisis served to make the presence of the Filipino community known to a larger segment of the town. This was perhaps not the best or preferred way for Filipinos to advertise their presence in the city, but the crisis was forced on them, and no other choice was available then. In this circumstance, mainstream or external factors structured the context and conditions under which a subjugated minority was compelled to make itself known while exercising its rights: the community was forced to appear in a position of weakness, as an underdog asking for help. Those who were aware of the Filipino presence in San Francisco were alerted by the crisis to the reality that the physical site of attachment of the community was about to disappear. This was a good-bye call signaling an unknown tomorrow full of uncertainty.

The destruction of the hotel did not occur overnight, but took place over a ten-year period. Its residential clientele had shifted from individuals in search of employment or employed in menial jobs in the city to retirees who were likely to spend the rest of their life at the hotel. On the one hand, management was much dissatisfied with its patrons, for the hotel was not profiting as much as it should; on the other hand, residents were forced to cope with a management neglecting to maintain the hotel's standards, with eviction notices, and, finally, with the closing of the building by the local police.[121]

When Milton Meyer, Inc. – a real estate corporation that owned the building in the late 1960s – threatened to place a parking lot over the hotel,[122] protests by hotel residents and outside sympathizers and activists nullified the Company's ability to eject its tenants. Mounting pressure from the community resulted in the sale of the hotel in 1974 to the Four Seas Investment Corporation, a Bangkok-based development company, controlled, according to William Moore, "by interests in Hong Kong and Singapore."[123] Thus, the problem could not be solved locally but was moved to the global arena. The new players were not American, but rather Asian capitalists. From then on, protests had to be directed against a Bangkok firm, and not against a local firm. This form of globalization of capital led to the marginalization of elderly Filipinos not only by people inside the United States but also by outsiders. It shows how local conflicts between two groups of citizens are sometimes solved by the *mediation of international actors and global capital*.

The destruction of the International Hotel structure did not lead to the collapse of all the institutions of the community. Those that owed their existence to the locale were unable to survive without attracting a different clientele. These institutions were no longer territorially based but served a larger community beyond Manilatown. For example, in 1987, ten years after the fall of Manilatown, the Manilatown Choir was still in existence. Similarly, a few other institutions created by the ethnopolis outlived Manilatown.

In a short conversation with an urban planner at the City Planning Landscape, I was able to get a sense of the viewpoint held by the municipal government regarding the reasons that had led to the collapse of Manilatown. For him,

> City hall saw the Manongs as a fringe group and not as property owners... This was land used by low-income people that prevented the expansion of the financial district. It was not a policy against the Filipinos, but a policy that was not to the advantage of poor people in general who were living in the area. In contrast, Chinatown has a character that one wanted to keep.

It will be useful to summarize here the several factors that militated against the survival of Manilatown.

- First, the unwillingness of educated and professional Filipinos to come and live in Manilatown resulted in the creation of an area for single men and poor urban dwellers. Had a commercial class been present, they would have made Manilatown more stable by transforming it into a permanent center of Filipino social life.
- Second, urban renewal was also a factor. To help upgrade the value of the hotels in the area in order to cater to the needs of incoming tourists, it further accelerated the demise of Manilatown by evicting the poor.

- Next, the fact that Filipinos failed to own the land and buildings in the area made the neighborhood vulnerable. They were dependent on the white businessmen who owned the hotels.
- Finally, the unwillingness of city hall to step in and to protect the residents from eviction made the survival of Manilatown nearly impossible. The city would have helped only if it had seen Manilatown as having the potential to bring in tax dollars like Chinatown did.

So far, I have addressed mostly local issues. Manilatown's global process of exclusion and marginalization also affected its stability.

The globalization of exclusion

The rules of governmentality under which the US occupying forces operated in the Philippines were rules of both inclusion and exclusion. Rules express an enduring paradox because their enactment *establishes a system of exclusion precisely because they are about inclusion*. According to this principle, what is not included is ruled out. In this sense, the US enterprise in the Philippines produced many individuals who became excluded at various levels from the mainstream system of power. This system of rules was itself a localized outcome of a globalized production imposed from without by an extraterritorial and global force, with global geopolitical strategies and hegemonic ambitions. It was out of this stratum of the excluded – influenced by globalized local conditions – that the Filipinos emigrated to California and initiated what grew up to be Manilatown.

Their exclusion in the United States also had a global connotation, since they were stigmatized and racialized as *colored foreign bodies* in contrast to the *uncolored bodies* of the socially constructed mainstream. Here the global process evolved as the immigrants – who were twice excluded, both at home and abroad – maintained ongoing relations with Filipinos in Hawaii and the homeland, and with diasporic individuals from San Francisco who later emigrated to these two sites. With this process, the transnational circuit was firmly established.

Manilatown was a perfect expression of a site caught in a circuit of global exclusion. This circuit was made up of the interaction between people living in San Francisco, the Philippines, and Hawaii. What they shared in common was the experience of their exclusion in the social formation where they were incorporated. In the sites where they were excluded, both socially and physically, they developed a *modus vivendi* that, on the one hand, included transnational relations for self-support, the sharing of information, the selection of spouses, financial aid, and the maintenance of family connections. On the other hand, they developed resistance strategies in order to both cope with their miseries and deal with the dominant Euro-American community.

By "global exclusion," I mean a system of practice that operates transnationally and rules people out of specific conditions of existence on the basis of a dominant ideology. This definition implies that one must distinguish process from content. Exclusion may affect only one aspect of one's life. One may be included from some areas while being excluded in others. For instance, Filipinos were not excluded from attending the Anglo-Catholic Church in San Francisco, although they might have been asked to sit in the back seats. They were also structurally included in the labor force as a source of cheap labor. Thus, they were included at one level but excluded at another, which prevented them from attaining positions of power.

I do not see the globalization of exclusion as a homogenized system constructed from above by a unitary global system, but as a series of systems with global and local connections. As there are diverse systems of globality, so are there diverse modalities of the behavioral expression of the globalization of exclusion.

Manilatown resulted from a double process of exclusion that emanated from the *non-citizen status* of its residents. Unlike the Chinese and Japanese immigrants, Filipino immigrants had not been citizens in their own country, but rather had been *colonial subjects* resident in a country that failed to become an independent republic until the mid-twentieth century. Since citizenship is based on the principle of inclusion/exclusion, with the included enjoying more rights than the excluded, Filipinos' inability to acquire American citizenship (the result of racist state practices) prevented their full integration into mainstream American society.

Their immigration was a movement from non-citizen status in a colonial environment to non-citizen status in an independent federal union. Translated into practical terms, this means that they were not entitled to the same rights as citizens. Outside the realm of citizenship, Manilatown – the residential site of a non-citizen population – became a site in a transnational circuit that facilitated the global circulation of marginalized Filipino immigrants.[124]

The exclusion of the global

It may sound odd to speak of the exclusion of the global, since the global can be constructed as including the whole world. Such a view reflects an etymological way of approaching the issue, however, not an analytical slicing of the totality. Furthermore, it does not imply the exclusion of the global by the local if one could imagine a local that is totally located outside the framework of the global. The global can be excluded only if one speaks of a universe of globalities. I find this line of argument most useful in interpreting the Filipino data.

I see the world as made up of diverse circuits of globality, interconnecting niches that are organized according to their internal logic and that interact, cooperate, and compete with each other. In this universe, some globalities dominate others: I can think of financial networks that influence and help shape the economic infrastructure of many countries, if not the world. These contrast with the reality of ethnopolitan transnational connections. Other global networks are less dominant, since they reach only family members and therefore can influence only a specific universe.

I speak of the exclusion of the global in three ways: first, the exclusion of a global network by another global network on the basis of specialization and not hostility, simply because of different orientations. This can be referred to as profession-specific or class exclusion, but not as racial or ethnic exclusion. Not only Filipinos in Manilatown but also poor whites, whose meager means prevented them from participating in class-based global networks, were excluded. However, exclusion of the latter must be seen as *passive exclusion,* since they could eventually meet the requirements for membership.

Global exclusion is *active* when the act to rule out is intentional, or intentionally built up in the process. A global network can function in a closed circuit, preventing whole categories of people from joining in for whatever reasons. An exclusion can be intended to prevent such an entity from being part of a specific global process. For example, segregation on the basis of race prevented Filipinos from joining whites' networks.

Another type of exclusion is hybrid in the sense that it implies inclusion at one level and not the other. In the global political economy of the United States, Filipinos were included at the bottom of the process but excluded from the managerial level.

Still another form of global exclusion results from the indirect consequences of different forms of globality. An ethnic group may not be targeted, but globalization may work to its disadvantage regardless. This speaks to the interconnectivity of the globe and the fact that the process can affect every unit that is part of any of the multiple global networks.

The fact that the global can be included in a global network and excluded in others tells us a bit about the complexity of mapping out the universe of globality. When power is added to the making of the process, then the exclusion of such a global network may push it to a marginal positionality.

On a global scale, exclusion is a process different from marginalization. Not all of those excluded are considered marginal: exclusion implies a process of separation, but not necessarily of inferiorization and subalternization. However, in the case of the Filipinos *racialized exclusion* also meant inferiorization.

How does racialized exclusion become marginalized and globalized? There are three ways this can happen. First, hegemonic racial ideology affects multiple sites, as in the case of the empire and colonial domination. The dominant system imposes its racial categories on others, both at home and abroad. This was singularly the case in the US occupation of the Philippines, where European racial views served as a barometer for Manilatown and the Philippines. Here the same ideology (notwithstanding its local coloration and variations) equally affected diverse sites. Second, racialized exclusion is globalized when a dominant ideology uses its multiple sites of interaction to shape the ways it deals with local entities. Here, globality shapes the production of locality. Third, globality is achieved when the influence of the dominant sector is internalized and it affects the transnational relations of the excluded. To the extent that Manilatown residents imposed on their family left behind racial categories they had acquired from Anglo-Americans, this constitutes a case of global racialized exclusion.

In a context of multiple globalities, the exclusion of one by the other is the tapestry through which interactional units can be framed and understood. The global is not homogeneous; the idiosyncracies of human behavior allow room for the included and excluded.

The globalization of marginality

"Marginality" refers here not to the strategies of resistance by the excluded, but to the process whereby an individual or institution – and for that matter an ethnopole – becomes either included at the bottom of a dominant system or entirely excluded from it. So, marginality implies the existence of two entities and the process by which they are linked to each other to produce an uneven outcome.

Marginality is different from the concept of exclusion since one may be marginalized by inclusion as well. In the specific instance of Manilatown, the ethnopole was included in the territory of the United States, but at the bottom of the social structure. Thus, it was subject to *marginalization by inclusion,* as opposed to *marginalization by exclusion.* However, since Filipinos were excluded from the citizenship that would have allowed them to be upwardly mobile, they were included at one level and excluded at another. Thus, they encountered a double, or hybrid, process of marginalization: spatial marginality which confined them to non-white areas, and social marginality, prevented them from enjoying the same rights as the whites.

Marginality can also be understood as the process by which an individual or institution stands at the border of two worlds; this is the marginalization found at the social borderland, where one does not quite belong to either side, but is instead related to both. This is the situation of the *diasporic ethnopole,* or *diaspolis,* that occupies the borderland between the homeland and the country of adoption. Such ethnopolitans are completely assimilated to neither the country of adoption nor the homeland, because socially they live outside of both.

The process of disqualification and inferiorization often provides the justification for the outcome. The dominant system disqualifies and inferiorizes them in order to marginalize them, because it calculates the cost of integration to be much higher socially and economically than the potential returns from this form of long-term investment. If decoupled, social costs are considered higher than economic profits.

Naturally, the globalization of marginality is effected in the borderland situation since the ethnopole lives its marginality while maintaining relations with both the homeland and other diasporic sites. While the marginal condition is produced by the dominant system, the transnational relations are part of the ethnopole's daily life. In this view, the ethnopole may not be kept solely as a local reality. This globalization is derived from a diasporic condition that can be either centralized or marginalized.

In the marginalization by inclusion, globalization comes into play to the extent that the dominant system uses its global connections to shape groups in its midst or relegate them to the margins of society. Here the globalization of the ethnopole is derived from the status of the dominant system to which it is subalternized. It is globally produced and its marginal content is reproduced over time with the ability of the dominant system to maintain its global connections.

In an instance of marginalization by exclusion, globality becomes a factor as transnational linkages are maintained to deal with rejection. Since these marginalized people maintain global connections, their locally produced marginality attains a global status.

The globalization of marginality emanates either from the actions of the dominant system or those of the dominated system, or it is co-produced by both the dominant power and diasporic spatiality. These outcomes are influenced by the nature of the relations of power.

In the case of Manilatown, one must also include that these were racialized processes. Not only was this marginalization globally produced, but it was racialized as well. Globalized marginality is said to be racialized when the race factor shapes the outcome in a dominant-dominated situation. The Filipinos and their ethnopole were marginalized precisely because they were constructed as non-white foreigners in a country where whites had constructed themselves hosts for everyone else (including the Native Americans).

The marginalization of the global

An analysis of Manilatown reveals the fact that both the local and the global can be marginalized. The local can be marginalized by another local reality or by a global entity in the same way that the global can be marginalized by both the global and the local. When a Filipino was prevented from renting or buying an apartment or house in a white neighborhood, it was likely the result of a local form of marginalization by way of exclusion.

In this section, I am interested in examining the marginalization of the ethnopole by the local and the global. The global is said to be marginalized by the local when the former plays a dominant role *vis-à-vis* the latter. Local labor conditions were a factor in shaping the marginality of Manilatown as a global ethnopole. These conditions affected the local outcome that was itself part of a global process.

The marginalization of the global by the global implies here the existence of diverse forms of globality. The dominant US occupying forces were a major factor in the marginalization of the Filipinos at home and in the production and marginalization of Manilatown. Manilatown was further marginalized by Chinatown, itself a global ethnopole: a global ethnopole marginalized another global ethnopole. In the first instance, the marginalization of both the mainland and the ethnopole was engineered by the same global entity, while in the second only the Manilatown ethnopole was directly affected by the process of marginalization effected by Chinatown.

When the process is seen from the angle of social identities, the marginalization of the global may also proceed from its social location between the social space of the homeland and that of the country of adoption. Here marginalization proceeds from the temporal lag resulting from the fact that it would take time to achieve assimilation, if that is the goal of the ethnic group, and from the need to maintain transnational relations with the homeland.

The marginal status of the global ethnopole is shaped by its spatial location between two social spaces (the country of adoption and the homeland), the dominant global apparatus that channels immigration to the United States, the immigrants' integration prospects, and sectoral globalities, as in the case of Chinatown, that further influence the outcome. Both local and global processes interplay in the production of the ethnopole's marginality.

Filipinos' marginality was defined by their immigrant condition and lack of citizenship, by their diasporic status *vis-à-vis* the homeland, and by their hostile attitude toward the Marcos administration, which viewed them as political opponents. Located in the margins of both Philippine and American social systems, the Manongs were able to carve out a living and re-create a space reminiscent of the homeland. Manilatown became the expression of both their longing for the homeland and a symbol of their exclusion from mainstream American society.

Given Manilatown's status as a marginalized global ethnopole, I see five essential conditions that critically affected its attempt to root itself in the area like Chinatown:

- First, the ability to own land and houses, as a way of forming a residential core, is a priority for stability. A stable neighborhood is made up of home owners who care about their property and who are ready to protect their investment at any cost.
- Second, the community must be able to develop a business sector that caters to the needs of the residents and other clients.
- Third, it must develop cultural institutions, such as language schools, churches, and newspapers, that help stabilize the population; this is of prime importance for the reproduction of the ethnopolis over time.
- Fourth, it must have good relations with city hall. An important element in the collapse of the ethnopole was city hall's lukewarm

response to the plight of the poor Manongs. Whereas city government had been active in maintaining Chinatown as a tourist attraction, it had little interest in Manilatown, viewing it more as a source of problems than as a source of income for the city's coffers.

- Finally, the community received no political help from the homeland. The opposition politics concerning the homeland government divided the community and prevented some Filipinos with families still in the Philippines from participating in the social activities of the ethnopole. As a result of this political estrangement, the homeland government did not provide any meaningful assistance to help prevent the eviction of Filipinos from this site. As a result, since Filipinos did not constitute an influential ethnic political group, they were unable to get much help from city hall.

Manilatown was a marginalized community that could not reproduce itself over time, for the reasons mentioned above. Moreover, it could not prevent the outmigration of its members to other areas, nor could it attract new members from the Filipino commercial elite or stop the gentrification of the neighborhood. Finally, it also failed to project an identity different from that of Chinatown, which led outsiders to believe that it was unable to attract the tourist crowd.

5
The Ethnopole as a Global City

Just as an ethnopole can be deglobalized, as we have seen in the case of Japantown analyzed in Chapter 3, it can also be reglobalized. *Reglobalization* is the process by which an entity either relinks itself or is relinked to extraterritorial sites after it has willingly or unwillingly gone through a process of deglobalization. Such a reglobalization can be achieved through a routine process of relinking, or it may be engineered, sponsored, or shaped as such by an external unit. In its forward and backward linkages, the process is not different from that of globalization. When it is achieved as a *sui generis* or self-induced phenomenon, without the mediation of another entity, we term it *raw globalization*. It is known as *cooked globalization* when it is led from without or planned from within.[125] These categories, however, are not mutually exclusive. While raw globalization may become cooked by way of amplification and formalization, cooked globalization may also be transformed into raw globalization with time, through a routinization of the process and by informalization. The global ethnopole is traversed by these two types of globalization; they cohabit in this same spatial niche, somehow interacting with and reinforcing each other.

I find the concept of raw and cooked globalization analytically productive because it induces us to consider human agency as being central to the globalization process. It also forces us to distinguish between two sets of mechanisms, each with its own rationale, and to ponder the relationship of one to the other in the production of the globalization process. Raw globalization suggests that which is unprocessed, natural, and spontaneous, while cooked globalization presupposes formalization, planning, and order – that is, it is not something that just happens without or against the intervention of human agency.

In this chapter I will examine the raw and cooked globality of Japantown from the double angle of corporate Japantown and that of the ordinary citizens who call the ethnopole their hometown. To accomplish this goal, I will deconstruct Japantown into the global facets that shape its character as a global ethnopole.

There are various forms of globality that make up the global ethnopole: the economy is simply one aspect. For an ethnopole to be global, it is not necessary for all of its facets to be global. However, global connections of one unit may influence other units as well. An analysis of the global ethnopole therefore requires the disentangling of these various aspects to see how they are connected to outside sites and to each other.

In this scheme of things, an ethnopolis is not defined as "global" simply because of its disparate individual connections with other countries or because of the impact of international events on community life (if these were the essential criteria, most ethnopoles would be defined as global). It is defined as "global" because the multinational connections it entertains are sustained over time, shape local social conditions, and are important in the everyday life of the community.

Cooked globality through corporate takeover

The year 1968 was a milestone in the history of Japantown because it was the year that the reglobalization of the ethnopole was inaugurated and celebrated. Until then the ethnopole had been governed by a raw form of globality, as individuals engaged in transnational relations and transactions on a regular but individual, sporadic basis. Japantown's renovation as a global city, or its reglobalization, was engineered to present Japantown as an ethnic showcase, one that both symbolized friendship and *rapprochement* between the United States and Japan and welcomed Japanese businesses and immigrants to the area. It is a cooked form of globality because it was rationally designed to accomplish those purposes and to produce the following outcomes: to entice Japanese businessmen and women to invest in Japantown and establish either headquarters or subsidiaries of their operations there, to renew or rekindle the interest of Japanese Americans in the new Japantown, to help strengthen social and commercial ties between San Francisco and Tokyo–Osaka, and – with the redesign of the area to give it a more prominent Japanese appearance – to entice more tourists to Japantown. The new Japantown is also an example of theme-park-ization of the ethnopole: its appearance was remade to attract tourists and to provide them with an exotic site where they can entertain themselves and, at the same time, feed the diasporic and mainstream economy by purchasing goods.

The renovation of Japantown was spearheaded by city officials as a sign of reconciliation and friendship that would lead to renewed commercial transactions and social relations with Japan. The city was well aware that an injustice had been done to Japanese Americans – US born and immigrants – by their incarceration during World War II and their subsequent losses of property – and that a subdued postwar Japan was not the same as the tigerish and belligerent prewar Japan. It was also aware that the Japanese quarter in the Western Addition was in a dilapidated state and needed renovation. Thus, in the midst of these local and international concerns, the San Francisco Redevelopment Agency, in collaboration with Japanese American business and civic leaders, came up with a plan for the renovation of Japantown. However, a good chunk of the money for the reconstruction of the site came from Japanese who had been invited to invest in Japantown. Thus, this renovation scheme included the participation of local (city agencies and Japanese-Americans), national (Japanese Americans in Hawaii), and international (Japanese businesses) actors.

The rebirth of Japantown was, indeed, a global event since both Japanese businesses and the Japanese government collaborated with the local government in making it a reality. It symbolizes an important site of Japanese investment in San Francisco. Okita notes that financial help for the construction of the Japan Trade Center, the most commercial and visible spot in Japantown, came from Japan:

> National-Braemer, Inc., headed by people from San Francisco and Hawaii, approached Kinki Nippon Railway Company Limited of Japan to invest in Nihonmachi. On October 11, 1961, Kinki incorporated as a business, Kintetsu Enterprises Company of America, and in 1962 National-Braemer received permission from the Japanese Government for Japanese capital to be invested in the Japan Trade Center.[126]

The architectural design of the Japan Trade Center was also a global project: its binational design team was composed of the second-generation Japanese American Minoru Yamasaki, who served as the main architect, and Professor Yoshiro Taniguchi of Tokyo, who designed the Peace Plaza and Peace Pagoda.[127] The Peace Pagoda was a gift donated to Japantown by the people of Japan.

The global aspect of the ethnopole is reflected in the organization of the space/place itself. As Feldman puts it,

> While the Japan Center embodies the sleek sophistication of modern Japan, Buchanan Mall resembles a timeless rural village...[The Buddhist Church on Pine Street is] a replica of one in Kyoto...The intimate tea room, designed by a consultant to the Japanese Imperial Household, was built in Kyoto, then dismantled and reassembled in the Nichibei Kai Cultural Center on Sutter Street.[128]

The Japan Trade Center, the life blood of the ethnopole, is composed of three commercial buildings that serve as business sites for a variety of Japanese shops, which attract both the local population and tourists from far away. It is here that the global status of Japantown can be gauged, because the most important buildings belong to Japanese investors. For example, Tasamak Plaza, the Kinokuniya Building, and the Kintetsu Building, which constitute the Japan Trade Center, are all owned by Japanese corporations and are subsidiaries of companies whose headquarters are in Japan. According to Hanford,

> Kintetsu Enterprises Company of America, a subsidiary of Kintetsu Corporation of Japan, is still the Center's key anchor...Kintetsu owns and manages the deluxe Raddison Miyako Hotel and the Kintetsu Shopping Mall...the Best Western Miyako Inn and the Japantown Bowl.
> Kinokuniya Book Stores of America, the largest Japanese bookstore chain in the US and a subsidiary of the largest bookstore chain in Japan,...owns the [Japan Trade] Center's Kinokuniya Building, a two-level shopping mall, and the shop-lined Webster Street Bridge connecting the Kinokuniya and Kintetsu Buildings.
> Union Bank (Bank of Tokyo)...owns the portion of the Center which houses its Japantown branch and retail space above the branch.
> Tasamak Corporation, a Japanese investment group...owns Tasamak Plaza, a two-level shopping mall adjacent to the Raddison Miyako Hotel.[129]

Through foreign ownership of the principal buildings, the Japan Trade Center has been made into a satellite of investors or corporations in Japan. This heavy dependence on Japan – for policies, transfer of managers, salaries, and merchandise – makes the center vulnerable in its negotiations to shape its local/global character, since it must accommodate these foreign interests, but it also makes possible the constant transnational flow of goods, capital, communications, and people between Japan and Japantown.

What is important to notice is not only the fact that these buildings are owned or managed by Japanese, but also the border-crossing practices their operators are engaged in. These operators maintain the "Japanness" of the neighborhood by the stores they sponsor and the goods and products from Japan they stock and sell. The taste for Japanese things is nurtured here because it is the central marketplace for some Japanese products. While the transnational relations of some businesses are mostly between Japantown and Japan, for others these include transnational relations between Japantown and diasporic Japanese communities in Canada, Brazil, or Europe, or wherever the store's headquarters is located. For example, a flower arrangment school at the Japan Trade Center brings Japanese instructors in and sends out students and associates to Japan for classroom instruction. However, one furniture shop in Japantown was found to be a subsidiary of a firm headquartered in Italy.

Although these subsidiaries have some autonomy in handling local matters, central planning is by and large done in Japan. Transfers of Japanese managers to Japantown are decided by the headquarters and the rhythms of transnational visits for consultation with the headquarters or the San Francisco subsidiaries are also decided and approved by Japan. In most of the cases, the manager of a subsidiary store in Japantown is likely to be a first generation immigrant who was transferred to occupy this new position, and who previously had worked for the company in Japan.

The above examples indicate that an ethnopole can be defined as global when it is a node in a border-crossing economic or business network. In this instance, the node is connected to San Francisco as a financial command center, but primarily to Japanese businesses in Japan and in other American cities, and to other Japanese diasporic sites as well. Its globality is made possible because of its linkage with transnational and global economic institutions outside Japantown. I call this form of international incorporation *nodal globality*.

One of the main features of the Japan Trade Center is the book shop (whose name I will withhold) that attracts Japanese tourists and locals. Established in Japantown in 1969, it is a subsidiary of a Japanese company, founded in 1927 and headquartered in Tokyo's Shinjuku district. As the largest Japanese bookstore in California, it monitors the operations of small units in the chain stores in the western United States. A parent company in New York monitors its two operations on the East Coast – in New York and New Jersey. This expanding bookstore is part of a multinational operation with stores in six US cities (Costa Mesa, Los Angeles, San Francisco, San Jose, Edgewater (New Jersey), and Seattle (Washington), and in Indonesia, Malaysia, Singapore, Taiwan and Thailand. In addition, it maintains business offices in New York and London.[130]

The bookstore makes available to the public Japanese books, magazines, and videotapes, and books on Japanese Americans and other Asian American groups. After several visits to the bookstore, I have estimated that 20 percent of the books are in English and about 80 percent of all the books and other items, such as magazines, are in Japanese. A few Chinese comic books (about 200) from Taiwan are stocked here for sale as well. Since the store is the main distribution center of Japanese books, it is a central site of attraction and a meeting place for Japanese Americans in the Bay Area.

The bookshop enhances the global status of the ethnopole because it is part of a global sectoral network. This entity is global because of its linkage to a command center in Japan that controls and manages a global network. Central and peripheral globality are two modes of incorporation that characterize one's position in a border-crossing network. Globality is said to be central when it reflects the *control center* of an international operation, and peripheral when it symbolizes the location of a unit that plays a subsidiary role in the network.

Thus the decision to offer specific books to the local community is made not solely by the San Francisco management, but can be influenced by the headquarters or any unit in the global network that comprises the bookstore as a multinational operation. Furthermore, four out of the five bookstore managers are from Japan, and one is from the United States. These individuals had worked in Japan and were transfered as a promotion or other circumstance to the Japantown subsidiary store. In the past, managers have been transferred back to Japan to work there for the company after they had completed their terms in San Francisco.

The above example indicates that the ethnopole is engaged in yet another type of globality. Since the bookstore is engaged in its transnational relations in a specific sector of the global economy, and since this influences the global shape of the ethnopole, we call this *sectoral globality,* to distinguish it from a more general form of globality.

The banking system, with its border-crossing people and money, provides an example of another form of transnationality. The Bank (whose name I will withhold) is another subsidiary institution that owns a piece of the Japan Trade Center. Emerging from the merger between Union Bank and the Bank of California that took place on April 1, 1996, it has since become a subsidiary of the Bank of Tokyo–Mitsubishi, Ltd., which is the largest bank in the world. The Bank is part of a global network of banking institutions with several branches and offices in California, Oregon, Washington, New York, and Texas, and overseas facilities mainly in cities along the Pacific Rim, – such as Bangkok, Bombay, Cebu, Guam, Hong Kong, Jakarta, Kuala Lumpur, Manila, Saipan, Seoul, Singapore, Taipei, and Tokyo – and other international branches in São Paolo and the Cayman Islands.

As a subsidiary of a Tokyo-based banking institution, the management of this local operation is closely monitored by its headquarters in Japan, whose managers visit Japantown to inspect the books, assess situations, and manage good relations between the two sites. Transfers of certain personnel are decided by headquarters. For example, the manager of the Japantown branch was transferred from Japan to San Francisco to head the operation in the city.

The globality of these multinational entities is formal, is recognized and monitored by the states involved, and is policed by the headquarters. It is a cooked globality that has an impact on the families of the employees who also come along to the new site and who, in turn, must maintain relations with their own parents at home. As one moves from the formal institution to informal family arrangement, one sees how cooked globality may engender raw globality, and how it may generate a highly skilled and elite migration controlled by the headquarters–subsidiary relations.

Japantown houses a subsidiary of a Japanese flower arrangment institution whose headquarters is located in Kyoto, Japan. From New York, where it was established earlier, the school was relocated to Japantown in 1970. This overseas subsidiary coordinates the activities of forty chapters in the United States and Canada and sells to its members and the public at large, flower arranging supplies, including containers and books. In addition, the San Francisco office arranges for Japanese flower arranging teachers to come to the United States and provide instructions to its members, to lead workshops, and give demonstrations. Likewise, it also arranges study tours for people to visit the main headquarters in Japan and enroll in the courses it offers. Through its magazine, the Japantown subsidiary informs its clientele and members about forthcoming study tours in Japan. The company imports from Japan goods such as *kenzan* ("frogs"), scissors, containers, vases, books, and pamphlets, so that members can have easy access to these flower arranging supplies. Likewise, certificates delivered by the subsidiary come from the headquarters in Japan.

The subsidiary makes a little bit of money from membership fees, sales, and chapter contributions, but the bulk of the money used to run the operation comes from Japan. The money made by the center is mostly used to cover costs for the publication of the magazine, postage, and miscellaneous items, and to pay for travel fares and accommodation for professors visiting from Japan. Thus, Japan is the life-blood of this operation: it receives its money, supplies, and visiting professors from Japan. I refer to this form of transnational interaction as *dependent globalility* because one pole in the global process depends on another.

The Cherry Blossom Festival, which takes place in the spring, is a festive event that celebrates the global status of Japantown. It is an international event because of the array of people it brings to the area. In 1997, the festival also celebrated the fortieth anniversary of the San Francisco–Osaka Sister City Association. In addition to the large numbers of performers from Japan, and more specifically from Osaka, there was also an official delegation made up of Osaka's Honorable Mayor Takafumi Isomura and city council members. Fujiyasu Kimono – a major company based in Japan that has been providing free kimonos to the Cherry Blossom Queens for the past thirty years – was represented by its president Seishichi Ato.

The annual festival is held to both renew residents' consciousness of the homeland and to renew ties with Japan. Japanese participation is paramount in the success of the event. Business leaders from Japan, as well as their subsidiary companies in the United States and Canada, are represented, and they display their floats. The mayor of Osaka and the mayor of San Francisco serve as grand marshals for the parade. The parade is a celebration of the localization of globalization.

The identification of Japantown with a global city status evokes the idea that the ethnopole is global in several different ways. The ethnopole is global when it becomes the site of a multinational event such as the Cherry Blossom Festival. This annual event meshes together the Japanese, Japanese Americans, and other Japanese diasporans into a global family: it is a global homecoming event. The festival projects and actualizes the global connections of the local community. This high point of globality comes about because individual Japanese and groups of Japanese citizens participate in it, and Japanese businesses take part in it, either by sending representatives from Japan or US subsidiaries or by underwriting expenses incurred. This event manifests the *spatial globality* of the ethnopole and is a symbol of the *localization of globality*.

Hence, three modalities of globality can be identified in Japantown thus far: *Circumstantial globality* refers to the ephemerality of a transnational practice and occurs as an event detached from the routine of everyday life in the enclave. *Cyclical globality* refers to the recurrence of a border-crossing practice that lacks permanence and that is repeated annually or seasonally. *Permanent or sustained globality* indicates the routinized and ongoing flow of such a practice. Each of these forms contributes in its own way to the makeup of the enclave as a global ethnopole.

One of Japantown's hotels has served as a conduit through which the ethnopolis maintains transnational relations with the Japanese community in Brazil – the largest settlement after Japan. For the past five years, a representative of the hotel has been going to São Paolo, more specifically to Liberdade – where the community has its strengths, including its museum – in search of potential clients in order to entice them to visit San Francisco by informing them about the happenings in Japantown and wiring the two communities together. Until then, these two communities had ongoing relations with Japan, but not so much with each other. Now Japanese Brazilians annually visit Nihon Machi and stay at one of the hotels. It was estimated that about 2.7 percent of the hotel revenue in mid-1990 came from the Japanese Brazilian clientele as a result of this connection.

The Hotel (whose name I will withhold) is part of a Japanese chain. Its representative advertises mostly the Japantown location, but also indirectly the location in Los Angeles and the ones in Japan. A key individual can serve as a *node in the working of transnational relations*, and that node can be a *center of a global process*. An individual node can become the center of a global network just as a firm's headquarters can serve as a node of a global network.

Thus, the ethnopole is global in four different ways: it is an initiating node connecting parts of border-crossing networks; it is the point of destination of activities initiated elsewhere; it is a mediating mechanism through which both local and global actions find their complementarity, and it is all of these things at various levels.

The Hotel's revenue from its Japanese clientele has fluctuated between 10 percent and 35 percent of its total revenue, depending on the state of business in Japan – whether it is in a recession or inflation period – or the state of United States–Japan relations. Geopolitical crises impact the density of transnational relations in the ethnopole. The global aspects of businesses have immediate repercussions on their success in Japantown. When the yen is stronger than the dollar, the importation of books and magazines costs the bookstores more and adjustment must be made. In contrast, recession in the Japanese economy means fewer Japanese tourists and less profit for the Japantown businesses. A major sector of the Japantown economy depends on Japan; it makes profit or loses money according to the economic climate in Japan. This portion of the ethnic economy *navigates inside a transnational economic system*. The global ethnopolis has a transnational economic basis that sustains it.

Of the Japanese and individuals of Japanese descent who use the Hotel on a yearly basis, about 60 percent are Japanese students and 10 percent are corporate; 20 percent are Japanese Americans or Canadians and 10 percent are Japanese from Brazil and other countries including Mexico. Other Asian countries do business with the Hotel, too: it has welcomed guests from Malaysia, Korea, Taiwan, Singapore, and the Philippines. There is a *temporal order* in these transnational visits that links Japantown to Asia. For example, the Taiwanese, I was told by a staff member, prefer to pay the low winter rates, while Singaporeans prefer to come during the summer. So, *temporality is a factor in disentangling these transnational connections*. Between 1989 and 1994, the Hotel's revenue gathered from the Asian clientele varied between 12 percent and 21 percent.

In addition to temporality, there is the question of *density*. For example, the relations of the hotels are not simply to individuals, but also to companies and agencies. As a staff person states,

> The company organizes the tourist package, and then they call the hotel to see if we want to be part of it – do we have space or do we want to do the business, and can we give a special rate. So we discuss and decide if we want to do it. And if we decide that we are going to have too much business during that period, we won't want to do it; then we have to tell them. If we feel like it is our own company, the second largest tour operator out of Japan, we have to do it. So, we will do five rooms or we will do this and that. But when we are "hungry", we go to them and say, "can you do a package?"

These formal and cyclical transnational relations lead to tourist visits and profits by both hotels and local merchants. These global practices of local businesses are sometimes mediated by the hotels on which they depend for tourist dollars and they demonstrate how transnational relations of one unit can affect other units in the ethnopole.

Some units are globalized because of the global practices they engage in. For example, the Hotel is a global operation and the clients and staff reflect that global and multicultural dimension: clients come from various parts of the world inside and outside Japan, including Mexico, Germany, France, the United Kingdom, Korea, and Singapore. Among the staff are Japanese, Koreans, Chinese, Anglos, and Latinos – people who can speak the languages of the guests. The restaurant at the Hotel serves Chinese food during the day and Japanese food at night when the Japanese cooks take over.

A globalized transaction generated by a unit may impact another unit. For example, since the Japantown Bowl in Japantown belongs to Kintetsu, when a bowling group comes to town, it stays at the Hotel, which is also owned by the company. This is another example of *cooked globality*, in which an agency does the transnational packaging and this benefits other businesses in the network. These prefabricated forms of globality bring a different dynamic to transnational relations. They are planned in advance to produce net gains or a certain outcome. Hence the notion of *planned globality* with rationality as its pillar.

The enduring legacy of raw globality

The various forms of cooked globality discussed exist side by side with different types of raw globality, a process that occurs informally. Japanese Americans have engaged in this kind of global connection ever since their return from the internment camps after World War II. Raw globality is materialized in three distinct sites: in old immigrants who are engaged in transnational relations in a sporadic way; in new immigrant families, some of whom are here to stay and some of whom intend to return to Japan later; and family firms that maintain ongoing global relations for business purposes.

Family firms constitute an important element in the ongoing process of raw globality. These are institutions that have developed business contacts for the purpose of buying Japanese products and reselling them in Japantown, or that are engaged in exporting goods to Japan. What is interesting to note is that there is an evolution in the *direction of global flows* pertaining to the operation of these firms: the direction of global flows is not fixed, but at times reverses itself. A businesswoman recalls that when she began selling Japanese prints in

Japantown, she would go to Japan to buy them. However, since many Japanese prints were collected after the war by Westerners, it is now easier to purchase them in the United States. In the recent past, Japanese collectors and buyers have come to Japantown to purchase Japanese prints from her store.

The bulk of raw globality is carried out through family relations and is heavier and more regular among first-generation immigrants because of family left behind. Raw globality occurs through telephone, fax, e-mail, snail mail, periodic visits, and remittances that students received from their parents in Japan. It is sometimes materialized as a permanent flow through the institutionalization of *multinational family organization,* since family members live in different countries and are engaged in border-crossing relations. Multinational family organization is the *transnational locus* where family members with different class status – as a result of living in different countries with different opportunity structures – *interact with each other through border-crossing practices.*

Because the Japantown data traverses four generations, it provides important clues on *generational transnationality.*[131] It indicates that transnationality functions transgenerationally, as youngsters are visited by aunts and uncles from Japan and they spend time with relatives whenever they accompany their parents to Japan. Sometimes the immigrant heir to family land is the main connection that makes the generational transnational factor an enduring one. The following case pertaining to a third-generation Japanese American attests to this. Joe, who grew up in Japantown, says,

> My father was born here. He eventually became the oldest male heir in Japan, and even though he had no interest in reclaiming the land it was still in his name because he became the oldest male heir. My mother's father came here in 1892 and my father's father came here in 1910...I think that my sister and several cousins served to strengthen and reawaken the linkage with our family in Japan. My aunt was born here but was sent back to live in Japan, and she stayed in Japan and married a Japanese national. She stayed there during the war. My sister lived in Japan for a year and she established a stronger relationship with both sides of our family back in Japan. I think that strengthens it and it continues. I don't think that it is as strong as it once was, but I think we still consider them family. We do have family there, aunts, uncles, and cousins who came from Japan to visit...My cousin is getting married this weekend and

my aunt has flown all the way from Japan to be here. So, it is going to serve as a family reunion.

Raw globality is not exclusive to the first generation of immigrants. Second and third generations are also involved in it because of family in the old country with whom they still maintain contact, not only because of consanguineal relations but also because of the intricacies of rules of inheritance. The above example clearly indicates some mechanisms that sustain the working of generational transnationality.

The data so far tends to point to a specific form of globalization that is less generalized than the globalization of the city itself. One may speak, then, of *ethnic or family globality* to refer to the attachment of an ethnopole to a network of binational, transnational, and global relations. It follows the circuitry of the homeland and diasporic sites.

Local dynamics of global practices

In this case of Japantown, reglobalization led to structural rearrangement in the local community. It brought key globalized institutions to the area – the Japanese Consulate, Kintetsu, Kinokuniya, and Tasamak – and reinforced the status of local institutions. It also reglobalized existing institutions and events such as the Cherry Blossom Festival. Reglobalization does not mean simply a "relinking" or "reconnection" with an overseas site, but also local reorganization because the dynamics of globalization implodes the local social structure itself as a consequence of the process.

As cooked globalization materialized in the form of a circumscribed group of institutions, one would not expect these to affect each other without also affecting the preexisting global practices in the ethnopole. Because of the nature of the informal political process and these institutions' dependence on the local clientele for the success of their operations, their introduction in the milieu has contributed to the social reshaping of the ethnopole. This impact is more visible in the corporate world they establish in the enclave that more formally links the ethnopole to Japan and the mainstream business sector of San Francisco. While this formal corporate world does not completely marginalize the preexisting informal political structure, it certainly competes with it for dominance in the ethnopole's relations with the world outside its local bounds.

What is important to notice is how global connections feed local relations. At a time when Japanese American residents were moving out of a rundown enclave, the globalization of businesses meant that the enclave would survive as a new business center. No doubt, the Japan Trade Center gave a new vitality to the enclave by providing an infrastructure that supports the performance of this cooked form of globality. Here is an instance where global relations impact the survival of the enclave, local space, and fluctuating demographics – all at once.

The construction of the Center brought to Japantown not only the subsidiaries of large corporations but also family businesses. According to the general manager of one of the three buildings in the Center, more than 90 percent of small businesses in the unit under his supervision were owned in 1997 by first generation Japanese immigrants. He spoke of one Japanese resident who owns four retail shops in Japantown and who goes back to Japan twice a year to refurbish supplies and visit his family there. His sister, who is in charge of another store he owns in Tokyo, helps with ordering supplies for the Japantown outlets.

According to the president of the Japanese Merchants' Association, which comprises a membership of about 100, more than 70 percent of the businesses at the Center are owned by first-generation Japanese immigrants and Japanese Americans. He estimated that there are about 140 merchants in Japantown, one-quarter of whom do not belong to the association. About 20 percent are Koreans, 5 percent Chinese, and the rest Vietnamese and others. Out of the Japanese group, 30 percent are Japanese Americans. Thus, the majority of the small businesses are independently owned by first-generation immigrants who had money with them to establish their stores.[132]

Larger Japanese businesses in the ethnopole attract clients not only for their operations but also for the smaller stores. Japanese tourists who come to visit and regular clients who buy Japanese goods in the Japan Center naturally purchase other household items sold by Japanese-American stores in the neighborhood. In a sense, the former bring the tourists in for the latter. This example shows how microglobalization has a trickle-down effect on other institutions in the neighborhood stores.

As a result of the construction of the Japan Trade Center that brought more tourists to the area to use the facilities (stores, hotels, banks, travel agencies, and restaurants), local businesses have adapted their outlets to new immigrant and visitor tastes in order to survive. Now local stores sell non-Japanese goods as well to please the new clientele. Tourists from Japan, other US cities, and other countries (Brazil and Canada, for example) constitute a primary market for some stores. In a sense, Japanese businesses have become mixed enterprises, selling Japanese and American goods to Japanese tourists and local consumers. Globalization has reshaped the content of the local stores and has transformed them into *global entities that rely on an international clientele (tourists) for their success.*

The globalization of Japantown becomes evident in its function as a tourist center. It brings tourists to the area who use the facilities (stores, hotels, banks, travel agencies, restaurants). They constitute a primary market for some stores. We have three sets of tourists: Japanese from Japan, Japanese from other states (e.g. Hawaii) and from other countries (e.g. Brazil and Canada).

The stores have their temporal rhythms pertaining to transactions with their local and global clientele: a *permanent* clientele (neighbors and tourists); a *regular* but not permanent clientele (those Japanese who live in the Sunset district); and an *irregular* clientele consisting of those who live in the suburbs and who show up for certain events. Here again, globalization implodes in the local stores to shape the contours of their economic transactions.

With the creation of the Japan Cultural and Trade Center, the demographics of Japantown had dwindled. As a result of the reglobalization of the enclave, three different groups have emerged, in addition to the old-timers who returned to the area after the war. These three groups are mainly Chinese and Korean immigrants, the new Japanese immigrants who have established their shops here, and the employees of corporations such as Kintetsu Enterprises of America.

This new form of globalization has also brought disjuncture. For example, there is a floating Japanese managerial population in Japantown. Transferred here from Japan, they may be transferred back at the end of their terms in the United States. These binationals are less integrated with the rest of the Japanese American population because they consider themselves Japanese and see their future in Japan. Some are given this overseas job as part of their training and upward mobility so that, should they become managers at the headquarters in Japan, they will have a better understanding of overseas operations.

By attracting people to the area, the incoming Asian population made it possible for businesses to survive and aided in the vitality and survival of the ethnopole as a whole. Further, immigration may eventually lead to the transformation of the enclave into an Asiatown. The Japanese Americans of Japantown are well aware of this possibility and are making plans so that the total eclipse of the Japanese population does not occur in the near future.

In the face of this possible greater gentrification, the Japanese Merchants' Association, "tries to lure businesses from Japan to the area,"[133] according to Muto, since it is more difficult to convince Japanese Americans to open small stores in Japantown. Yamamoto says that

> Japan's very success has meant less and less Japanese immigration to America... The Japanese population of San Francisco increased by exactly one person between the 1980 and 1990 census.[134]

Actually, it is in reaction to the flight of Japanese-American-owned businesses that it became necessary to bring Japanese in as a way of counteracting what some Japanese Americans perceived as the rush of Korean businesses into the area. The perception that Koreans will soon colonize Japantown because of their sheer numbers – whether realistic or not – is a common concern shared by many Japantown residents.

Several mechanisms – both global and local – have already led to a degree of gentrification in Japantown. Gentrification occurs because of the law of the market. Those who have money can purchase vacant houses for sale. Some believe this is how Koreans have been able to gain a foothold in the community, because they tend to have more money than the old-timer Japanese American citizens. However, gentrification also happens because members of the younger generation who have entered professions find jobs elsewhere in the mainstream labor market and do not resettle in Japantown. Furthermore, Japantown has gentrified because of city and federal policies. The Japanese American Religious Federation, having built a residence complex with federal money for low-income and older people, could not, by law, select exclusively Japanese Americans to move in. So, blacks, whites, and other ethnics were brought in. A few older individuals who were not living in Japantown came back so as to be part of the community and live among their own people.

Globalization of the enclave means the multiethnic composition of its population – in this case, Koreans, Chinese, Filipinos, and Asian Indians – and their transnational relations with their homeland. This is not a *globalization of homogeneity*, but rather a *globalization of gentrification*, by which I mean that the transnational linkage each group maintains with its homeland is reflective of the population composition of the enclave and of the new immigrants who come to the area. While *globalization of homogeneity* refers to a sedentary population where immigration of other groups is minimal or non-existent, *globalization*

126 *The Global Ethnopolis*

of gentrification implies conflict and interaction between new residents and old-timers, between the majority group in the enclave and other ethnic groups. The dominant presence and visibility of one group may become at times a source of tension in the ethnopole. Sometimes the tension is a reenactment of old animosities that existed between the groups prior to their immigration to the United States, as in the case, for example, of the animosity between Koreans and Japanese.

Thus, the ethnopole is global as a gentrified enclave because of the diversity of its population composition (Japanese, Chinese, Filipinos, Koreans, and Asian Indians) and the transnational relations each of these ethnic groups maintains with its homeland. I call this *demographic globality*.

The Japanese Consulate was once located inside Japantown and projected as a subsidiary or extension of the Japanese government. It helped to attract people to the area, both tourists and businesspeople. But this identification was perceived by some as a possible impediment to the local community's development in the event of a conflict between the two governments. The symbol of friendship could easily turn into one of conflict. The consulate moved out of Japantown precisely at the time when Washington and Tokyo were verbally fighting about trade protectionism. Its relocation protected the neighborhood from this kind of transnational tension, which was strongly felt at the local level.

Local tension sometimes has a global dimension as well, as occurs when such tension is fed not only by local interaction among the groups but also by events that happen in any of the groups' homelands with immediate repercussions in the enclave. For example, in the early 1990s Japanese government officials blamed African Americans and other minoritized groups for all the ills in the United States; this fueled tension between Japanese Americans and African Americans. Although Japanese American leaders dissociated themselves from the Japanese officials' derogatory racial remarks, these still had a negative impact on the local scene and enclave.[135]

At other times tension and resentment arise precisely because an individual uses the transnational factor as a way to construct another person's identity so as to minoritize him or her. The *Western Edition* reported an incident that occurred during the mayoral campaign pitting Willie Brown against the incumbent mayor Frank Jordan. Jordan's staff, in an effort to be in the good graces of Richard Wada of the Japanese American Democratic Club commiserated with him over the death of "your Emperor." "What are you talking about? He is not my

Emperor, I am an American," said Wada.[136] This incident demonstrates how far the global has influenced our perception of the local, and the different positionalities of its local inscription.

Logics of rules

The ethnopole is also made global by the intersection of transnational processes that it houses. We have already alluded to the intersection of people (Koreans, Chinese, Asian Indians, Japanese, and Vietnamese), goods (Japanese, Chinese, and Korean products sold there), capital (via the banking system) and communications (telephone, fax, e-mail). The intersection of the logics of rules is another important factor that constitutes the globalization of the ethnopole.

In postcolonial literature, the notion of "rules" is often dissected in terms of technologies of governance. Thus, colonial governmentality develops a series of strategies of domination that insures the survival of the regime. This is not an explicit context of coloniality, and the rules described here refer to a different form of governmentality: the internal logics that govern the ethnopole.

These rules of governance are anchored in the ethnopole and produced by three sectors, each with its internal logic and global agenda. The governance of the polity which rests with city hall concerns itself with order, integration (that is, the harmonious articulation of the ethnopole with the rest of the city), and the transformation of the enclave into a "theme park" for the purpose of providing an atmosphere for tourists to enjoy. These rules of governance address Japantown's needs in the context of the larger city and for the common good of a greater population. Although formulated with the input of the ethnopolitans, they are legislated by an outside body that concerns itself with larger issues of governance. The rules of city hall, with its global (tourism) and local (welfare of the enclave) orientation, are major factors in the shaping of everyday life in the ethnopole.

The corporate world of Japantown has also developed its own set of unwritten rules that provides a rationale for its actions. The logic of this apparatus must be sought in the transnational orientations of the players. The very location of the Japantown stores induces them to cater to foreign tourists, and, of course, to local buyers as well. However, as subsidiaries of overseas headquarters firms, they are naturally engaged in transnational transactions. Unlike city hall, which seeks the common good, their main orientation is profit-maximization. Thus in this specific sector, transnationality is undertaken first and foremost to make a profit, and this is the major rule of governance that explains the dynamics of the corporate world of Japantown.

The non-profit grassroots system is another sector, with its local and global agenda, that influences everyday life in the ethnopole. The logic of rules here is also different from those of the sectors mentioned above. The rationale of these rules is to intervene on behalf of the poor, the elderly, and the newly arrived immigrants. For example, the Committee against Nihonmachi Eviction (CANE) was founded to provide the necessary correction or opposition to those forces behind the eviction of old-timer residents to make room for the commercial buildings of Japantown. However, globalization has contributed to the success of some of these grassroots organizations through donations they receive from the corporate structure of Japantown, and because of this largesse, the stance of the grassroots to the business community has changed from one of outright rejection to acceptance and tolerance, albeit with a healthy dose of suspicion. These grassroots organizations provide needed services to their constituents. However, their concerns embrace not only the local, but also the global as they network with overseas individuals and organizations. For example, in 1985, with the help of local grassroots organizations, five survivors of the atomic bomb that destroyed Hiroshima and Nagasaki staged a protest at the Peace Plaza pleading for nuclear disarmament and reminding us of the holocaust inflicted by our government on the Japanese people.[137] What they sought was a platform on which to broadcast their global message, and Japantown provided such a venue. Another good example is the support that San Francisco Japantown's activists give to Japanese Peruvians' efforts to get redress from the US government because of their harsh experiences in US detention camps during the Second World War.

The proposition that the ethnopole can be constructed as a global city has been analyzed in this chapter along with the modalities of raw and cooked globality. The data shows how the ethnopole is traversed by a multiplicity of forms of globality and how in turn these forms have shaped its global contours. In Chapter 6, I will address the global spatial infrastructure that sustains the global ethnopole.

6
The Global Space of the Ethnopole

Because the ethnopole is a site of residence of a diaspora, and because of the globality of its interactional relations, it evolves in a global space composed of two mechanisms of spatial formation: a *global heterospace* and a *global ethnospace*. The global heterospace refers to spatial interaction between the ethnopole and extraterritorial sites of otherness, and the global ethnospace refers to the spatial relationship between the ethnopole and the homeland and other diasporic sites. In other words, the global space of the ethnopole is a limited domain that can be spatially circumscribed and mapped out. And it is important to do so if the argument of the ethnopole as a global city is to be sustained.

Through its diasporic residents the ethnopole maintains ongoing relations with extraterritorial sites; an analysis of this global map will show how ethnopolitan globalization is spatialized. The global ethnopole cannot be properly understood without unveiling the global space that serves as its infrastructure. The ethnic yellow pages – collections of advertisements published in book form and focused on ethnic businesses and ethnic audiences – provide the raw data for unveiling the global space of the ethnopole. Described by Howe as "a compartmentalized and concise form of capitalism,"[138] the ethnic yellow pages serve as a key advertising strategy of businesspeople who make money not only in the local ethnopole but in its extraterritorial tentacles as well. The ethnic yellow pages redraw the global marketing sphere of the ethnopole by connecting the local market to overseas clients, producers, distributors, and employees, and in the process produce transnational transactional spaces.

These transnational spaces of interaction, intersection, and interrelation are indeed spatial corridors that connect multilocal sites to each other in multiple transactional encounters. An analysis of the ethnic yellow pages allows us to distinguish the following sites of spatial globality:

- The sites of location of advertisers indicate and define the global market arena that these global actors who advertise in the ethnic yellow pages belong to. Sometimes, these advertisers are managers of subsidiary firms whose headquarters are overseas.
- The readership that the ethnic yellow pages target comprises local buyers, foreign tourists, and overseas clients. This is the clientele whose purchases provide the necessary backup for the ethnic enterprises to prosper.
- The ethnic yellow pages reflect the globality of products, since some of these are manufactured elsewhere and imported to be sold in the ethnopole. This indicates that a transnational space links the site of production to the site of consumption.
- The ethnic yellow pages reflect the transformation of local stores into global entities because they advertise to attract foreign tourists and depend on international clients for their success. As such, they refurbish their inventory to meet the tastes and demands of that international clientele.
- Businesspeople from outside the community advertise in the ethnic yellow pages to tap into a specific global niche and transnational transactional spatial corridor. Local politicians and overseas government officials also use this medium to reach their expatriates or diasporic constituents and feed them political propaganda. No matter what, advertising in the ethnic yellow pages provides one with global exposure, given their international circulation.
- The global space of the ethnopole is shaped by social actors and is continually being unmade and remade. It is a stratified space based on the inclusion/exclusion process, that is, on the distinction between those who make use of it and those who do not. It is also stratified in terms of access and temporality of use, that is, by those who regularly buy the products it advertises and those far away who acquire them sporadically.[139]
- Both the advertisers and the publishers are involved in the projection and construction of global space. While the global space projected by advertisers corresponds to their target niches, the global space projected by the publishers is less restrictive. However, it does not correspond to an actual global space, but a constructed one, because of the dynamics of the population movement over which it has no control.

The distinction made by Keyman between *inherited space* and *projected space* is instructive in that it unveils the dynamics of spatial relations.[140] The space that the advertisers project, which becomes the inherited space of the publishers, may not coincide with the space projected by the yellow pages. This outcome may in turn influence the projected space of the advertisers as they refurbish their stocks to meet the needs of a new and unexpected clientele. The logic of the global space of the ethnopole can be understood through an analysis of the Chinese, Japanese, and Filipino yellow pages.

Genesis of the ethnic yellow pages

The ethnic yellow pages came into being as an intermediate space that mediates the needs of diasporic, mainstream, and overseas clients. They provide homeland, diaspora, and mainstream businesses with an outlet in which they can engage in global competition, that is, compete for a share of the global ethnic market. The ethnic yellow pages is a localized global site that further turns the ethnopole into a globalized local site.

There was a history of yellow pages publishing in the United States prior to the publication of the ethnic yellow pages; ethnics have always been aware of their existence and continue to use them. In some cases, the content of this medium is adjusted to meet the cultural sensibility of the ethnics. This medium is not an ethnic creation, but rather is published by mainstreamers in an effort to expand their market targets or transactional economic spaces by drawing clients from specific ethnic communities. In other words, mainstream economic spaces are expanded to include ethnic economic enclaves for the purpose of profit-maximization.

The publication of a yellow pages that catered to non-white clients first came about in the mid-1960s with the influx of large groups of people from the Third World to the United States. Right around this time, the American yellow pages industry was involved in reaching out to these new groups and in developing ethnic market targets. For example, Southern Bell and NYNEX published Hispanic yellow pages geared to this specific group. They were not advertising Hispanic businesses to mainstream clients, but rather mainstream businesses to potential Hispanic customers. But since advertising involves more than just the use of the ethnic language, the messages, colors, and signs were coded to attract the attention of prospective ethnic clients. This top-down approach contrasts with the bottom-up approach of ethnic advertising, which solicits mainstream businesses to advertise in their yellow pages.

While in some cases, an ethnic yellow pages is a franchise of the mainstream yellow pages undertaken to reach ethnic customers, in other cases these are ethnic ventures carried out by diasporic entrepreneurs. In California, almost every Asian American group has its own yellow pages: *Japanese Telephone and Reference Directory* (304 pages); *The Japanese Business Directory and Guide: Telephone Guide* (512 pages); *Thai Yellow Pages* (314 pages); *The Filipino Directory: USA, Canada, Philippines* (612 pages); *Tasvir Persian-American Yellow Pages* (704 pages); *Chinese Yellow Pages* (1156); *Vietnamese Business Directory* (752 pages); *Korean Business Directory* (566 pages); *Bridge USA: Telephone and Maps: Japanese Business Telephone Directory* (1034 pages); *Chinese Consumer Yellow Pages* (1888 pages). In the case of the Chinese yellow pages, more mainstream American businesses are advertised than ethnic businesses, thereby introducing Chinese American patrons to American products and facilitating penetration of the enclave economy by mainstream businesses. In contrast, the Japanese yellow pages advertises more ethnic than mainstream American businesses.

The ethnic yellow pages, a post-Civil-Rights-movement phenomenon, are proliferating in the United States in general and in California in particular. Most are published by ethnic entrepreneurs (Chinese, Thai, Vietnamese, Japanese, Filipino, Korean, Iranian, Haitian, Cuban) who have realized that there is a potential market in these ethnopoles, and whose aim is to connect the United States, the homeland, and ethnic businesses to diasporic and transnational clienteles. While ethnic businesses have always advertised in ethnic newspapers, the yellow pages comprise the first systematic and large-scale attempt at targeting the ethnic enclave, the homeland, and other diasporic sites all at once. As an advertising medium, the ethnic yellow pages differ from ethnic radio and ethnic newspapers because the former reaches a more global audience; their advertisements also last longer as people keep the book as a souvenir or to enhance their personal library, thus making it an easy reference to share with overseas family and visiting friends.

Unlike the mainstream American yellow pages, which dominate the market in any given city because of their inclusiveness, the ethnic yellow pages, in some cases, compete among themselves for clientele. In the same ethnopole, there may be more than one yellow pages in circulation, as publications do not confine themselves to any single community but have a local, national, and transnational content.

For example, the same Filipino yellow pages that is largely circulated in Los Angeles and Manila is also the most popular one in San Francisco because it advertises for businesses in all three locations.

The following edited statement made by a key managerial staff member of one of the ethnic yellow pages publications gives us a sense of the implosion of the global through mass migration in the genesis of such a business and telephone directory:

> We started in 1988. At that time, there was only the *Asian yellow Pages*. They had started three or four years before, using mostly American sales agents to contact Chinese merchants. But that strategy did not work as well as they would have liked. They were getting low renewal rates, so they were forced to find new clients every year. We showed up at the request of our Los Angeles parent company; it is a franchise, we got right down to working with the local communities through the owner, Mr. Wang [fictional name], who was a representative of a foreign-owned commercial enterprise. He already had some contacts with the local business people, and through them we were able to beat our competition because we were Chinese-community based, whereas they were running it only as a business. Granted we were also running as a business, but we had higher exposure; and from that, it expanded based on the growth of the Chinese community in the Bay Area.
>
> We realized that in the past, the merchants were mostly Chinese people whose families had come during the gold rush. So, they were usually Cantonese, and if not first generation, then already second to third generation. They were very conservative. They didn't have the spending power, neither did they want to advertise. But then as Los Angeles got bigger, more Chinese from Taiwan and China began to come over; there were more business owners and more consumers with stronger buying power. We caught a wave and took off from that. There were also two other books that came out at the same time; but because they had limited resources and were quite isolated from the community, within two years they were gone. In contrast, we made an effort to go out and participate in different Chinese events, and to establish relations with businesses.
>
> Two years after we started, we realized that selling to Chinese merchants would not be enough. The market was simply not large enough to sustain the big book. At that time, the sales team from the competing yellow pages jumped ship and came over to our company. It was at that juncture that we began to revolutionize the sales

strategy of the yellow pages. We began to target American businesses, increasing their awareness of the buying power of the Chinese community and educating them on marketing techniques that would work on Chinese consumers; due to this, the ads they placed in our book brought in a lot of Chinese buyers to their establishments, and so they liked it. As a result, the number of American ads began to increase, and it was easier to target other American businesses.

Today we have two teams, one that targets American businesses and another that targets Chinese businesses. The methodology is different, due to the cultural difference between the American and the Chinese. And so, we are here today.

Already in the process of foundation, the homeland connection was invoked through the immigrants who were resettling in San Francisco. This influx made a difference both in terms of the initial process and the success of the operation. The mediating role of a representative of the Overseas Chinese Committee of the Republic of China, which facilitated the business contacts through his own network of acquaintances, was also central in the early expansion of this yellow pages and its establishment as a viable economic venture. Thus, the creation of this Chinese yellow pages was not simply a local process, but had transnational implications and ramifications as well.

There is a marked progression in the conception of the Filipino yellow pages, which started as a local concern and later moved on to address national demand and homeland needs. In a sense, the national and global imposed themselves on the local. With the addition of national and global business addresses, the local concerns have taken on a global dimension. A staff member provides his insider view of the evolution of the Filipino yellow pages:

We started as a group of journalists who had a newspaper and who wrote about the community, and we kept getting questions like "where do I find this restaurant?", and "where can I find this Filipino place and this video store?" and stuff like that. So, we kept answering them, and finally a group of us got together and made up a book with a set of ads, and printed the book so people wouldn't have to be calling us. We thought maybe it would be a good service to the community. You know, to consolidate all of the Filipino businesses in one place, put together all of this information for people who are trying to settle in the United States. Actually, it was targeted to the new immigrants.

We saw the need, so we came up with the directory that includes not only Filipino-based businesses but also mainstream companies. Then eventually people in other cities were saying "Hey we need one of these." So we started expanding from Los Angeles to the rest of the United States. Then some of the communities in Canada said that they needed one as well. So we included Canada in our publication.

Sometimes the fact that globality invades the process is not primarily because the yellow pages links the ethnopole to extraterritorial sites, but rather because it is located in a transnational reading space so as to help newcomers adapt to American society. For instance, the Japanese yellow pages is believed to be read mostly by monolingual first generation immigrants from Japan.

Whatever the genesis may be, both mainstream and ethnic entrepreneurs use the yellow pages to deal with the buying power of an expanding market among the newly arrived immigrants and the ethnic enclaves. The yellow pages leads the mainstream to survey the needs and geographical distribution of the ethnics in order to target them as potential buyers or clients and to develop yellow pages in their homeland language. In the case of the ethnic entrepreneurs, the ideology is that of economic empowerment and ethnic solidarity, and they see the publication of their yellow pages as providing a tangible backup to the slogan "buy from your own people". For the mainstream, it is an expansion of the market. For the ethnics, it is a matter of keeping the money inside the ethnic group, giving more visibility to the enclave economy, drawing clients from the mainstream to the ethnic stores, and, in the process, empowering the ethnic enclave.[141] This ethnic ideology is still pervasive even when the yellow pages publish ads for mainstream businesses and thus allow them to penetrate the ethnic market.

Content of ethnic yellow pages

An ethnic yellow pages can be read as a geographical document because of the way in which it addresses the spatial question. It provides a detailed geography of sites: religious, medical, commercial, social, political, local, and transnational. It is published to allow users to navigate inside this local/global space. As such, it provides direction, orientation, signs, and geographical information that is both categorized and hierarchized.

While the main purpose of the ethnic yellow pages is to provide some publicity for businesses, it is sometimes used as a telephone book, listing a few private home numbers. It also provides information pertaining to the integration of immigrants in American society, and serves as a vehicle to transmit important political information from the homeland government. Yellow pages are popular precisely because of the extra, essential information they provide in the national language of the homeland that everyone in the ethnopole can readily access.

The content of the ethnic yellow pages is well summarized by a staff member who helps edit one of them. What he says is representative of the others as well:

> Commercials will be very high, maybe 80 percent, and maybe with 10–15 percent for general information and 5 percent for new immigrants. That's because the nonprofit organization that helps new immigrants is usually very conservative on their budget in advertisement, so their space is smaller.
>
> Merchants seek other services, in our ads for them. They advertise with us because we have a very large reader base. We try to provide useful information, other than the advertisements, that the Chinese community can use; for example, one of the more popular whitepage sections is the DMV auto driving test form. About six years ago, we used to print the entire test form, until the DMV informed us that a lot of people were passing who did not know what to do. So, understanding the situation, we changed the way that particular section was laid out.
>
> Consulates keep in contact with us because we have information as to their operation hours, the types of services they provide, and their telephone numbers. So, we keep in touch with consulates from China, Hong Kong, and Taiwan.

Each ethnic yellow pages has three components: it is an information resource book for new immigrants and monolingual ethnics; it is a business directory that provides information on stores and service centers; and it provides general information on the homeland and from government officials.

The Filipino yellow pages published in Los Angeles contains general information on the history of each province of the Philippines, statements by several government officials, a political message from the president of the Republic, another political message from a Filipino member of the Canadian Parliament directed to his Filipino Canadian constituencies and overseas friends, and invitations from provincial governors to Filipinos living abroad to invest at home and to contribute to the economic development of the country. In effect, an outsider reading the directory would learn a great deal not only about the businesses being advertised but also about the nation's history and social conditions and the government's current plan of action.

Although Pacific Bell's yellow pages offers a more thorough listing of all the government offices, the ethnic yellow pages list only the consulates, a couple of immigration numbers, and the Department of Justice. By being focused on immigration, it reflects the different needs of the ethnic readership. Thus, the differences between these two business directories is more in terms of clientele and language used than in terms of layout.

Market target

The primary market target of the Bay Area's ethnic yellow pages is Northern California. Based on their clientele, the publishers have developed a cognitive map of the history of the population of the region. Their pages reflect their knowledge of the targeted population rather than the actual history and geography of the group. The publisher of one of the Chinese yellow pages states:

> There's an interesting mix of Chinese in the Bay Area. For San Francisco and Oakland, it's mainly Cantonese. Since the gold rush, their family and friends have moved here when they come over. They like to consider themselves as the oldest group of Chinese in America. For the Fremont and Santa Clara region, most are first generation college graduates from Taiwan and China. They study the sciences and then go on to work as engineers in Silicon Valley's large corporations.
>
> In terms of shop owners, the Cantonese have more businesses here. Engineers have become a larger buying power. In San Jose, there are a lot of Korean Chinese or Vietnamese Chinese immigrants. They are usually Chinese people who have gone to Korea or Vietnam before coming here. For instance, though they speak both Vietnamese and Chinese, as a community they are more familiar with Vietnamese. But they advertise in Chinese in our book. Then, there are the peninsula Chinese who own import/export and other types of businesses. So, there is very much a mix of Chinese in the Bay Area.

With the collapse of Manilatown, the Filipino directory now concentrates on the new business enclave in Daly City. According to Manuel, (fictional name),

> Although Stockton was predominantly Filipino, a lot of them, after they had made their fortune, started buying property in south central San Francisco and Daly City. And that's where they have moved to. I know of several families that used to live in Stockton but now reside in Daly City. I would say that Daly City will become a Filipino town of sorts, for it now has a large Filipino concentration.

For the Japanese directory, the market target is influenced by considerations of cost, manpower, and logistics. Richard (fictional name) says, "We only cover Northern California... You see, as our main office is in San Francisco, we would have to verify all the numbers. So it would be hard to do on a large scale."

By and large, the ethnic yellow pages targets the ethnic population in the enclave but is also aimed at ethnic and diasporic niches throughout the nation, other countries, and, to a lesser extent, even the homeland. In this marketing strategy, the target is focused on the ethnics and not the mainstream or foreigners. Although each ethnic business may prefer to have a more open market so as to make more profit, the medium needed would become too cumbersome in order to meet the needs of the non-ethnics. Such a directory would have to publish ads in a multiplicity of foreign languages.

Thus, the language of the yellow pages is both user-friendly and limiting, with ads and additional information written mainly in the ethnic language.[142] The medium of communication by itself limits other potential clients' ability to read the ads. Only those individuals able to read the language may take advantage of the ads. As I was told by a staff person working on the Chinese yellow pages,

> We usually stick with Chinese, and because there are different dialects, we tend to use Mandarin as the standard. Mandarin is even more recognizable now that Hong Kong is back to China. It is also the written common denominator. People from Taiwan and China read Mandarin, and people from Hong Kong often read Mandarin although their dialect is slightly different. Even with China – Shanghai and Santong and other areas of China – each has its own dialect. So our Chinese staff often need to know three or four different dialects even though the primary written language we use is Mandarin.

The Filipino yellow pages is written in English because the business language of the Philippines is English. Some portions are in Tagalog or Filipino when the subject matter requires it or when the Filipino companies prefer it.

The language used may make it more difficult and more costly for a reader to access the ethnic yellow pages. Non-members of the group may need a translator to use it. For non-English speakers, mainstream advertising creates a similar problem. One person notes,

> One of my partners had a Chinese girlfriend, and one day at her parent's house in the Sunset, he discovered there was a guy in the community who was translating Macy's Sunday ads in the Chronicle in Chinese and charging people $1 apiece. There was a line around the block to buy these translations.[143]

To facilitate access, some ethnic yellow pages publish ads in English and provide translations in the language spoken by monolinguals in the ethnopole.

The ethnic yellow pages advertise for American and diasporic businesses, businesses that belong to other ethnic groups in the enclave, diasporic businesses in other countries, and homeland businesses. As one may infer, these yellow pages are not confined to the local ethnopole, but advertise for both American and ethnic businesses in other states as well. However, because the ethnopole is a commercial center of attraction, it occupies a prominent place in terms of ads directed to its business operations.

The publisher of one of the Chinese yellow pages estimates that close to 60 percent of the ads advertise for American businesses, while only 39 percent are geared toward Chinese businesses both at home and abroad, and about 1 percent of the ads are placed by other ethnics, such as Vietnamese or Koreans who have businesses or own stores in Chinatown. These other ethnics are often Chinese who migrated from Vietnam or Korea and who identify with their previous country of adoption. In regard to these ethnic Chinese, the composition of the yellow pages reflects both the business environment and the marketing strategies of the publishers. A member of the publishing team of one of these operations notes,

> We tried, but in terms of different ethnics, there still was that boundary. It was easier for American businesses to want to work with Chinese buyers, but another way was needed for Korean business owners who wanted to sell to Chinese.

The market target for those who advertise in the ethnic yellow pages is the particular ethnic clientele they seek. While American businesses have used the regular yellow pages or the specialized yellow pages published by Pacific Bell, an ethnic yellow pages presents them with a new outlet. Mainstream businesses have tried various ways to penetrate this market to get new clients. For example, using the Chinese yellow pages means that they must decide whether the ads should be in English only, in English with Chinese translation, or in Chinese only. Some have experimented, moving from one strategy to another depending on projected net returns, which can lead to unexpected problems.

Other ethnic merchants, such as Koreans or Japanese, face a dilemma when they publish ads in the Chinese yellow pages because they cannot access their own ethnic groups with such ads written in English or Chinese and not in their own ethnic language. Again, because the ads are printed in English or Chinese, this limits the size of their readership to those who can read the language. For Koreans or Japanese who wish to access their own community, they must publish their ads in either the Korean or Japanese yellow pages.

Thus, the ethnic yellow pages provide market niches that are very much reader-based. Publishers make a conscious decision to sell or advertise to one particular group of readers, making the publication convenient solely for those readers. New immigrants comprise a large portion of the readership:

> We found out that the majority of the readers are new immigrants who have just come here. As their English is not proficient, they can use our book as a guide. Second generation Chinese tend to use the guide less because, by then, they are able to use the Pacific Bell yellow pages, which covers more. We found that housewives tend to use the book a little more, although we have a lot of Chinese businesspeople using our book as an index or contact source for their business needs. Our popular sections are for attorneys, auto repairs, and doctors. Insurance and travel agent sections are very competitive.

Immigrants patronize immigration lawyers mainly for help in changing their status or in navigating through commercial and trade laws. These attorneys may either speak the ethnic language or belong to law firms who have ethnic lawyers on their staff. The category "medical doctors" provides a more inclusive section than one finds in the mainstream yellow pages. Here acupuncturists, Chinese herbal-medicine doctors, traditional Chinese doctors, and plastic surgeons are among those most sought after by Chinese readers. These practitioners, able to speak the ethnic language, are familiar with the cultural background of the clients as well and can relate to clients in a way that non-Chinese practitioners cannot.

Competition

The ethnic yellow pages vie to remain the main outlet for advertising in the ethnople, since their success and longevity depends on their prominence among the ethnic business community. To achieve their goals, they must compete with other media – not so much with television, radio, and newspaper advertising, which being daily outlets, do not compete in the same category. Rather, Pacific Bell's yellow pages and other ethnic yellow pages circulating in the San Francisco Bay Area provide the most competition.

It is important to analyze the ways in which the ethnic yellow pages assess the impact of competitors and the niches they try to establish in order to remain on top. The following narrative gives us a glimpse of how the actors involved perceive both the mainstream and ethnic yellow pages that they compete with:

> For Oakland, there is a very localized directory. It is not as thick, is published only once a year, and focuses mainly on Oakland's Chinatown and its surrounding businesses. That market does not really concern us. As that directory is fairly small, their rates are small, and those advertisers using them are more concerned with spending less money. The other yellow pages, the Bay Area yellow pages, headquartered in Houston, is harder for us to figure out – how they are selling – because they don't have a regular sales force. As the owner is in Houston, he flies out to meet with the sales team only once every couple of months. They have a very high turnover rate for salespeople, making it hard for us to pick out who on their sales team is actually selling. Sometimes, they will lower their rates to less than 50 percent of our rates or even give out their ads for free. So, we are not sure how they are making a profit, since the cost of producing a book is relatively standard. As we are producing the same type of directory, we wonder how could they not charge clients for producing their book. However, as they are very prosperous in other areas (Houston and Seattle), there is a possibility that they came out here to try out the market and, after a year and a half, they are reluctant to fold. There is always a three-year time-period for any product

to grow, so they are possibly still waiting it out. Also, as their owner is not in the San Francisco Bay Area, we use their lesser degree of involvement with the community as our strong point: "We are here, we can serve you."

We've also talked to Pacific Bell, who also tried to publish a Chinese yellow pages with a small market and discovered that it would be both more time consuming and costly for them to print a Chinese yellow pages than to focus solely on their yellow pages. Their rates were roughly three to four times higher than ours. Conversely, if we decided to print a mainstream yellow pages, our cost would have been so high that we would have to raise our rates to match the operational expenses involved with a large company. Some of our sales people are still using a bartering system, where the client will pay cash for half the amount and the other half is service rendered for one thing or another – it is a policy hard to justify once you are as big as Pacific Bell. So, they tried and saw that it did not work, and that was that.

There are two forms of competition at work here: competition between the ethnic and the mainstream yellow pages that target ethnic groups; and competition among ethnic yellow pages publishers to earn the heart and soul of the ethnic business community. The mainstream, by sponsoring one ethnic venture against others, may shift the balance of the competition. There is, then a national influence on the local competition, but there is also an international or global influence. To the extent that subsidiary-firms located in an ethnopole sponsor one ethnic yellow pages rather than another they alter the local competition scene.

Advertisers

The success of the ethnic yellow pages depends on the ability of the managers to attract and retain the advertisers as a steady clientele. But advertizers' interest in buying space depends on the yellow pages' ability to reach a sizable number of prospective clients. So coverage is an important factor here. Wide coverage, however, requires some research to identify sites and locate advertisers and clients.[144] Since mainstream American companies that advertise in the ethnic yellow pages are either local or national businesses, it is necessary to understand the rationale of such a practice:[145]

> If there were a large enough Chinese population in the San Francisco area where we could publish just one book for the San

Francisco area, I think we would do so. In terms of revenue, Pac Bell could get enough revenue from just one city, whereas we have to pool the entire Bay Area just to get enough revenue to justify our operation. In terms of outreach, I am not sure if our sales managers have thought that far; we do have national accounts, but they are usually firms like Sears, Macy's, Safeway, and Roundtable Pizza. As large chains, they see the Chinese community as a source of buying power. When they buy advertisements with us, they go through a single medium that has control over the Chinese yellow pages in the Pacific Region, the West Coast Region, and they will buy one ad that covers everything.

The strategy for locating clients is similar to that of the mainstream yellow pages: they buy lists of potential customers or canvass newspapers in search of new operations.[146] This constant search through newspapers listings is *sine qua non*, because new businesses – potential clients – may open up at any time. Says a staff person,

> We actually buy mailing lists from Pacific Bell, and the other source is the Chinese newspapers. We have sales agents that sit and read the newspapers because they want to see what is new. We have been around for ten years, and our sales team knows whenever there is a new business that just came out.

Advertisers have specific needs, and unless they are met, they are unlikely to use the same medium again. They have the option of using the radio or newspaper for their publicity. By and large, the ethnic yellow pages fare well in terms of keeping their clientele: the renewal rate for the three ethnic pages (Filipino, Japanese, and Chinese) is above 80 percent, which indicates the satisfaction of a large group of patrons. One informant states,

> I think we have an 85 percent renewal rate. So clients come back about 85 percent of the time. But from what I understand, the previous book – although that was about 10 years ago – got only about a 50–60 percent renewal rate. Our book is covering around twelve hundred pages every year, plus or minus about one hundred pages. We found that to be pretty consistent. And so I think at this point, we have reached market saturation.

The large size of the Chinese yellow pages is partly the result of the publishers' strategy to develop two different teams, one American and one Chinese, to go after the clients. The informant says that this is a necessary step because of the two business cultures one has to deal with:

> We were pretty much forced to have two teams, one to sell to American businesspeople and one to the Chinese business owners. But when I go overseas, I see the yellow pages, and it is a different kind of yellow pages. Our book is very much influenced by the Pacific Bell yellow pages, although, on the selling side – I was told anyway – it is closer to overseas: very cost conscious and very bargain-driven.
>
> Advertisers call us sometimes, but usually we call them. Our sales force is very aggressive. Usually by the third day of their grand opening, we already have three people from our sales force that have already contacted them. It is almost a race for the sales team to reach the new business, because our regulations state that the person who first contacted the business is responsible for the sale. If the person cannot close the deal within the given time, then we open up the account for other sales executives.

Distribution

The ethnic yellow pages are distributed not only in the local communities, but also in the countries of origin.[147] Shermach states that Chinese tourists have access to the yellow pages through local restaurants, travel agencies, consulates, and relatives who return from trips to the United States and bring the books to their homeland. One informant describes his company's strategy for distributing the books in Northern California:

> We try to look for markets where a lot of people would go every week as distribution points. For more rural areas like Marin, Danville, and Fremont, we would place them in restaurants that Chinese people would frequent. We usually put about 300 or 400 books and check every week to make sure that there is an adequate stock. For areas like Chinatown or San José, where the Chinese population is much denser, in the markets we put several thousand books at a time, and usually one or two weekends later, the piles would be gone and we would restock. As time went on, we would have distribution points that are published in our book and in our advertisements in the newspapers, and we would also advertise on TV, Chinese television – and radio where the distribution points

are – and tell them that they can go to those establishments (who are usually our advertisers) and pick up our directories there.

In contrast, the Filipinos distribute their books through specific outlets in the United States, Canada, and the Philippines:

> In Canada, we have a contract with Montreal and Ottawa. In the Philippines, we distribute our books in Manila, the capital city, and in Cebu. In the United States, we distribute in Los Angeles, Chicago, Hawaii, Las Vegas, the Maryland-Virginia-Washington hub, San Diego, the Bay Area, and we are currently negotiating with Silicon Valley. Also, we drop off these free yellow pages in restaurants, eateries, and banks – basically wherever we have a reasonable expectation that it will go to a Filipino crowd or Filipino businesses.
>
> Actually, more than 50 percent of the calls we get requesting these books are from tourists. Our normal circulation has been mostly limited to ethnic outlets. For example, a majority of Filipino tourists wanting to go to Disneyland and Universal Studios and shopping will use it.

Unlike the other yellow pages that are distributed free of charge, the Japanese yellow pages of San Francisco is not given but sold to people. The rationale I was given is that "it is a business and therefore people would buy it because they need it." Copies are distributed in the Japanese bookstores in San Francisco and San Jose and in Japanese banks. One such bank usually buys one thousand books every year to distribute to customers free of charge. The Japanese consulate makes copies available to visitors as a way of providing needed information to Japanese tourists.

Local and global reach

The global and local reach is constituted by the geographical sphere of influence of the ads, the locations of the businesses that place ads, and the residences of the clients or patrons. Although locally produced, the yellow pages are used by people in Northern California and beyond.[148] In a sense the yellow pages help to define the globality of the ethnopole because they identify extraterritorial sites that comprise the ethnopole's global spatial infrastructure.

Yellow pages advertising focuses mainly on the city where the ethnopole is located and sites surrounding it. Names and addresses of merchants are verified every year to ensure the reliability of what is published. Both the Chinese and Japanese yellow pages emphasize Northern California, while the Filipino yellow pages tend to be more global. There are reasons for this different approach. Chinese and Japanese have specific yellow pages books for specific regions. For example, they each have separate books for Los Angeles and Southern California. One informant says,

> For our book, it is a Northern California issue, so the coverage is limited to the area our sales people could reach. It is also the area where there is a more dense population of Chinese. So, north of the Bay Area, say Marin County, we have fewer clients, because the Chinese population there thins out. That's not necessarily the Chinese buying population; it is just that there are fewer Chinese business owners up north, east past the Oakland mountain range, and south of San Jose. Beyond that – Morgan Hill and Gilroy – though there would be a Chinese population there, they're buyers, not business owners. So, it would be harder for salespeople to go all the way down to Morgan Hill for one client. They would rather go down when there are three or four clients so that they can service them all at once.

The Filipino directory published in Los Angeles distributes its ads in three major sections: one each for the United States, Canada and the Philippines. One staff member notes,

> We have a base in the Philippines as well, geared towards, what Filipino businesses are exporting to the United States and Canada. As it turns out, from the original purpose of extending to the Filipino communities, the Philippines operation now reaches the Filipino communities in Canada as well.

The Filipino staff person makes a distinction between the geography of buyers and that of business owners, though, for distribution purposes, he must include both. In this sense, the distribution provides a much larger view of the global space issue. He says, "We do have readers writing to us and requesting the yellow pages...In our Northern California book, we cover from Vancouver to Washington, DC, New York, Atlanta, and other states."

The global reach is constructed along three axes: the extraterritorial area covered, the international locations of the readers, and the international locations of businesses who advertise in the pages. The global/transnational connections are made through subsidiary–headquarters relations, multinational corporations, and import–export firms. The rationale of this multilayered practice is provided below. As an informant describes it,

> The global reach usually consists of food products (like cookies). We found that for those clients there is a significant buyer who would like to have certain products here for one reason or another. So, though they come here to set up a manufacturing plant, their advertising decisions are still made by the company in China, Hong Kong, or Taiwan. Another major field is airlines, who, seeing the Chinese population go back frequently, advertise with us very prominently. Other services include the air cleaners. As Chinese style of cooking tends to generate more grease or smoke than American cooking, many Chinese homeowners discover that their house has become greasy after two years of cooking. So, they will buy a Chinese-made air cleaner, which is more powerful and is geared towards the exhaust of more grease and smoke. Besides these, other businesses are very localized.

Readers outside the United States do request copies of the book by mail, which is an indication that these individuals find it useful. It is estimated that an average of about two dozen requests are made every year from Canada and other Pacific Rim countries. However, the book is also known in other countries through tourists or former residents of the ethnopole who take copies with them to their new residences and share them with friends. Such yellow pages books are very popular in China. Auto dealers' sections are especially popular because they make it possible for retailers there to contact merchants here.

Some of the people who have had access to the book in their home countries make contact with these merchants once they come here as tourists; there is a nascent international clientele being served by the ethnic yellow pages. The Japanese nourish their tourist clientele by publishing information catering to them. One staff member says, "Japanese tourists like their golf, and we have the golf associations' section."

Of the three, the Filipino directory is more formalized along a global line, maintaining two offices, one in the United States and the other in the homeland, in a headquarters–subsidiary type of relation that enhances the transnational flows of communication, clients, and products. An informant says that, "We have a manager in the Philippines operating in our subsidiary office there, but the headquarters of the operation is over here." As a matter of fact, on the day this conversation took place in Los Angeles, we learned that the CEO of the company that publishes the directory was in the Philippines visiting the overseas office.

The global heterospace of the ethnopole

The ethnopole is involved in transnational relations with overseas entities in addition to the homeland and other diasporic sites. While these relations tend to be more business-related than personal or familial, they nevertheless account partly for the globality of the ethnopole. In fact, they link the ethnopole to extraterritorial sites that enhance its globality.

Not all the stores in Japantown are owned by Japanese. For example, a furniture shop owned by an Italian company serves as a subsidiary of a headquarters firm in Italy. Products sold in the store are presumably imported from Italy. The success of this store depends a great deal on the relations it maintains with the foreign operation. Thus, it further links Japantown to Italy, acting as a node in the global networking space of this ethnopole.

The hotels in the ethnopole play an important role in the expansion of the global heterospace as well and are a good example of transnational relations. For example, the managers of these hotels maintain ongoing relations with travel operators in Europe and Asia, agents responsible for luring the tourists in. These tourists come in, use the facilities, patronize local stores and hotels, and buy gifts in the ethnopole, thus feeding the local economy in many different ways. Some stores depend on tourists for their survival and cater to tourists' needs and tastes. Even stores that used to primarily serve the local population now add new items to their stock to meet tourists' demands – the tourist presence has helped to reshape the contents of these local stores. In a sense, these local stores have become *global entities,* for they depend on a global clientele for their survival. Not only do the tourists sustain the local economy by patronizing them, but they also indirectly provide jobs to the locals hired to staff some of these institutions.

Another arena that expands the global heterospace of the ethnopole is the presence of other ethnic groups and residents (both Anglos and non-whites). For the sake of argument, I will concentrate here on the non-white population in the ethnopole, and more particularly on the Koreans. Lured by the prospect of business ventures, Korean merchants have established stores in the enclave, and they compete with local merchants for clientele. Their presence has hybridized the Japanese-American commercial sphere in the enclave, and this further globalizes the ethnopole in other directions, since they maintain transnational relations with the homeland.

This global heterospace is a necessary and central component to the global space of the ethnopole. It grows inside the enclave, it connects the enclave to the world, and it is the space where the ethnic and foreign meet, and, in the process, form a hybrid entity. Heterospace is intrinsic to the making of the globalized local space, which is spatially multidirectional because it expands by going beyond the boundaries of the global ethnospace.

The global ethnospace of the ethnopole

The global ethnospace of the ethnopole comprises a universe made of the homeland, the enclave and other diasporic sites. This universe is a global spatial infrastructure through which various sites are linked directly or indirectly to each other through political, commercial, familial, religious, and social relations. It is a socially constructed space whose geographical boundaries are known. Within this infrastructure, various transnational spatial forms are developed among diasporic sites and between the homeland and diasporic sites.

One may speak of the global ethnospace as comprising transnational commercial, religious, political, familial, and social spaces, each of which incubates, nurtures or is shaped by specific transnational projects. In this light, one may also argue that the global ethnospace is crisscrossed by an array of transnational spaces as well. This spatial crisscrossing can be seen in the way in which the ethnic yellow pages are used by Filipino politicians. For example, President Fidel Ramos uses the Filipino yellow pages to invite the diaspora to invest in the country. As he puts it, "The Philippines is back in business, here in the heart of a booming Asia, and those who invest in the country now will go with us to the top."[149] Letters from the vice president of the Republic of the Philippines, the president of the Philippines Chamber of Commerce and Industry, the president of the League of Governors, the mayor of the City of Baguio, the member of Parliament for Winnipeg North (Canada), and the ambassador of the Philippines to Canada are indicators that these individuals want to reach the diaspora, to inform its residents of what the provinces are doing, to get the confidence of these expatriates – who can influence with their money and telephone calls the outcomes of provincial elections, who can project a positive image of the country abroad, and who invest and use their tourist dollars in the country. Of course, these politicians are consolidating their bases of support by reaching out to these overseas and virtual electorates. The Filipino member of Parliament is also using this medium to reach out to his electorate and fans in Canada and indirectly projecting the image of success of the diaspora. His message in the yellow pages shows that the Filipino presence is not simply a matter of two nations – the United States and the Philippines – but has a global scope.

Global commercial ethnospace links the ethnopole to businesses and clients in the Philippines and in various diasporic sites. These are transnational economic spaces that are always in the making and remaking, as old businesses fade away and new ventures appear.

Social and familial ethnospaces are multivariate because of their diverse points of connection and crisscrossing. One thinks here of family relations, transnational grassroots organizations, and civic associations, with their ongoing diasporic projects in the homeland.

Conclusion

The Chinese, Japanese, and Filipino yellow pages are part of a general trend of entrepreneurial activities in the diasporic communities in the United States. In most of the large cities, ethnic businessmen advertise in yellow pages that cater to their communities. A clear distinction must thus be made between the mainstream yellow pages that target specific ethnic groups and publish ads in their language, and the ethnic yellow pages that advertise for mainstream businesses. The mainstream yellow pages expands its business by penetrating the ethnic market and is less interested in advertising for ethnic businesses; the ethnic yellow pages publishes ads for both groups and in the process provides mainstream businesses access to ethnic clients. A double spatial phenomenon is at play here: *spatial expansion* in the case of the mainstream scenario and *spatial globalization* in the case of the ethnics.

Ethnic yellow pages target a specific market niche: diasporic clients in the United States and overseas and homeland buyers. While the American yellow pages tends to advertise for stores inside the city, the ethnic yellow pages advertise for stores across the nation and for overseas stores as well. In the process, they produce a global space punctuated by economic sites that inform readers about the locations of businesses, the kinds of products sold, and the size of the diasporic economy. Furthermore, they divide the ethnic market arena into zones and hierarchize them by allotting more advertisements for stores in the ethnopole than for those located outside its boundaries. Such a hierarchy is reflective of the population density in the ethnicized informal urban system.

The clientele that uses the yellow pages is very segmented in terms of place of residence and time of use. It comprises the daily clients who live in the enclave, the weekend clientele that comes from the larger ethnic community in the city and its surroundings, and the tourist clientele. When an ethnic yellow pages (e.g. Chinese) advertises for other ethnic businesses (e.g. Korean, Vietnamese, or Indian) in the neighborhood, it collapses various ethnic spaces into a single commercial panethnospace.

While prospective mainstream clients come to mainstream stores to buy things that are on sale, a sale strategy is not regularly used by diasporic merchants in the ethnopole. The ethnopole does not rely on the "sale" tactic to bring people in, but rather on the church, the ethnic fair, New Year celebrations, political protests, humanitarian services, family associations, yellow pages advertising, and specialty stores. These events have both a celebrating as well as commercial aspect. Thus, the mainstream and the ethnic use different strategies or existing channels to attract people to their stores.

I find major differences between the mainstream and the ethnic yellow pages pertaining to their ecumenism and distribution strategies:

- First, the mainstream advertises for businesses located in each city, thus each city has its yellow pages. These yellow pages advertise for stores in a bounded space.
- Second, the mainstream commercial book is inclusive and does not focus on any specific ethnic group; it is made available to the general public.
- Third, the mainstream yellow pages tends to be exhaustive – it covers everything (just send in your money and we will publish your ads). In contrast, the ethnic yellow pages are particularistic and focus on a specific ethnic clientele. While the mainstream uses the English language for its advertisements, the ethnopole uses the ethnic language, with signs revealing clearly its ethnic target.
- Fourth difference that signals a distinction between the two types of yellow pages has to do with their distribution to the public. Ethnic yellow pages are simply placed in strategic locations in the ethnopole for people to pick up. In contrast, the mainstream yellow pages

is distributed through a system of attachment-advertisement, which I distinguish from the *inclusion-advertisement* system. The latter is the process by which an ad is inserted in a medium of communication so as to attract the attention of the reader. Ads published in newspapers fall under this category. In contrast, by attachment-advertisement I mean the process by which an ad or a group of ads is presented as an appendage to a medium of communication. The mainstream yellow pages falls under this category, being distributed freely as an appendage to the telephone directory.

- While the mainstream yellow pages concentrates on the commercial space of the city, the ethnic yellow pages address a much larger space, going beyond the limits of the city. Clients are called on to navigate a global market. As we have seen in the Filipino case, three national markets – the United States, Canada, and the Philippines – are transnationally linked in a global market arena. This yellow pages provides a clue as to the social construction of global space that comprises global sites that are transnationally linked. The directory informs us that there is not just one global space, but rather global spaces, depending on one's structural, cultural, ideological, or gendered position in society.

In this light, the global space of the ethnopole is likely to be different from the global space of the nation-state, because these two universes do not completely coincide with each other. One may speak then of scales of spatial globality. I believe this analytical distinction is crucial in understanding the kind of global space created and produced by different localities. In a sense, it's another way of looking at global space from the bottom up, or focusing on the microspaces of globalization.

7
The Global Ethnopole in the Global City

The focus of this book on the global ethnopole develops a new approach to the study of the urban ethnic community or the immigrant enclave by paying as much attention to its local as to its transnational relations and global articulations. It unveils the global dimension of the local place as something intrinsic to its everyday life.[150] This globality, with its multitude of temporalities, is not imposed on the local, but instead has always been part of its trajectory. Such a global process affects segments of the local community differently, because of the different ways the latter becomes embedded in the former. There is much diversity in the expression of that globality at the local level as a result of multiple temporalities of social action, spatial practices, generational positions, and class status. Thus, the ethnopole is a vivid spatial expression of the social reproduction of the articulation between the global and the local.

Throughout this book, the emphasis has been to read the ethnic enclave as a global ethnopole, thereby expanding our inquiry into areas that have been assumed but not yet explored. I have argued that the emphasis on the local at the expense of the global has led to a biased understanding of the space of place. Introducing this global aspect better reveals the complexity of the site. The previous chapters have described these local and global relations in their multiple angles. This concluding chapter will further theorize, systematize, and operationalize the location of the global ethnopole in the global city and what it entails, so as to better reveal the globalization process of the American transnation.

Space making

Disentangling the structural location of the ethnopole inside the global city is complicated by the fact that its three key variables are constantly changing: the ethnopole with its relations with the global city and the homeland, the global city with its crisscrossing and border-crossing transnational relations that constitute its makeup, and the homeland which has become a transnation. The boundaries of what constitute local versus global practices are blurred because of the various ways the local implodes in the global and the global in the local.[151] This perspective helps explain why understanding local space making is important in our effort to analyze the hybrid constitution of the ethnopole.

The role of space in the making of the ethnopole is central to the process because it provides an infrastructure for the expression of social relations. It is the niche where racial ideologies become embodied as racial practices as a result of the encounter between the guest-immigrants and the host-community. So "space making" in the global ecumene is contingent with "race making" as a form of practice for achieving global hegemony.

One speaks of the global making of ethnic space to indicate that it is not simply a local production; nor is it unbound. Ethnopoles did not evolve as accidents of history, but rather as a result of local and global forces. These global forces resonate in the localized global city, which sets the constraints within which the global ethnopole evolves. *Disciplinary mechanisms* developed by the dominant sector of society have been used to contain and control the boundaries of the ethnopoles and their residents' spheres of activities. Here space is *ideological* (the production of hegemonic versus subaltern ideologies to justify the spatial order of things), *geographical* (the location of the dwellers outside of or in the margins of mainstream space), *social* (the position of the dwellers in a hierarchy of status sites), *racialized* (the demarcation of white space from non-white space), and *ethnicized* (the location of the enclave in an hierarchy of ethnic positions). It is worth identifying and examining both the diverse disciplinary mechanisms that have been used by the city in the production and reproduction of segregated ethnic space, and the transnational relations that the dwellers have developed to resist the ghettoization of their ethnopole:

- The *mechanism of segregation* is the main strategy used to separate the insiders from the outsiders. Although insiders/outsiders can be distinguished in many different ways and for many different reasons, in the case of ethnic groups race is the major factor.[152] Segregation insinuates that the foreign factor is inferior, hence the reference to the global.

- Perhaps one of the most severe obstacles to racial integration was the *mechanism of housing discrimination* that prevented non-Euroethnics from living outside the ghettoized space allocated to them.[153] This form of discrimination entails not only *de facto* segregation, but also the incorporation and incarceration of individuals in a place outside of which they are not welcome. Housing discrimination is a tool used to form communities of subaltern, second-class citizens and to make visible those citizens' outsider status. In this strategy, the state ties the status of the non-white to specific localities. Such localities therefore provide an infrastructure for the expression and social reproduction of one's subaltern status. Housing discrimination indicates the locus of the insertion of the global in the local without indicating the modalities of the transnationality process. It shows the effects of disciplinary mechanisms on the global as it collapses in a specific place into the local. This form of globality is not an unbridled process that penetrates the local at every point, but rather its insertion is controlled and choreographed at specific locales. Housing discrimination did not play itself out outside the global–local context, but rather served as a tactical instrument to domesticate the global in the local.

- The early Asian immigrants were not welcome to settle where they pleased in San Francisco, but rather were forced to develop their neighborhoods in the physical margins of the city.[154] In so doing, they created "spaces of difference" or "islands of externalities." Through the *mechanism of spatialization* developed by the mainstream to marginalize the non-Euroethnics, the dominant sector of society reincorporates them at the bottom of the spatial structure of the city. To their subaltern racial status is attached the subaltern status of their space of difference. The mechanism of spatialization domesticates the global once more by directing it to a place whose status is below that of the places of the Anglos. Thus, one observes how the hierarchy of global space can be inverted at the point of its insertion in the local space. In other words, the principle that rules the grammar of global space can be transcribed or adapted to meet the desiderata of local space. For example, while wealth can be the main criterion in the hierarchization of global space, race may become the main criterion at the local level. It is a space different

from that of the mainstream, a place where the foreign is implanted in our midst.
- Another extreme way in which the mainstream isolates non-Euroethnics from the rest of society is through the *mechanism of quarantinization*. Not only the quarantinization itself is important, but also the fact that the city contemplates the idea, projects a space of representation, discusses the potential outcome, and thereby publicly humiliates the residents of such an ethnic enclave. Quarantinization locates, separates, medicalizes, and downgrades the status of the group.[155] Such a dramatic step is often undertaken to prevent the spread of an epidemic, as in the case of Chinatown in the late nineteenth century. However, the explanation for the epidemic of the disease was not given in terms of germ theory, but rather in terms of race. Here the insertion of the global in the local led to its essentialization. The residents' Chineseness was blamed for the occurrence and spread of the epidemic.
- The space of the ethnic group is seen by the mainstream as a microcosm of the homeland, and the vocabulary the mainstream uses to describe it is meant to indicate the satellite nature of the enclave *vis à vis* the homeland; hence it is nicknamed "little Africa" or "little Canton" or "little Tokyo." This reterritorialization reveals the global expansion of the overseas homeland and, at the same time, the subalternization of its extraterritorial tentacles. These guest communities – by allusion to their foreignness – are made inferior to prevent them from becoming host-communities or from transforming the host-community into a guest-community, thereby reversing the hierarchical order of things. Minoritizing the guests prevents the homeland from having any legitimate hegemonic claim on the host country. Hence the *mechanism of minoritization* by *miniaturization* has both a local dimension that inferiorizes and subalternizes, and a global dimension that prevents the colonization of the host-community by the guests.
- The mainstream miniaturizes the ethnopole in the way it refers to diasporic sites. This reference is not to a local but rather to a global reality, the existence of the homeland. As noted earlier, the ethnopole is read as a microcosm of the entire country. The *mechanism of miniaturization* implies that global connection and recognition and transnationality because of the relations it implies. Chinatown is not simply a symbol of China, but an enclave that maintains its Chineseness precisely because the residents maintain relations with their relatives and business partners, and have developed interests

in the affairs of the homeland. However, as Bauman reminds us, "communities are not nation-states in miniature."[156]

- Through the *mechanism of stigmatization*, negative aspects of the locale, such as filth, prostitution, disease, delinquency, gangs, and criminal activities in general, are singled out and amplified. These issues are not explained in terms of oppression, discrimination, and poverty, but rather as the inability of the people to assimilate and to become American. Such stigmatization is carried out in the domain of social representation as well, in order to insinuate the outsider status of the group. What matters here is not the interpretation but the representation by the mainstream, who has access to the media and controls the corridors of power. Ethnic residents are not stigmatized as homegrown individuals, but as foreigners, hence the global aspect of the stigmatization process.

- Racism is a central factor in segregated space making and is seen here as a process; and one may speak of "racial formation" to explain the problem.[157] The residents of the ethnopole are seen by the mainstream as if they belong to one ethnic group. Thus, the homogenization of the enclave is "cooked" from without and not from within. The *mechanism of racialization* speaks to issues of difference, interaction, and integration, and it moves the problem from the local to the global, that is to the global racial reference, where all local references make sense. It is a different kind of globality that does not refer necessarily to the homeland, but rather to racial ascription on a global scale. It is a globality that refers to universality.

- Through the *mechanism of exoticization*, the space of difference is highlighted by way of magnifying and amplifying the foreign aspect of the ethnopole. It is seen by the mainstream as a spectacle site, to be used also for the enjoyment of incoming tourists. Indirectly, this means that city hall would prevent its modernization to insure its reproduction as an exotic site. Exoticization implies global spatial continuity between the homeland and the ethnopole.

- While the previous mechanisms were constructed from without by the mainstream, the *mechanism of diasporization* is a construction of the ethnopole in its interaction with both the homeland and the host-community.[158] It is the process by which the group reconstitutes itself abroad and establishes modes of relations with the homeland. While adjusting to the space of the host-community, the diaspora occupies an in-between structural space linking itself to the homeland. By definition, a diaspora is a global social formation.

- There is a temporal dimension to the adaptive trajectory of the ethnopole. Sometimes it is subtle and has to do with the rhythm of life. At other times it is more visible because it interferes with the structure of the week or the year. In other words, the temporalities of the mainstream do not coincide with those of non-Western and non-Christian immigrants. The making of segregated space is related to one's ability to maintain these different temporalities so as to prevent complete assimilation. I refer to this global process as the *mechanism of temporization*.
- To render effective the segregation factor, social mechanisms had to be developed to enforce the spatial distance. For example, through the *mechanism of business discrimination*, the Anglo community made it difficult for Chinese to engage in the laundry business by preventing them access to commercial licenses, as reported in the *Yick Wo v. Hopkins* case.[159] At other times, Chinese were forced to pay taxes not imposed on other groups. This two-tier taxation system prevented fair competition with Anglos. Just as the space in which they were allowed to operate was marginalized, the businesses they were allowed to operate were also marginalized.
- The disciplining of the body is a very radical way of controlling a person's life. The *mechanism of bodily regulations* was developed to curtail the freedom of movement of Chinese immigrants in San Francisco. Such regulations were operative outside the enclave and had no purpose other than to confine the ethnics to their quarter. An example of such a disciplining practice was the ordinance that forbade Chinese from carrying baskets held on two ends of a pole on their shoulders in the city.[160]
- While the mechanism of bodily regulation simply made certain practices illegal, the *mechanism of dishonorization* goes one step further by invading and shaping the body and influencing its physical outlook. The queue-cutting ordinance, which ordered the cutting of a prisoner's hair to no more than one inch from the scalp, was created for that purpose.[161] The attempt here was to deglobalize the body by way of localizing it.
- Through various *mechanisms of marginalization and exclusion*, the mainstream has sought to isolate the ethnopole in order to prevent it from attaining any position of power in the city. In this context, social exclusion is supposed to reinforce spatial marginalization. The study of the global ethnopole examines the insertion of the global in the local and, more specifically, how some aspects of the global can be marginalized at the local level.

- The system is held together by *mechanisms of social control*. Through ordinances and social practices, the Anglo segment of society creates three spaces: the mainstream space or space of power; the space of the others, or the subaltern space; and the space of difference that maintains the separation between the two.[162] In this light, the legal system is used by the mainstream as a means of control and not necessarily as a means of justice when the mainstream deals with the "others." In this context, the maintenance of hegemony takes precedence over justice.

Confronted with the mechanisms of exclusion imposed by city government and the mainstream community, residents of the enclave engaged in processes that would lead to their desegregation. In the nineteenth century, they hired white lawyers to represent them, since they were barred from representing themselves; they relied on missionaries and preachers to speak positively about them to the mainstream community; they organized social institutions as solidarity mechanisms and places of refuge in a hostile environment; and they used their quarters as bases for cultural creativity, economic pursuits, and political resistance.

Space making involves a series of mechanisms of control and countermechanisms of resistance that have both global and local content in their representation of reality, implementation of strategies, and counterhegemonic pursuits. This analysis of space making attempts to explain the global aspects of the ghettoization of ethnic place within the boundaries of the global city.

Space collapsing

The collapse of the ethnopole may also shed light on the globalization process. It is not enough to study globalization in the routine life of the ethnopole; it is just as important to study the global aspects of its decline. In the instances discussed in this book in which an ethnopole collapsed, neither could be explained simply in terms of local issues. Under what circumstances does an ethnopole collapse?

In the case of Manilatown, it collapsed because new immigrants were not settling in the ethnopole but instead went to Daly City; this caused a slow reduction in the size of the ethnopole, making it vulnerable to public pressure. The capitalist players who closed the International Hotel and forced the Filipinos out were part of a multinational corporation with tentacles outside the city limits. Once evicted, they were dispersed to live wherever they could find cheap places to rent. The collapse of the ethnopole did not accompany the deglobalization of the residents: it was an instance of collapse without deglobalization. One may call this process the *dispersion model*.

In contrast, the collapse of Japantown occurred because of actions of the homeland. The cause of the residents' eviction – the Pearl Harbor event, in which they did not participate – was external and foreign to them. This external cause brought about the collapse of their ethnopole. Thus, this collapse was accompanied by deglobalization, since the people were incarcerated and could not maintain ongoing relations with the homeland because of war between the two nations. One may call this process the *detention model*.

Another scenario that describes the collapse of an ethnopole is that of the displacement of Greektown in Chicago so that the University of Illinois could occupy its place.[163] Here, the collapse of the ethnopole meant its relocation and reterritorialization without deglobalization, and it was accomplished for the common good of the citizenry. One may call this process the *relocation model*.

The fourth possible scenario involves the collapse of the ethnopole because of outmigration and gentrification. Chile Town collapsed in the nineteenth century because its residents migrated to, and were assimilated in other neighborhoods in, San Francisco, and the ethnopole did not attract new migrants from the homeland. One may call this process the *assimilation model*.

The last scenario describes the collapse of Little Italy in San Francisco. By midcentury, Little Italy was the informal capital of the Italian community in Northern California because of its cultural institutions, its business district, its fairs and festivals, and the sizable number of people of Italian descent who lived there. However, with migration of the second generation to the suburbs and other parts of town, the overflow of Chinatown inside Little Italy, and gentrification in general, the neighborhood has lost its distinct Italian personality. One may call this process the *gentrification model*.

Ethnopole and state relations

The relations of the ethnopole with the homeland have not been homogeneous, and their ups and downs affect and are affected by the ethnopole's relations with the global city. I want to analyze next how these different types of ethnopole–state relations influence the relations of the ethnopole to the city.

Ethnopole–state relations have taken diverse shapes, which I will transcribe in terms of models so that we can better understand the involution of the ethnopole within these different parameters. In the course of the history of these ethnopoles, the United States either has made it clear that some immigrants were no longer welcome and thus were invited to return home, has conveyed strong signals to the homeland state to stop sending immigrants to the United States, or has taken the extra step to develop repatriation policies for the return of immigrants to their homeland. I refer to this process as the *repatriation model;* it indicates the reincorporation of the immigrants into the homeland. In this model the residents may be either willing or unwilling to participate in the scheme, and the model suggests that in some cases they had no alternative. Some fought to stay in the country while others voluntarily returned home. The model also involves the willingness of the sending state to welcome the ethnics back to their native land.

Such a repatriation policy reflects either domestic tension or tension in the relations between the sending and the receiving state. Repatriation becomes then the expression or outcome of international relations between states. The consequences for those in the ethnopole are many, ranging from a growing feeling of vulnerability to family separation. When the tension is domestic, it is likely to be the result of the local mainstream community's attempts to take jobs away from the immigrants and thereby marginalize them further by reducing their ability to earn a living. Such a situation affects the ethnopole–state relations because it places a burden on the sending state's ability to reincorporate returned citizens in the labor structure of the home country. Here the strain between state and ethnopole is caused by the interference of the receiving state. Such a policy affects not only those in the sending state who can no longer migrate to reunite with families or search for employment, but also the ability of the ethnopole to attract more people, which indirectly may influence its growth and development both in terms of demographics and commerce. One example of this was the repatriation of the Filipinos proposed by the US government in the 1930s as a way of getting rid of them so that the government would not be responsible for their welfare.

Ethnopole–state relations can also be studied in the economic realm. Economic relations are two-way relations that benefit both entities, and sometimes one more than the other. As already indicated, diasporic businesses depend on the homeland for products to be sold in the ethnopole to tourists and locals. Since these items are made only in the homeland or are cheaper if bought there, these relations tend to benefit the ethnopole and are necessary to maintain its exotic business atmosphere. This *economic model* provides insight in terms of the economic transactions it unveils in these transnational relations.

The state at times uses the diaspora as a provider of additional foreign currency. This money is exchanged in the purchase of goods, as in the case of the merchants, and allows the country to export more goods to the United States through the business ventures of import–export houses of commerce, through the remitttances sent by overseas relatives, through the money they bring back when they visit the homeland, through additional taxes levied on departing immigrants, and through the manipulation of formal and underground exchange rates.[164] In any of these practices, foreign currency circulates in the homeland as a result of the diaspora's relations to the mainland.

The third model places the diaspora and the homeland in opposition to each other. I refer to this model as the *political opposition model* to indicate that the ethnopole is involved in resistance movements or organizations whose goal is to overthrow the homeland regime.[165] The relations are hostile because the homeland government wants to silence the expatriate opponents to prevent them from destabilizing the regime, and the ethnopole wants its demise. These relations affect the ethnopole in many ways. The ethnopole finances opposition forces in the homeland, is placed under surveillance in the receiving state because of these political activities, and becomes as well a spying ground for the homeland's regime. In this context, the political structure of the ethnopole is dominated by the opposition, which tends to silence those whose allegiance is to the homeland regime. Political opposition brings about political divisions in the community as the ethnopole becomes a platform for dissident politics.

In the *ethnic model*, the ethnopole uses the homeland to strengthen its ethnic status abroad. In this case, one claims an ethnic status to show one's relationships with an ancestral homeland. The recognition of the connection is important in order to claim specific language rights – for example, bilingual education – and to showcase the peculiarities of the culture, as in the celebration of ethnic festivals.

In situations where the state considers the ethnopole as its extension and the ethnopole agrees, relations between state and diaspora are seen as relations inside a continuum. I refer to this continuum as the *transnational model* to indicate that the ethnopole is involved in an amicable way in the development of the homeland, and that the homeland has good ongoing relations with the ethnopole. In this model, the ethnopole is involved in homeland politics to improve things in the ancestral country. This can include local projects developed in the villages and collaboration between grassroots organizations to foster democracy, improve human rights, and sustain local initiatives. Communications with the homeland synergize these communities with each other.

Globality

The identification of the ethnopole inside a container city in the globalizing world brings forth the idea of a dynamic situation with the following ramifications:

- Seen as a *process and an outcome*, the ethnopole participates in the globalization of the city because of its location inside this social formation, the relations it maintains with it, and the homeland to which it is still connected. As a corollary, one may also say that the global relations the ethnopole is engaged in also feed the city. The microgeography of global ethnopoles reveals that these local sites are engaged in global processes that shape their relations with the city that contain them. In turn, their relations with the city influence the modalities of their global interaction. So, the globality of one feeds the globality of the other and vice versa. This is why the dynamic of this process cannot be understood fully without consideration of these two poles.
- These two entities do not have fixed positions, but are *constantly changing*. This implies that the two influence each other in such a way that the behavior of the ethnopole can be understood only to the extent that one understands its relations with the city in which it is spatially enclosed. It also indicates that the relations of the ethnopole with the homeland are influenced by the fact that the ethnopole is located in a global city, and these relations in turn influence the city. Likewise the relations of the city with the homeland take into consideration the needs of the ethnopole. For example, relations between the city of San Francisco and its sister-city Osaka involve Japantown in the process.
- Both the city and the ethnopole are traversed by *transnational currents*. These transnational relations are not identical: they crisscross rather than coincide. The ways in which they influence each other may not be clear-cut. However, the transnationality of the city impacts and is impacted by the transnationality of the ethnopole for which it serves as a container.

- Because of the transnationality factor, the city does not totally contain the ethnopole, but rather provides it a *context* within which it can express its transnationality. The city as place does not coincide with the city as space. Therefore the space of the city is much larger that the place it occupies, because it is a site that connects various sites related to it through transnational relations.
- Relations between the ethnopole and the city are influenced by *transnational practices* that both are engaged in. These relations are not simply the outcome of their presence in the same site, but rather are shaped by the fact that both the ethnopole and the city are influenced by the transnational relations that transnationalize the content of the transnational practices they are engaged in. The two global poles are transnationalized not simply because they are intertwined with each other, but also because they are part of larger frameworks that encompass extraterritorial sites and actors.
- In a sense, the ethnopole displays characteristics opposite of those of the global city as a "command center for finances." In fact, the global ethnopole is a *system of subsidiaries* with headquarters-institutions either in the homeland or elsewhere in the city. We have seen in the case of Japantown that the headquarters of the local firms are in Japan (Tokyo and Osaka). Thus, this system of subsidiaries is a locus that feeds the local process of globalization.
- Globalization affects the *economic structure* of the ethnic neighborhoods. This occurs because the products the homeland provides satisfy the market needs of a clientele that seeks these items – which cannot be found elsewhere, or can be found but only at a higher price because of transportation costs. Tourists, who constitute a segment of the ethnopole's clientele are also a result of globalization. Inside the ethnopole, some individuals are able to find work because of this international clientele that sustains the market. The employment of some is a direct result because they produce things and interact with foreign producers and clientele. Others are employed indirectly: they supply labor and products to meet the demands of local stores. This is a polar economic system because of the triple interaction of the mainstream, the transnational economy, and the local neighborhood economic practices. I call this polar economy a *diasporic economy* because it demonstrates that the diaspora intervenes to develop a new economic system, and because its globality/transnationality has its characteristics distinct from those of the global city. A polar economy such as this is linked to the mainstream economy through various means. Chief among

them is the cheap labor it provides to mainstream customers and industry, sometimes in the form of sweatshops and cheap services to mainstream clientele. Cheap services are one arena where one can follow the linkage of the ethnopole to satellite clusters, as work is sometimes performed there and brought back to the ethnopole to finalize the transaction.

- The connection of the ethnopole to any other sites within its network of sites may be beneficial to all involved. For example, Silicon Valley's connection to Japan brings tourists in who may visit Japantown and use Japanese facilities and services in downtown San Francisco. This shows how an enclave can be used to feed the transnational economy of which it is a part. What one sees here is that the global ethnopole is a symptom of the inability of the nation-state to *patrol, control, and protect its borders.*
- One may speak of an *emerging global ethnopolitan system* corresponding to Sassen's notion of "transnational urban systems"[166] – that is, one characterized by the existence of subsidiaries whose headquarters are in the homeland, by reliance on the homeland for products sold in the ethnopole, by the central role of the ethnopole in the functioning of sister-city relationships, by the harmonization of ethnopolitan time with that of the homeland for the celebration of major cultural and national events, and by multiple transnational relations with other diasporic sites.
- In this global logic, the spatial relations of the ethnopole with the city must be seen in terms of the intersection of two urban systems: those of the city with other cities, and those of the ethnopole with other ethnopoles, on one hand; and those of the intersection of the city as part of a transnational urban system with the ethnopole that is part of a transnational ethnopolitan system, on the other. In these two sites of intersection, the character of the ethnopole is defined and its identity revealed.
- The strength of an ethnopole's relations with the homeland may determine its *hierarchical position* in the national and transnational ethnopolitan systems. That is, the relationship may transform the ethnopole's central status to satellite status or may disarticulate the entire system by assigning central status to some and satellite status to others.
- Because these relations traverse *different spatial borders and time zones*, space and time are important factors in disentangling the constitution of the ethnopole. What we see here is an expansion of the space of the city through the relations of the city with other

sites and through the relations of the ethnopole with other sites as well. The complexity of the relations is impacted by the fact the *space of the city* is larger than the *place of the city* so the *space of the ethnopole* is larger than the *place of the ethnopole*. The city also becomes the site where different cultural time zones resonate with its different week systems (e.g. those of Muslims and Jews), different New Year celebration periods (e.g. Chinese, Tibetan, Iranian, Ethiopian), and different years depending on whether solar or lunar calendars are used and all of that because of the existence of different global ethnopoles in its midst.

Above that, it is important to understand that the relations of the city to the ethnopole occur in a *global context* and cannot be fully understood outside of these parameters. Both the ethnopole and the city are globalized and should be seen not as locally bound, but rather as globally expanding.

Notes and References

1. To get a sense of these neighborhoods, see D. Cinel, *From Italy to San Francisco* (Paolo Alto: Stanford University Press, 1982); B. J. Godfrey, *Neighborhoods in Transition* (Berkeley: University of California Press, 1988); D. P. Gumina, *The Italians of San Francisco, 1850–1930* (New York: Center for Migration Studies, 1978); I. Narell, *Our City: The Jews of San Francisco* (San Diego: Howell–North Books, 1981); James Sobredo, "From Manila Bay to Daly City: Filipinos in San Francisco," in James Brook *et al.* (eds), *Reclaiming San Francisco* (San Francisco: City Lights Books): 273–86.
2. See Ron Kelley, Jonathan Friedlander and Anita Colby, *Irangeles: Iranians in Los Angeles* (Berkeley: University of California Press, 1993): 59; and Timothy P. Fong, *The First Suburban Chinatown* (Philadelphia: Temple University Press, 1966).
3. In *Imagined Communities*, Anderson (1992: 187) sees these locales as

    new versions of [thereby] "old" toponyms in their lands of origin ... What is startling in the American namings of the sixteenth to the eighteenth centuries is that "new" and "old" were understood synchronically, coexisting within homogeneous, empty time. Vizcaya is there alongside Nueva Vizcaya, New London alongside London: an idiom of sibling competition rather than of inheritance.

4. See Mark Abrahamson, *Urban Enclaves: Identity and Place in America* (New York: St. Martin's Press, 1996): 19–32.
5. See Jacob Riis, *How the Other Half Lives* (New York: Sagamore Press, 1957): 91; Thomas Kessner, *The Golden Door: Italian and Jewish Immigrant Mobility in New York City 1880–1915* (New York: Oxford University Press, 1977): 130.
6. See Edwin Steiner, *On the Trail of the Immigrant* (New York: F. H. Revell, 1906): 175.
7. See William V. Flores, "Citizens vs. Citizenry: Undocumented Immigrants and Latino Cultural Citizenship," in William V. Flores and Rina Benmayor (eds), *Latino Cultural Citizenship: Claiming Identity, Space, and Rights* (Boston: Beacon Press, 1997): 264; Joann Biondi, "Miami's Caribbean Enclaves; Little Haiti and Little Havana Reflect the Culture, Food and Music of their Islands," *New York Times*, 140, Sect. 5 (Sunday, February 1991): XX8(N), col. 1; Scott Harris, "'Little India' (Pioneer Boulevard, Los Angeles)," *Los Angeles Times* v 111 (Tuesday September 1, 1992): B1, col. 2; Harold Gilliam and Phil Palmer, "The Face of San Francisco," *San Francisco Sunday Chronicle*, (October 1, 1961); J. K. Yamamoto, "Changes in J-Town: San Francisco's Japantown is still the Heart and Soul – if not the Physical Center – of the Japanese American Community," *San Francisco Bay Guardian* (East Bay edn) 27(6) (November 11, 1992).
8. Michel S. Laguerre, "Technologies of Minoritized Space," *IURD Working Papers Series*, 681 (Berkeley: Institute of Urban and Regional Development; University of California at Berkeley, 1997).

168 *Notes and References*

9. To frame this issue in the context of the city's history, politics and urban development, see Mel Scott, *The San Francisco Bay Area: A Metropolis in Perspective*. (Berkeley: University of California Press, 1959); William Issel and Robert Cherny, *San Francisco, 1865–1932: Politics, Power and Urban Development*. (Berkeley: University of California Press, 1986); R. E. DeLeon, *Left Coast City: Progressive Politics in San Francisco (1975–1991)*. (Kansas City: University of Kansas Press, 1992).
10. See James Duncan and David Ley (eds), *Place/Culture/Representation*. (New York: Routledge, 1993): 6; K. Anderson, "Cultural Hegemony and the Race-Definition Process in Chinatown, Vancouver: 1880–1980," *Environment and Planning D: Society and Space*, 6 (1988): 127–49.
11. See "The Big Uproar Over Little Havana," *New York Times* (Friday, October 26, 1990): A8(N), A12(L), col. 4.
12. On the commercial aspect of these neighborhoods, see Colette Marie McLaughlin and Paul Jesilow, "Conveying a Sense of Community along Bolsa Avenue: Little Saigon as a Model of Ethnic Commercial Belts," *International Migration*, 36(1): 49–63, 1998.
13. For Smith (1995: 254), these diasporic enclaves are "different forms of reterritorialization as a collective response to displacement and deterritorialization."
14. See "Little India in Artesia: Why Not?" (editorial), *Los Angeles Times*, 111 (Sunday, September 6, 1992): M4, col 3.
15. For a geographical survey on ethnic San Francisco, see Brian J. Godfrey, *Neighborhoods in Transition: The Making of San Francisco's Ethnic and Nonconformist Communities*. (Berkeley: University of California Press, 1988).
16. See, for example, Saskia Sassen, *The Global City: New York, London, Tokyo* (Princeton: Princeton University Press, 1991). Donald Lyons and Scott Salmon, "World Cities, Multinational Corporations, and Urban Hierarchy: The Case of the United States," in Paul Knox and Peter J. Taylor (eds) *World Cities in a World System* (1993) (Cambridge: Cambridge University Press): 115–131.
17. On the definition of microglobalization, see Jorg Durrschmidt, "The Delinking of Locale and Milieu," in J Eade (ed.), *Living the Global City: Globalization as a Local Process*, (London: Routledge, 1997): 56–72.
18. On globality and the local–global distinctions, see M. Featherstone (ed.), *Global Culture* (London: Sage, 1990); Martin Albrow, *The Global Age* (Stanford: Stanford University Press, 1997); Rob Wilson and Wimal Dissanayake (eds), *Global/Local* (Durham: Duke University Press, 1996).
19. Ann Game, "Time, Space, Memory with Reference to Bachelard," in Mike Featherstone, Scott Lash and Roland Robertson (eds), *Global Modernities* (London: Sage, 1995): 195.
20. David Harvey, *The Condition of Postmodernity* (Cambridge: Blackwell, 1989): 303.
21. Mike Featherstone and Scott Lash, "Globalization, Modernity, and the Spatialization of Social Theory: An Introduction," in Mike Featherstone, Scott Lash and Roland Robertson (eds), *Global Modernities* (London: Sage, 1995): 4.
22. Roland Robertson, "Glocalization: Time–Space and Homogeneity–Heterogeneity" in Mike Featherstone, Scott Lash and Roland Robertson (eds), *Global Modernities*. (London: Sage, 1995): 26 and 30.

23. Jan Nederveen Pieterse, "Globalization as Hybridization," in Mike Featherstone, Scott Lash and Roland Robertson (eds), *Global Modernities* (London: Sage, 1995): 51.
24. On the role of Little Havana in the Formulation of US foreign policy, see Ruben Berrios and Lillian Thomas, "Taking Orders from Little Havana (US Embargo Against Cuba)," *Bulletin of the Atomic Scientists*, 50(5) (September–October, 1994): 20.
25. Becker ('The Course of Exclusion', PhD, University of California, Berkeley, 1936, p. 154) notes that

> hoping to change the school board's ruling, the President early in 1907 invited Mayor Schmitz and the board members to Washington to discuss the treatment of Japanese school children in San Francisco...The matter was resolved when the Board of Education rescinded its action.

This action was undertaken by the federal government because "there is a fear that Japan may take offense at some happening and strike without warning, as she did against Russia" (*San Francisco Examiner*, Friday, February 1, 1907).
26. Martin Albrow, "Traveling Beyond Local Cultures: Socioscapes in a Global City," in J. Eade (ed.) *Living the Global City: Globalization as a Local Process* (London: Routledge, 1997): 53.
27. Roland Robertson, "Mapping the Global Condition: Globalization as the Central Concept," in Mike Featherstone (ed.), *Global Culture* (London: Routledge, 1990): 19.
28. Z. Mlinar "Introduction," in Z. Mlinar, *Globalization and Territorial Identities* (Aldershot: Avebury, 1992): 1–15.
29. David J. Keeling, "Transport and the World City Paradigm," in Paul L. Knox and Peter J. Taylor (eds). *World Cities in a World System* (Cambridge: Cambridge University Press, 1995): 115.
30. David J. Keeling, "Transport and the World City Paradigm": 118.
31. See, for example, Anthony D. King (ed.), *Culture, Globalization and the World System* (Minneapolis: University of Minnesota Press, 1997); Roland Robertson, *Globalization: Social Theory and Global Culture* (London: Routledge, 1992). Ulf Hannerz, *Transnational Connections* (London: Routledge, 1996).
32. There are several good books on the history of San Francisco's Chinatown and Chinese in California; among them, see G. Victor and Brett de Bary Nee, *Longtime Californ': A Documentary Study of an American Chinatown.* (Stanford: Stanford University Press, 1986); Judy Yung, *Unbound Feet: A Social History of Chinese Women in* San Francisco (Berkeley: University of California Press, 1995); and Charles J. McClain, *In Search of Equality: The Chinese Struggle Against Discrimination in Nineteenth Century America* (Berkeley: University of California Press, 1994); Sucheng Chan, *This Bittersweet Soil: The Chinese in California, 1860–1910 (*Berkeley: University of California Press, 1986); and Gunther Barth, *Bitter Strength: A History of the Chinese in the United States, 1850–1870* (Cambridge, Mass.: Harvard University Press, 1964); Stanford Lyman, *Chinese Americans* (New York: Random House, 1974); C. M. Loo, *Chinatown: Most Time, Hard Time.* (New York: Praeger, 1991); and Chin-Yu Chen, "San Francisco's Chinatown: A

Socio-Economic and Cultural History, 1850–1882," PhD Dissertation, University of California at San Diego (1992).
33. Thomas Wong, *San Francisco Chinatown: The Core Area, Conditions and Trends*, (San Francisco: Cameron House, 1995); Christopher Lee Yip, "San Francisco's Chinatown: An Architectural and Urban History," PhD Dissertation, University of California at San Diego (1985); and Connie Young Yu, "A History of San Francisco Chinatown Housing," *Amerasia Journal* 8(1) (Spring: Summer, 1981): 93–109.
34. Gerry Kearns and Chris Philo, "Preface," in Gerry Kearns and Chris Philo (eds) *Selling Places: The City as Cultural Capital, Past and Present* (Oxford: Pergamon Press, 1993): ix; Katherine Bishop, "San Francisco's Chinatown is Struggling to Save its Soul: Chinatown's Uniqueness is Being Threatened by Tourists," *New York Times*, 140 (Monday, December 27, 1990): A(N), A1(L), col. 5; and Jan Lin (1998) *Reconstructing Chinatown* (Minneapolis: University of Minnesota Press).
35. See Michel S. Laguerre, *The Informal City* (London: Macmillan, and New York: St. Martin's Press, 1994).
36. On the business sector in Chinatown, see Bernard Wong, *Ethnicity and Entrepreneurship: The New Chinese Immigrants in the San Francisco Bay Area*. (Boston: Allyn & Bacon, 1998).
37. San Francisco Department of City Planning, *Commerce and Employment in Chinatown* (San Francisco: Department of City Planning, 1984); Special Chinatown Reports, *San Francisco Magazine* 111(6), (June, 1996): 22–35.
38. "In Search of Empowerment: San Francisco's Chinese Community Strives for a Voice in the City," *San Francisco Business* (July, 1985: 6–10).
39. On New York's Chinatown's informal political structure, see Kwong (1987).
40. On the history of this important political institution in Chinatown, see Him Mark Lai, "Historical Development of the Chinese Consolidated Benevolent Association/Huiguan System," *Chinese America: History and Perspectives* (1987): 13–51.
41. Even before President Nixon's visit to China, there was substantial trade between China, Hong Kong, and Taiwan; see for example, Teh-Pei Yu, "Economic Links Among Hong Kong, PRC, and ROC – With Special Reference to Trade," in Jurgen Domes and Yu-ming Shaw (eds), *Hong Kong: A Chinese and International Concern* (Boulder: Westview Press, 1988): 110–126.
42. On Vietnamese refugees in the New York and Los Angeles Chinatowns, see Seth Mydans, "Chinese Refugees from Vietnam Thrive in Chinatown," *New York Times* (11 February 1984): 29, 32; "Vietnamese of L.A. C-Town," *Asian Week*, (30 November 1984): 24.
43. For an interesting and useful study of Chinese Vietnamese in San Francisco, see Joe Chung Fong, "The Development of the Chinese-Vietnamese Community in San Francisco, 1980–1988," MA Thesis, University of California-Los Angeles (1988). For other important empirical studies of the Vietnamese population in the Bay Area, including San Jose, see Caroline Valverde, "The Foundation and Future of Vietnamese Politics in the Bay Area," MA Thesis, San Francisco State University (1994); Steven J. Gold, *Refugee Communities: A Comparative Field Study* (London: Sage, 1992); and James A. Freeman, *Hearts of Sorrows: Vietnamese American Lives* (Stanford: Stanford University Press, 1989).

44. On the multiple layers of Chinese transnationalism, see Aihwa Ong, "On the Edge of Empires: Flexible Citizenship among Chinese in Diaspora," *Positions* 1(3) (1993): 745–80; Aihwa Ong, "Limits to Capital Accumulation: Chinese Capitalists on the American Pacific Rim," in Nina Glick Schiller *et al.* (eds), *Perspective on Migration Towards a Transnational* (New York: New York Academy of Sciences, 1992); and Aihwa Ong, and Donald M. Nonini *The Cultural Politics of Modern Chinese Transnationalism* (New York: Routledge, 1997).
45. Joseph Conforti, "Ghettos as Tourism Attractions," *Annals of Tourism Research*, 23(4) (1996): 830–42; and Mike Davis, "Chinatown (Part II): The Internationalization of Downtown Los Angeles," *New Left Review*, 164 (1987): 65–86.
46. K. K., "Editorial: Nihonjin-Machi Mondai [The Japanese Town Issue]," *Shinsekai* (May 17, 1906).
47. K. K., "Editorial," *Shin Sekai*, (May 17, 1906).
48. K.K., "Editorial," *Shin Sekai*, (May 17,1906).
49. K. K., "Editorial," *Shin Sekai*, (May 17, 1906).
50. H. A. Millis, *The Japanese Problem in the United States* (New York: Macmillan, 1915): 70.
51. Carey McWilliams, *Prejudice: Japanese Americans: Symbol of Racial Intolerance*. (Boston: Little, Brown, 1945): 76.
52. Bradford Smith, *Americans From Japan* (New York: J.B. Lippincott Co., 1948): 221.
53. Bradford Smith, *Americans From Japan* (New York: J.B. Lippincott Co., 1948): 226.
54. Harry H. L. Kitano, "Housing of Japanese Americans in the San Francisco Bay Area," in Nathan Glazer and Davis McEntire (eds), *Studies in Housing and Minority Groups* (Berkeley: University of California Press, 1960): 183.
55. Suzie Kobuchi Okazaki, *Nihonmachi: A Story of San Francisco's Japantown*. (San Francisco: SKO Studios, 1985): 36.
56. Midori Nishi, "Changing Occupance of the Japanese in Los Angeles County, 1940–1950," PhD Dissertation, University of Washington (1955): 45–47.
57. Evelyn Nakano Glenn, *Issei, Nisei, War Bride: Three Generations of Japanese American Women in Domestic Service* (Philadelphia: Temple University Press, 1986): 29–37.
58. On Japanese American history, see William Petersen, *Japanese Americans: Oppression and Success* (New York: Random House, 1971); Harry H. L. Kitano, *Japanese Americans: Evolution of a Subculture* (Englewood Cliffs, New Jersey: Prentice-Hall, 1976); Yuji Ichioka, *The Issei: The World of the First Generation Japanese Americans, 1885–1924* (New York: Free Press, 1988); Roger Daniels, *Asian America: Chinese and Japanese in the United States since 1850*. (Seattle: University of Washington Press, 1988); Roger Daniels, *The Politics of Prejudice: The Anti-Japanese Movement in California and the Struggle for Japanese Exclusion* (Berkeley: University of California Press, 1962); Yamato Ichihashi, *Japanese in the United States* (Paolo Alto: Stanford University Press, 1932); Hilary Conroy and T. Scott Miyakawa (eds), *East Across the Pacific: Historical and Sociological Studies of Japanese Immigration and Assimilation* (Santa Barbara: ABC-Clio Press, 1972); David J. O'Brien and Stephen S. Fugita, *The Japanese American Experience* (Bloomington: Indiana University Press, 1991); Peter Irons, *Justice at War: The Story of the Japanese*

172 Notes and References

      American Internment Cases (New York: Oxford University Press, 1983); Audrie Girdner and Anne Loftis, *The Great Betrayal: The Evacuation of the Japanese Americans During World War II* (London: Macmillan, 1969); and Ronald Takaki (1989) *Strangers from a Differrent Shore: A History of Asian Americans*. (Boston: Little, Brown).
59. Midori Nishi, *Changing Occupance of the Japanese in Los Angeles County*: 21.
60. Bradford Smith, *Americans From Japan*: 57.
61. Yuji Ichioka, *The Issei: The World of the First Generation Japanese Immigrants, 1885–1924* (New York: The Free Press, 1988): 62.
62. S. Muto "Generations of San Francisco Japantown," *Asia Week* (March 1991): 15.
63. Suzie Okazaki, "Nihonmachi: A Story of San Francisco's Japantown,": 29.
64. Daniels, *Asian America* (*University of Washington Press, 1933*): 126.
65. Bradford Smith, *Americans From Japan*: 221
66. Ivan H. Light, *Ethnic Enterprise in America: Business and Welfare among Chinese, Japanese and Blacks* (Berkeley: University of California Press, 1972): 66 See also Tetsuya Fujimoto, *Crime and Delinquency Among the Japanese Americans*. (Tokyo: Chuo University Press, 1978): 131–3.
67. Suzie Okazaki, "Nihonmachi: A Story of San Francisco's Japantown": 85.
68. Leonard Austin, *Around the World in San Francisco* (Stanford University: J. L. Delkin, 1940): 7.
69. *Hokubei Mainichi* (July 23, 1995).
70. Suzie Okazaki, "Nihonmachi: A Story of San Francisco's Japantown": 63.
71. Ulf Hannerz, *Transnational Connections* (New York: Routledge, 1996): 18.
72. Maya Angelou, *I Know Why the Caged Bird Sings* (New York: Bantam Books, 1970): 177–8.
73. Romel Pascual, "Pilipino Towns," in Anatalio C. Ubalde (ed.) *Filipino American Architecture, Design, and Planning Issues* (San Francisco: Flipside Press, 1996): 41–58.
74. Carole Herminger, "Little Manila: The Filipinos in Stockton Prior to World War II," *Pacific Historian*, (Spring, 1980): 24.
75. Carole Herminger, "Little Manila": 27.
76. Casiano Pagdilae Coloma, "A Study of the Filipino Repatriation Movement," BA Thesis, University of Southern California (1939).
77. Carey McWilliams, "Introduction," in Carlos Bulosan (ed.), *America is in the Heart* (Seattle: University of Washington Press, 1973): xiv.
78. Carey McWilliams, *Brothers Under the Skin* (Boston: Little, Brown): 240.
79. Kirk Grayson "The Filipinos," *The Annals of the American Academy of Political and Social Science*, 223 (1942): 45.
80. H. Brett Melendy, "California's Discrimination Against Filipinos 1927–1935," in Roger Daniels and Spencer C. Olin, Jr. (eds), *Racism in California* (New York: Macmillan, 1972): 146.
81. H. Brett Melendy, "Filipinos in the United States," in Akira Iriye (ed.), *The Asian American: The Historical Experience* (Santa Barbara: Clio Books, 1976): 101–28.
82. Luciano Mangiafico, *Contemporary American Immigrants: Patterns of Filipino, Korean, and Chinese Settlements in the United States* (New York: Praeger, 1988): 36.
83. Antonio J. A. Pido, *The Pilipinos in America* (New York: Center for Migration Studies, 1986): 71.

Notes and References 173

84. Lorraine Jacobs Crouchett, *Filipinos in California* (El Cerrito: Downey Place Publishing House, 1982): 36.
85. Carey McWilliams, "Introduction," in Carlos Bulosan, *America is in the Heart*: xv.
86. Cited in Fred Cordova, *Filipinos: Forgotten Asian Americans: A Pictorial Essay (1763-1963)* (Dubuque, Iowa: Kendall/Hunt, 1983): 135.
87. *The San Francisco Chronicle*, (February 13, 1942): 12.
88. Sonia Wallovits, "The Filipinos in California," BA Thesis, University of Southern California (1966): 77.
89. Lorraine Jacobs Crouchett, *Filipinos in California*: 62.
90. *The San Francisco Chronicle* (December 1971): 1
91. *The San Francisco Chronicle* (June 12, 1972): 61.
92. Roberto V. Valangca, *Pinoy: The First Wave (1898–1941)* (San Francisco: Strawberry Hills Press, 1977): 102.
93. Roberto V. Valangca, *Pinoy: The First Wave (1898–1941)*: 94.
94. Roberto V. Valangca, *Pinoy: The First Wave (1898–1941)*: 138.
95. Roberto V. Valangca, *Pinoy: The First Wave (1898–1941)*: 77.
96. *San Francisco Chronicle*, 11 (June 23, 1943): 3.
97. Roberto V. Valangca, *Pinoy: The First Wave*: 72.
98. Roberto V. Valangca, Pinoy: The First Wave: 72.
99. Carlos Bulosan, *America is in the Heart* (Seattle: University of Washington Press, 1973): 121.
100. Roberto V. Valangca, *Pinoy: The First Wave*: 66.
101. *San Francisco Chronicle*, 1 (1966): 25.
102. Roberto V. Valangca, *Pinoy: The First Wave*: 66.
103. Paul Groth, *Living Downtown: The History of Residential Hotels in the United States* (Berkeley: University of California Press, 1994).
104. Bruce B. Brugmann et al., *The Ultimate High Rise: San Francisco's Mad Rush Toward the Sky* (San Francisco: *San Francisco Bay Guardian*, 1971). On city politics during this era, see Richard Edward DeLeon, *Left Coast City: Progressive Politics in San Francisco (1975–1991)* (Kansas City: University of Kansas Press, 1992); Chester Hartman, *The Transformation of San Francisco* (Totowa, NJ: Rowman & Allenheld, 1984); John Mollenkopf, *The Contested City* (Princeton: Princeton University Press, 1983); Gray Brechin, "Progress in San Francisco: It Could Have Been Worse," *San Francisco Magazine* (October, 1983: 58–63; Richard Walker, "Landscape and City Life; Four Ecologies of Residence in the San Francisco Bay Area," *Ecumene*, (1995) 2(1): 33–64; Richard Walker, "Another Round of Globalization in San Francisco," *Urban Geography*, 17(1)(1986): 60–94; Richard Walker and the Bay Area Study Group, "The Playground of US Capitalism? The Political Economy of the San Francisco Bay Area in the 1980s," in Mike Davis et al. (eds), *Fire in the Heart* (London: Verso, 1990): 3–82; Richard Walker, "California Rages Against the Dying of the Light," *New Left Review*, 209 (1995): 42–74.
105. Rodolfo I. Necesito, *The Filipino Guide to San Francisco* (San Francisco: Technomedia, (1978): 23.
106. Carol D. Levine, "The City's Response to Conflicting Pressures: A Case Study of the International Hotel," MA Thesis (Social Science), San Francisco State College (1970).

107. On the politics of space in the Bay Area, see Anthony Ashbolt, "Tear Down the Walls: Sixties Radicalism and the Politics of Space in the San Francisco Bay Area," Doctoral Dissertation, Australian National University (1989); and Seymour Adler, "The Political Economy of Transit in the San Francisco Bay Area, 1945–63," Doctoral Dissertation, Department of City and Regional Planning, University of California at Berkeley (1980).
108. Ken Wong, "Filipinos Vow to Stay at International Hotel," *East–West* (June 4, 1969).
109. Roberto V. Valangca, *Pinoy: The First Wave*: 75.
110. Nelson Nagai, "Review of *The Fall of the I-Hotel*," *East Wind* (Winter–Spring 1985).
111. Vince Reyes, "Review of *The Fall of the I-Hotel*," *Ang Katipunan* (March 1984): 14.
112. *San Francisco Chronicle* (May 6, 1972): 12.
113. *San Francisco Chronicle* (November 16, 1974): 10.
114. Vince Reyes, "Review of *The Fall of the I-Hotel*," *Ang Katipunan* (March 1984): 14.
115. Emil DeGuzman, "International Hotel," *East–West* (January 6, 1971): 9.
116. Andy Gollan, "Filipino Eviction Protest," *Argonaut* (November 30, 1969): 1.
117. Carol D. Levine, "The City's Response to Conflicting Pressures,": 35.
118. Carol D. Levine, "The City's Response to Conflicting Pressures,": 31.
119. Carol D. Levine, "The City's Response to Conflicting Pressures,": 33.
120. Emil DeGuzman, "International Hotel," *East–West*, (January 6, 1971): 9.
121. Sherry Valparaiso, "Low Cost Housing Bill Defeated," *Ang Katipunan* (January–February 1976).
122. Emil DeGuzman, "International Hotel,": 9.
123. William Moore, "San Francisco Tenants Struggle to Stay Put," *The San Francisco Chronicle* (Thursday, October 24, 1974).
124. See, for example, Nerissa Balce-Cortes, "Imagining the Neocolony," *Critical Mass: A Journal of Asian American Cultural Criticism*, 2 (Spring, 1995): 95–120; Vicente L. Rafael (ed.), *Discrepant Histories: Translocal Essays on Filipino Cultures* (Philadelphia: Temple University Press, 1995).
125. Claude Levi-Strauss, *The Raw and the Cooked* (New York: Harper & Row, 1969).
126. David B. Okita, "Redevelopment of San Francisco Japantown," MA thesis California State University (1980): 34.
127. Louise Hanford, *Fact Sheet: Japan Center* (San Francisco: Hanford Associates, 1992): 3.
128. Ruth Duskin Feldman, "The Rebirth of San Francisco's Japantown," *Vista USA, The Magazine of Exxon Travel Club*, (Fall 1988): 9.
129. Louise Hanford, *Japantown: A Brief History*. (San Francisco. Hanford Associates, 1996): 3.
130. Louise Hanford, *Fact Sheet: Kinokuniya Bookstores* (San Francisco: Hanford Associates, 1996): 1–2.
131. For analyses of transgenerational identity among Japanese Americans, see Christie W. Kiefer, *Changing Culture, Changing Lives: An Ethnographic Study of Three Generations of Japanese Americans* (San Francisco: Jossey-Bass, 1974); and Jere Takahashi, *Nisei/Sansei: Shifting Japanese American Identities and Politics*. (Philadelphia: Temple University Press, 1997).

132. "Of the 170 businesses in Japantown, only 60 percent are now owned by Japanese Americans, according to Yukio Murata, president of the Japantown Merchants Association. Most of the others are owned by businesses in Japan. Korean-owned businesses total about 10 and Chinese fewer than half a dozen." K. Connie Kang, "Japantown: A Community Losing its Identity," *San Francisco Examiner* (September 14, 1987): B-4.
133. Sheila Muto, "3 Generations of San Francisco Japantown," *Asian Week* (March 8, 1991): 16.
134. J. K. Yamamoto, "Changes in J-Town," *San Francisco Bay Guardian* 27(6) (November 11, 1992): 32.
135. Sheila Muto, "Forum Stimulates Dialogue Between the Diverse Communities in the Western Addition," *Asian Week* (March 8, 1991): 16. See also, Dexter Waugh and Gregory Lewis, "Western Addition Tackles Racial Tensions," *San Francisco Examiner* (March 17, 1991): B-6.
136. Mark Rutherford, "Japanese Americans Come Out for Former Speaker," *Western Edition*, 2(13): 3, 1995.
137. Jim Kelly, "Plaza of Peace, Not in Pieces?," *San Francisco Progress* (June 19, 1985): A2.
138. Marvine Howe, "In Chinese or Persian, It's in the Yellow Pages," *The New York Times* (Monday, April 13, 1992): 11.
139. See Laura Buffoni, "Rethinking Poverty in Globalized Conditions," in John Eade (ed.), *Living the Global City: Globalization as a Local Process* (London: Routledge, 1997): 110–26.
140. E. Fuat Keyman, *Globalization, State, Identity/Difference: Toward a Critical Social Theory of International Relations* (New Jersey: Humanities Press, 1997): 39.
141. According to Johnson,

    Many of these publications serve as an introduction to American life, full of advice on how to obtain immigration papers or apply for citizenship or make long-distance calls. [They also contain information] about area schools, [provide] a sample driver's license test, a practice citizenship quiz and a listing of golf courses. (Johnson, 1995: 2–3).

142. On the role of language in ethnic advertising, see A. Guernica, *Reaching the Hispanic Market Effectively: The Media, the Market, the Methods* (New York: McGraw-Hill, 1982); S. Hernandez, "Choice of English vs. Spanish Language in Advertising," *Journal of Current Issues and Research in Advertising* 14 (Fall) (1992): 35–45; R. J. Harris *et al.*, "Language in Advertising: A Psycholinguistic Approach," *Current Issues and Research in Advertising*, 9(1) (1986): 1–26; Paul H. Johnson, "Advertising: Targeted Yellow Pages Offer Ethnic, Other Groups More than Just Listings in their Languages," *Los Angeles Times*, (Monday, 1995 December 11) Part D: 2; and S. Koslow *et al.*, "Exploring the Language Effects in Ethnic Advertising: A Sociolinguistic Perspective," *Journal of Consumer Research*, 20 (1994): 575–85.
143. Steve Ginsberg, "Chinese Media Group, #5: Ethnic Yellow Pages Ringing Up Growth," *San Francisco Business Times* 19(8) (October 21, 1994) Section 8: 7.
144. On the advertising process, see R. W. Jackson *et al.*, "The Yellow Pages as an Advertising Tool for Small Businesses," *American Journal of Small*

176 Notes and References

> *Business*, 10(4) (1988): 29–35; K. J. Kelly, "The Impact of Size, Color, and Copy Quantity on Yellow Pages Advertising Effectiveness," *Journal of Small Business Management*, 29(4) (1991): 64–71; and R. A. Rouse, "Yellow Pages Advertising: An Empirical Analysis of Attributes Contributing to Consumer Interest, Liking, and Preference," *Journal of Professional Services Marketing* 6(2) (1991): 35–44.

145. The use of the ethnic yellow pages by the mainstream to advertise businesses is significant. For example, Shermach notes that "fifty-seven percent of the Spanish Telephone Directory's ... advertisers are Anglos who cater to the Hispanic market with legal, medical, and retail services" (Shermach, 1994): 5.
146. Various yellow pages publishers use this strategy. For example, publishers of the Korean yellow pages in Houston draw most of their advertisers from the local Korean newspapers (Shermach, 1994): 5.
147. According to Shermach, "*Paginas Amarillas en Espanol de Texas* ... [is] distributed in Mexico and in advertising companies throughout the US" (Shermach, 1994): 5.
148. The Iranian Directory yellow pages does not concern itself only with one city. In addition to listings for Southern California, it publishes listings for "Northern California, Maryland, Washington, DC, and East Texas so Persian-speaking travelers can support Iranian businesses across the country" (Shermach, 1994): 5.
149. Fidel V. Ramos, "Message", in *The Filipino Directory: USA, Canada, Philippines* (Los Angeles: Phil-American Publishing Co, 1997): 14–15.
150. On the global/local articulation, see John Eade (ed.), *Living the Global City: Globalization as a Local Process* (New York: Routledge, 1997), and Rob Wilson and Wimal Dissanayake (eds), *Global/Local: Cultural Production and the Transnational Imaginary* (Durham: Duke University Press, 1996).
151. The literature on transnationalism clarifies this aspect of local practices among recent immigrants in the United States; see Linda Basch *et al.*, *Nations Unbound* (New York: Gordon & Breach, 1990).
152. Douglas S. Massey and Nancy A. Denton, *American Apartheid: Segregation and the Making of the Underclass* (Cambridge, Mass: Harvard University Press, 1993).
153. On housing discrimination, see Juliet Saltman, "Housing Discrimination: Policy Research, Methods, and Results," *Annals of the American Academy of Political and Social Science*, 441 (1979): 186–96, and George C. Galster, "Racial Steering by Real Estate Agents: Mechanisms and Motives," *Review of Black Political Economy*, 19 (1990): 39–63.
154. Chalsa M. Loo, *Chinatown: Most Time, Hard Time* (New York: Praeger, 1991).
155. Charles J. McClain, In *Search of Equality: The Chinese Struggle Against Discrimination in Nineteenth-Century Americas* (Berkeley: University of California Press, 1994).
156. Bauman, Z. "Searching for a Center that Holds," in M. Featherstone *et al.*, *Global Modernities* (London: Sage, 1995): 152.
157. On racial formation, see Michael Omi and Howard Winant, *Racial Formation in the United States* (New York : Routledge, 1994).

158. Michel S. Laguerre, *Diasporic Citizenship* (London: Macmillan Press, and New York: St. Martin's Press, 1998).
159. Charles J. McClain, *In Search of Equality*: 115–26.
160. Peter Kwong, *Chinatown, New York* (New York: Monthly Review Press, 1979).
161. Ibid: 25.
162. Michel S. Laguerre, *Minoritized Space: An Inquiry into the Spatial Order of Things* (Berkeley: Institute of Governmental Studies Press, 1999).
163. According to Kozaitis, "The Ravenswood area of Chicago's Northside... became the home of many of Chicago's immigrants when the 'Greek Town' of more than half a century at Haltstead was displaced in the 1960s by the construction of the University of Illinois at Chicago", see Kathryn A. Kozaitis, "Being Old and Greek in America," in Donald E. Gelfand and Charles M. Barresi, *Ethnic Dimensions of Aging* (New York: Springer, 1987): 179–95.
164. Peter Kwong speaks of "the KMT's manipulation of exchange rates, so that money sent home was worth several times less than its real value. The recipients in China suffered, and government officials made millions in the process", see Peter Kwong, *The New Chinatown* (New York: Hill & Wang, 1987).
165. G. Victor and Brett de Bary Nee, *Longtime Californ': A Documentary Study of an American Chinatown* (Stanford: Stanford University Press, 1986). Him Mark Lai, "The Kuomintang in Chinese American Communities before World War II," in Sucheng Chan (ed.), *Entry Denied: Exclusion and the Chinese Community in America, 1882–1943* (Philadelphia: Temple University Press, 1991): 170–212.
166. Saskia Sassen, *Cities in a World Economy* (Thousand Oaks: Pine Forge Press, 1994): 47.

Bibliography

Abrahamson, M. (1996) *Urban Enclaves: Identity and Place in America* (New York: St. Martin's Press).
Adler, S. (1980) "The Political Economy of Transit in the San Francisco Bay Area, 1945–63," Doctoral Dissertation, Department of City and Regional Planning, University of California at Berkeley.
Albrow, M. (1997a) *The Global Age* (Stanford: Stanford University Press).
Albrow, M. (1997b) "Traveling Beyond Local Cultures: Socioscapes in a Global City," in J. Eade, *Living the Global City: Globalization as a Local Process* (London: Routledge).
Anderson, B. (1992) *Imagined Communities* (London: Verso).
Anderson, K. (1988) "Cultural Hegemony and the Race-definition Process in Chinatown, Vancouver: 1880–1980," *Environment and Planning D: Society and Space*, 6: 127–49.
Ashbolt, A. (1989) "Tear Down the Walls: Sixties Radicalism and the Politics of Space in the San Francisco Bay Area," Doctoral Dissertation, Australian National University.
Asian Week (1984) "Vietnamese of L.A. C-Town,": 24, 30.
Austin, L. (1940) *Around the World in San Francisco* (Stanford University: J.L. Delkin): 7.
Barth, G. (1964) *Bitter Strength: A History of the Chinese in the United States, 1850–1870* (Cambridge, Mass.: Harvard University Press).
Basch, Linda *et al.* (1990) *Nations Unbound* (New York: Gordon & Breach).
Bauman, Z. (1995) "Searching for a Center that Holds," In M. Featherstone, S. Lash and R. Robertson, *Global Modernities* (London: Sage).
Becker, J. (1986) "The Course of Exclusion, 1882–1924: San Francisco Newspaper Coverage of the Chinese and Japanese in the United States," PhD Dissertation, University of California at Berkeley.
Berrios, R. and L. Thomas (1994) "Taking Orders from Little Havana (US Embargo Against Cuba)," *Bulletin of the Atomic Scientists*, 50 (5) (September–October 1994): 20.
Biondi, J. (1991) "Miami's Caribbean Enclaves: Little Haiti and Little Havana Reflect the Culture, Food and Music of Their Islands," *New York Times*, 140, Section 5" (Sunday, February 24, 1991): XX8 (N), XX8(L), col. 1.
Brechin, G. (1983) "Progress in San Francisco: It Could Have Been Worse," *San Francisco Magazine* (October): 58–63.
Brugmann, B. *et al.* (1971) *The Ultimate High Rise: San Francisco's Mad Rush Toward the Sky* (San Francisco: San Francisco Bay Guardian).
Buffoni, L. (1997) "Rethinking Poverty in Globalized Conditions," in J. Eade, *Living the Global City: Globalization as a Local Process* (London: Routledge): 110–26.
Bulosan, C. (1973) *America is in the Heart* (Seattle: University of Washington Press).
Card, Josefina-Jayme (1984) "Assimilation and Adaptation: Filipino Migrants in San Francisco," *Philippine Sociological Review*, 32(1–4): 55–67.

Chan, S. (1986) *This Bittersweet Soil: The Chinese in California, 1860–1910* (Berkeley: University of California Press).
Chen, Chin-Yu (1992) "San Francisco's Chinatown: A Socio–Economic and Cultural History, 1850–1882," PhD Dissertation, University of California at San Diego.
Cinel, D. (1982) *From Italy to San Francisco: The Immigrant Experience* (Paolo Alto: Stanford University Press).
Coloma, C. P. (1939) "*A Study of the Filipino Repatriation Movement*," BA Thesis, University of Southern California, Los Angeles.
Conforti, J. (1996) "Ghettos as Tourism Attractions," *Annals of Tourism Research*, 23(4): 830–42.
Conroy, H. and T. S. Miyakawa (eds) (1972) *East Across the Pacific: Historical and Sociological Studies of Japanese Immigration and Assimilation* (Santa Barbara: ABC-Clio Press).
Cordova, F. (1983) *Filipinos: Forgotten Asian Americans: A Pictorial Essay (1763–1963)* (Dubuque, Iowa: Kendall/Hunt).
Crouchett, L. J. (1982) *Filipinos in California* (El Cerrito: Downey Place Publishing House).
Daniels, R. (1962) *The Politics of Prejudice: The Anti-Japanese Movement in California and the Struggle for Japanese Exclusion* (Berkeley: University of California Press).
Daniels, R. (1988) *Asian America: Chinese and Japanese in the US Since 1850* (Seattle: University of Washington Press).
Davis, M. (1987) "Chinatown (Part II)? The Internationalization of Downtown Los Angeles," *New Left Review*, 164: 65–86.
Davreux, Françoise (1981) "La Minorité Chinoise de San Françisco: De la Société du Ventre à Celle de l'Oeil," *Ethnopsychologie*, 36(1): 53–68.
DeGuzman, E. (1971) "International Hotel," *East–West* (January 6): 9.
DeLeon, R. E. (1992) *Left Coast City: Progressive Politics in San Francisco (1975–1991)* (Kansas City: University of Kansas Press).
Department of City Planning (1985) *Chinatown: An Area Plan of the Master Plan of the City and County of San Francisco* (San Francisco: Department of City Planning).
Duncan, J. and D. Ley (eds) (1993) *Place/Culture/Representation* (New York: Routledge).
Durrschmidt, J. (1997) "The Delinking of Locale and Milieu," in J. Eade (ed.), *Living the Global City: Globalization as a Local Process* (London: Routledge, 1997): 56–72.
Eade, J. (1997) *Living the Global City: Globalization as a Local Process* (London: Routledge).
Espiritu, Y.L. (1995) *Filipino American Lives* (Philadelphia: Temple University Press).
Featherstone, M. (ed.) (1990) *Global Culture* (London: Sage).
Featherstone, M. and S. Lash (1995) "Globalization, Modernity, and the Spatialization of Social Theory: An Introduction," in M. Featherstone, S. Lash and R. Robertson (eds), *Global Modernities* (London: Sage).
Feldman, R.D. (1988) "The Rebirth of San Francisco's Japantown," *Vista USA, The Magazine of Exxon Travel Club* (Fall): 9.
Flores, William V. (1997) "Citizens vs. Citizenry: Undocumented Immigrants and Latino Cultural Citizenship," W. V. Flores and R. Benmayor (eds), *Latino Cultural Citizenship: Claiming Identity, Space, and Rights* (Boston: Beacon Press).

180 Bibliography

Fong, J. C. (1988) "The Development of the Chinese-Vietnamese Community in San Francisco, 1980–1988," MA Thesis, University of California-Los Angeles.
Fong, T. P. (1966) *The First Suburban Chinatown* (Philadelphia: Temple University Press).
Freeman, J. A. (1989) *Hearts of Sorrows: Vietnamese American Lives* (Stanford: Stanford University Press).
Fujimoto, T. (1978) *Crime and Delinquency Among the Japanese Americans* (Tokyo: Chuo University Press).
Galster, G. C. (1990) "Racial Steering by Real Estate Agents: Mechanisms and Motives," *Review of Black Political Economy*, 19: 39–63.
Game, A. (1995) "Time, Space, Memory with Reference to Bachelard," M. Featherstone, S. Lash and R. Robertson (eds), *Global Modernities* (London: Sage).
Garreau, Joel (1991) *Edge City: Life on the New Frontier* (New York: Doubleday).
Gillian, H. and P. Palmer (1961), "The Face of San Francisco," *San Francisco Chronicle* (October 1, 1961).
Ginsberg, S. (1994) "Chinese Media Group, #5: Ethnic Yellow Pages Ringing Up Growth," *San Francisco Business Times*, 9(8) (October 21), Section 8: 7.
Girdner, A. and A. Loftis (1969) *The Great Betrayal: The Evacuation of the Japanese Americans During World War II*, (London: Macmillan).
Glenn, E. N. (1986) *Issei, Nisei, War Bride: Three Generations of Japanese American Women in Domestic Service* (Philadelphia: Temple University Press).
Godfrey, B. J. (1988) *Neighborhoods in Transition: The Making of San Francisco's Ethnic and Nonconformist Communities* (Berkeley: University of California Press).
Gold, S. J. (1992) *Refugee Communities: A Comparative Field Study* (London: Sage).
Gollan, A. (1969) "Filipino Eviction Protest," *Argonaut* (November 30):1.
Grayson, K. (1942) "The Filipinos," *The Annals of the American Academy of Political and Social Science* 223.
Groth, Paul (1994) *Living Downtown: The History of Residential Hotels in the United States* (Berkeley: University of California Press).
Guernica, A. (1982) *Reaching the Hispanic Market Effectively: The Media, the Market, the Methods* (New York: McGraw-Hill).
Gumina, D. P. (1978) *The Italians of San Francisco, 1850–1930* (New York: Center for Migration Studies).
Hanford, Louise (1996a) *Japan Town: A Brief History* (San Francisco: Hanford Associates): 4p.
Hanford, Louise (1996b) *Fact Sheet: Japan Center, San Francisco* (San Francisco: Hanford Associates).
Hannerz, U. (1996) *Transnational Connections* (London: Routledge).
Harris, R. J. et al. (1986) "Language in Advertising: A Psycholinguistic Approach," *Current Issues and Research in Advertising*, 9(1): 1–26.
Harris, S. (1992) "'Little India' (Pioneer Boulevard, Los Angeles)," *Los Angeles Times*, 111 (Tuesday, September 1): B1, col 2.
Hartman, C. (1984) *The Transformation of San Francisco* (Totowa, NJ: Rowman & Allenheld).
Harvey, D. (1989) *The Condition of Postmodernity* (Cambridge: Blackwell).
Herminger, C. (1980) "Little Manila: The Filipinos in Stockton Prior to World War II," *Pacific Historian* (Spring): 24, 27.

Hernandez, S. (1992) "Choice of English vs. Spanish Language in Advertising," *Journal of Current Issues and Research in Advertising,* 14 (Fall): 35–45.
Howe, M. (1992) "In Chinese or Persian, It's in the Yellow Pages," *The New York Times* (13 April), Section D, Col. 1: 7.
Ichihashi, Y. (1932) *Japanese in the United States* (Paolo Alto: Stanford University Press).
Ichioka, Y. (1988) *The Issei: The World of the First Generation Japanese Immigrants, 1885–1924* (New York: The Free Press).
Irons, P. (1983) *Justice at War: The Story of the Japanese American Internment Cases* (New York: Oxford University Press).
Issel, W. and R. Cherny (1986) *San Francisco, 1865–1932: Politics, Power, and Urban Development* (Berkeley: University of California Press).
Jackson, R. W. *et al.* (1986) "The Yellow Pages as an Advertising Tool for Small Businesses," *American Journal of Small Business,* 10 (4): 29–35.
Jameson, Fredric and Masao Miyoshi (eds) (1998) *The Cultures of Globalization* (Durham: Duke University Press).
Johnson, P. H. (1995), "Advertising: Targeted Yellow Pages Offer Ethnic, Other Groups More than Just Listings in their Languages," *Los Angeles Times,* (Monday, December 11), Part D: 2.
K. K. (1906) "Editorial: Nihonjin-Machi Mondai [The Japanese Town Issue]," *Shinsekai,* (May 17).
Kang, K. C. (1987) "Japantown: A Community Losing its Identity," *San Francisco Examiner* (September 14): B-4.
Kearns, G. and C. Philo (eds) (1993) "Preface," in G. Kearns and C. Philo, *Selling Places: The City as Cultural Capital, Past and Present* (Oxford: Pergamon Press).
Keeling, D. J. (1995) "Transport and the World City Paradigm," in P. L. Knox and P. J. Taylor (eds), *World Cities in a World System,* (Cambridge: Cambridge University Press).
Kelley, R., J. Friedlander and A. Colby (1993) *Irangeles: Iranians in Los Angeles* (Berkeley: University of California Press).
Kelly, J. (1985) "Plaza of Peace, Not in Pieces?", *San Francisco Progress* (June 19): A2.
Kelly, K. J. *et al.* (1991) "The Impact of Size, Color, and Copy Quantity on Yellow Pages Advertising Effectiveness, "*Journal of Small Business Management,* 29(4): 64–71.
Kessner, T. (1977) *The Golden Door: Italian and Jewish Immigrant Mobility in New York City 1880–1915,* (New York: Oxford University Press).
Keyman, E. F. (1997) *Globalization, State, Identity/Difference: Toward a Critical Social Theory of International Relations* (Atlantic Highlands, New Jersey: Humanities Press).
Kiefer, C. W. (1974) *Changing Culture, Changing Lives: An Ethnographic Study of Three Generations of Japanese Americans* (San Francisco: Jossey-Bass).
King, A. D. (ed.) (1997) *Culture, Globalization and the World System* (Minneapolis: University of Minnesota Press).
Kitano, H. H. (1960) "Housing of Japanese Americans in the San Francisco Bay Area," in N. Glazer and D. McEntire (eds), *Studies in Housing and Minority Groups* (Berkeley: University of California Press): 178–97.
Kitano, H. H. (1976) *Japanese Americans: Evolution of a Subculture* (Englewood Cliffs, New Jersey: Prentice-Hall).

Bibliography

Knox, Paul L. and Peter J. Taylor (eds.) (1995) *World Cities in a World-System* (New York: Cambridge University Press).
Koslow, S. *et al.* (1994) "Exploring the Language Effects in Ethnic Advertising: A Sociolinguistic Perspective," *Journal of Consumer Research*, 20: 575–85.
Kozaitis, K. A. (1987) "Being Old and Greek in America," in D. E. Gelfand and C. M. Barresi (eds), *Ethnic Dimensions of Aging* (New York: Springer): 179–95.
Kwong, P. (1979) *Chinatown, New York* (New York: Monthly Review Press).
Kwong, P. (1987) *The New Chinatown* (New York: Hill & Wang).
Laguerre, M. S. (1994) "The Informal City" (London: Macmillan and New York: St. Martin's Press).
Laguerre, M. S. (1997) "Technologies of Minoritized Space," *IURD Working Papers Series*, 681 (Berkeley: Institute of Urban and Regional Development, University of California at Berkeley).
Laguerre, M. S. (1998) *Diasporic Citizenship* (London: Macmillan and New York: St. Martin's Press).
Laguerre, M. S. (1999) *Minoritized Space: An Inquiry into the Spatial Order of Things* (Berkeley: Institute of Governmental Studies Press).
Lai, H. M. (1987) "Historical Development of the Chinese Consolidated Benevolent Association/Huiguan System," *Chinese America: History and Perspectives* (San Francisco: Chinese Historical Society of America): 13–51.
Lai, H. M., (1991) "The Kuomintang in Chinese American Communities Before World War II," in Sucheng Chan (ed.), *Entry Denied: Exclusion and the Chinese Community in America, 1882–1943* (Philadelphia: Temple University Press): 170–12.
Levi-Straus, C. (1969) The Raw and the Cooked (New York: Harper & Row).
Levine, C. D. (1970) "The City's Response to Conflicting Pressures: A Case Study of the International Hotel," MA Thesis (Social Science), San Francisco State College.
Light, I. H. (1972) Ethnic Enterprise *in America: Business and Welfare among Chinese, Japanese and Blacks* (Berkeley: University of California Press).
Lin, Jan (1998) *Reconstructing ChinaTown: Ethnic Enclave, global change (Minneapolis : University of Minnesota Press)*.
Loo, C. M. (1991) *Chinatown: Most Time, Hard Time* (New York: Praeger).
Los Angeles Times (1992) "Little India in Artesia: Why Not?" (editorial), (September 6) Col.: M4.
Lyman, Stanford M. (1970) "Red Guard on Grant Avenue," *Trans-Action*, 7 (6): 21–34.
Lyman, S. (1974) *Chinese Americans* (New York: Random House).
Lyons, D. and S. Salmon (1995) "World Cities, Multinational Corporations, and Urban Hierarchy: The Case of the United States," in P. L. Knox and P. J. Taylor (eds), *World Cities in a World System* (Cambridge: Cambridge University Press): 115–31.
Mangiafico, L. (1988) *Contemporary American Immigrants: Patterns of Filipino, Korean, and Chinese Settlements in the United States* (New York: Praeger).
Massey, D. S. and N. Denton (1993) *American Apartheid: Segregation and the Making of the Underclass* (Cambridge, Mass.: Harvard University Press).
McClain, C. J. (1994) *In Search of Equality: The Chinese Struggle Against Discrimination in Nineteenth Century America* (Berkeley: University of California Press).

McLaughlin, C. M. and P. Jesilow (1998) "Conveying a Sense of Community along Bolsa Avenue: Little Saigon as a Model of Ethnic Commercial Belts," *International Migration*, 36(1): 49–63.

McWilliams, C. (1943) *Brothers Under the Skin* (Boston: Little, Brown).

McWilliams, C. (1944) *Prejudice: Japanese Americans: Symbol of Racial Intolerance* (Boston: Little, Brown).

McWilliams, C. (1973) "Introduction", in C. Bulosan, *America is in the Heart* (Seattle: University of Washington Press).

Melendy, H. B. (1972) "California's Discrimination Against Filipinos 1927–1935," in R. Daniels and S. C. Olin, Jr. (eds), *Racism in California* (New York: Macmillan).

Melendy, H. B. (1976) "Filipinos in the United States," in A. Iriye (ed.), *The Asian American: The Historical Experience* (Santa Barbara: Clio Books): 101–28.

Millis, H. A. (1915) *The Japanese Problem in the United States* (New York: Macmillan).

Mlinar, Z. (1992) "Introduction," In Z. Mlinar (ed.), *Globalization and Territorial Identities* (Aldershot: Avebury).

Mollenkopf, J. (1983) *The Contested City* (Princeton: Princeton University Press).

Moore, W. (1974) "San Francisco Tenants Struggle to Stay Put," *The San Francisco Chronicle* (Thursday, October 24).

Muto, S. (1991a) "3 Generations of San Francisco Japantown," *Asian Week* (March 8): 16.

Muto, S. (1991b) "Forum Stimulates Dialogue Between the Diverse Communities in the Western Addition," *Asian Week*, (March 8): 16.

Mydans, S. (1984) "Chinese Refugees from Vietnam Thrive in Chinatown," *New York Times* (11 February): 29, 32.

Nagai, N. (1985) "Review of *The Fall of the I-Hotel*," in *East Wind* (Winter–Spring).

Narell, I. (1981) *Our City: The Jews of San Francisco* (San Diego: Howell-North).

Necesito, R. I. (1978) *The Filipino Guide to San Francisco* (San Francisco: Technomedia).

Nee, V. G. and B. de Bary (1986) *Longtime Californ': A Documentary Study of an American Chinatown* (Stanford: Stanford University Press).

New York Times (1990) "The Big Uproar Over Little Havana" (October 26): A8, A12 (L), Col. 4.

Nishi, M. (1955) "Changing Occupance of the Japanese in Los Angeles County, 1940–1950, "PhD Dissertation, University of Washington.

O'Brien, D. J. and S. Fugita (1991) *The Japanese American Experience* (Bloomington: Indiana University Press).

Okazaki, S. K. (1985) *Nihonmachi: A Story of San Francisco's Japantown* (San Francisco: SKO Studios).

Okita, David B. (1980) *"Redevelopment of San Francisco Japantown,"* M. A. Thesis, Department of Public Administration, California State University, Hayward.

Omi, M. and H. Winant (1994) *Racial Formation in the United States*, (New York: Routledge).

Ong, A. (1992) "Limits to Capital Accumulation: Chinese Capitalists on the American Pacific Rim," in N. Glick Schiller *et al.* (eds), *Towards a Transnational Perspective on Migration* (New York: New York Academy of Sciences).

Ong, A. (1993) "On the Edge of Empires: Flexible Citizenship among Chinese in Diaspora," *Positions* 1(3): 745–80.

Bibliography

Ong, A. and D. Nonini (1997) *Ungrounded Empires: The Cultural Politics of Modern Chinese Transnationalism* (New York: Routledge).
Pascual, R. (1996) "Pilipino Towns," in A. C. Ubalde (ed.), *Filipino American Architecture, Design, and Planning Issues* (San Francisco: Flipside Press): 41–58.
Paugam, Serge (1966) *L'Exclusion: L'Etat des Savoirs* (Paris: Editions La Découverte).
Petersen, W. (1971) *Japanese Americans: Oppression and Success* (New York: Random House).
Pido, A. J. A. (1986)*The Pilipinos in America* (New York: Center for Migration Studies).
Pieterse, J. N. (1995) "Globalization as Hybridization," in M. Featherstone, S. Lash and R. Robertson (eds), *Global Modernities* (London: Sage).
Rafael, V. L. (ed.) (1995) *Discrepant Histories: Translocal Essays on Filipino Cultures* (Philadelphia: Temple University Press).
Ramos, F. V. (1997) "Message," *The Filipino Directory: USA, Canada, Philippines* (Los Angeles: Phil-American Publishing Co.).
Reyes, V. (1984) "Review of *The Fall of the I-Hotel*," *Ang Katipunan* (March): 14.
Riis, J. (1957) *How the Other Half Lives* (New York: Sagamore Press): 91.
Robertson, R. (1990) "Mapping the Global Condition: Globalization as the Central Concept," in M. Featherstone (ed.) *Global Culture* (London: Sage).
Robertson, R. (1992) *"Globalization: Social Theory and Global Culture* (London: Sage).
Robertson, R. (1995) "Glocalization: Time–Space and Homogeneity–Heterogeneity," in M. Featherstone, S. Lash and R. Robertson (eds), *Global Modernities* (London: Sage).
Rouse, R. A. (1991) "Yellow Pages Advertising: An Empirical Analysis of Attributes Contributing to Consumer Interest, Liking, and Preference" *Journal of Professional Services Marketing*, 6(2): 35–44.
Rutherford, M. (1995) "Japanese Americans Come Out for Former Speaker," *Western Edition*, 2(13): 3.
Saltman, J. (1979) "Housing Discrimination: Policy Research, Methods, and Results," *Annals of the American Academy of Political and Social Science*, 441: 186–96.
San Francisco Chronicle (1942) (February 13): 12.
San Francisco Chronicle (1943) (June 23): 11
San Francisco Chronicle (1971) (December): 1.
San Francisco Chronicle (1972a) (June 12): 61.
San Francisco Chronicle (1972b) (May 6): 12.
San Francisco Chronicle (1974) (November 16): 10.
San Francisco Department of City Planning (1984) *Commerce and Employment in Chinatown*. (San Francisco: Department of City Planning).
Sassen, S. (1991)*The Global City: New York, London, Tokyo* (Princeton: Princeton University Press).
Sassen, Saskia (1995) "On Concentration and Centrality in the Global City", in Paul L. Knox *et al.* (eds) *World Cities in a World-System* (New York: Cambridge University Press).
Scott, M. (1959) *The San Francisco Bay Area: A Metropolis in Perspective* (Berkeley: University of California Press).
Shermach, K. (1994) "Yellow Pages Publishers Find Niches Among Ethnic Groups," *Marketing News*, 28(2) (January 17): 5.
Sibley, David (1995) *Geographies of Exclusion* (New York: Routledge).
Smith, B. (1948) *Americans From Japan*, (New York: J.B. Lippincott Co.).

Smith, M. P. (1995) "The Disappearance of World Cities and the Globalization of Local Politics," in L. P. Knox and P. J. Taylor (eds) *World Cities in a World System* (Cambridge: Cambridge University Press): 249–66.
Sobredo, J. (1998) "From Manila Bay to Daly City: Filipinos in San Francisco," in James Brook, C. Carlsson and N. J. Peters (eds) *Reclaiming San Francisco: History, Politics, Culture* (San Francisco: City Lights Books): 273–86.
Steiner, E. (1906) *On the Trail of the Immigrant* (New York: F. H. Revell).
Takahashi, J. (1997) *Nisei/Sansei: Shifting Japanese American Identity and Politics* (Philadelphia: Temple University Press).
Takaki, R. (1989) *Strangers from a Different Shore: A History of Asian Americans*. (Boston: Little, Brown).
Tripp, M. W. (1980) "Russian Roots: Origins and Development of an Ethnic Community in San Francisco," MA Thesis, Department of Geography, San Francisco State University.
Valangca, R. V. (1977) *Pinoy: The First Wave (1898–1941)* (San Francisco: Strawberry Hills Press).
Valparaiso, S. (1976) "Low Cost Housing Bill Defeated," *Ang Katipunan*, (January–February).
Valverde, C. (1994) "The Foundation and Future of Vietnamese Politics in the Bay Area," MA Thesis, San Francisco State University.
Walker, R. (1995a) "Landscape and City Life: Four Ecologies of Residence in the San Francisco Bay Area," *Ecumene*, 2(1): 33–64.
Walker, R. (1995b) "California Rages Against the Dying of the Light," *New Left Review*, 209: 42–74.
Walker, R. (1996) "Another Round of Globalization in San Francisco," *Urban Geography*, 17(1): 60–94.
Walker, R. and the Bay Area Study Group (1990) "The Playground of US Capitalism? The Political Economy of the San Francisco Bay Area in the 1980s," in Mike Davis *et al.* (eds), *Fire in the Heart* (London: Verso): 3–82.
Wallovits, S. (1966) "The Filipinos in California," BA Thesis, University of Southern California.
Waugh, D. and G. Lewis (1991) "Western Addition Tackles Racial Tensions," *San Francisco Examiner* (March 17): B6.
Wilson, R. and W. Dissanayake (eds) (1996) *Global/Local : Cultural Production and the Transnational Imaginary* (Durham: Duke University Press).
Wong, B. (1988) *Ethnicity and Entrepreneurship: The New Chinese Immigrants in the San Francisco Bay Area* (Boston: Allyn & Bacon).
Wong, K. (1969) "Filipinos Vow to Stay at International Hotel," *East–West* (June 4).
Wong, T. (1995) *San Francisco Chinatown: The Core Area, Conditions, and Trends* (San Francisco: Cameron House).
Yamamoto, J. K. (1992) "Changes in J-Town: San Francisco's Japantown is Still the Heart and Soul – If not the Physical Center – of the Japanese American Community". *San Francisco Bay Guardian* (East Bay ed.), November 11, 1992.
Yip, Christopher Lee (1985) "San Francisco's Chinatown: An Architectural and Urban History," PhD dissertation, University of California at San Diego.
Yu, C. Y. (1981) "A History of San Francisco Chinatown Housing," *Amerasia Journal*, 8(1) (Spring-Summer): 93–109.

Yu, T. (1988) "Economic Links Among Hong Kong, PRC, and ROC – With Special Reference to Trade;" In *Hong Kong: A Chinese and International Concern*, edited by J. Domes and Y. Shaw (Boulder: Westview Press), pp. 110–26.

Yung, J. (1995) *Unbound Feet: A Social History of Chinese Women in San Francisco* (Berkeley: University of California Press).

Zhou, Min (1992) *Chinatown: The Socioeconomic Potential of an Urban Enclave* (Philadelphia: Temple University Press).

Index

Academy, x
Accumulation, 77
Activism, 38, 40
Acupuncturists, 140
Advertising, 140–2, 144, 147, 150–1
African American, 95
Agency, 15, 19, 33, 44, 48, 54, 56, 110
Alaska, 76, 81–1
Alien Land Act of 1913, 63, 70
Alliances, 39
Alterations, 48
American businesses, 134, 139
American New Year, 24
Angelou, Maya, 74
Annexation, 61
Antiglobalization, 71
Architecture, 48
Army, 84, 96
Asia, 42, 57, 59, 69, 148–9
Asian Americans, ix, 28, 76, 97, 155
Asiatown, 124
Asian Indians, 14, 125–6
Asian yellow pages, 133
Assembly Center, 73
Assimilation model, 8, 11, 108, 158, 160
Association, 31, 43, 66, 59–60, 150–1
Asymmetry, 7
Atlanta, 146
Attachment advertisement, 152
Austin, L., 67
Autonomy, 33

Babo, 5
Balce-Cortes, Nerissa, xi
Bangkok, 101
Bank, 12, 22, 46, 60, 67, 89, 145
Bank of America, 96
Bank of Tokyo, 116
Banking system, 116
Barrio, 13
Bauman, Z., 157
Bay Area, 20, 31–2, 37, 47, 133

Bay Bridge, 63, 67
Beacon Hill, 6
Beauty salons, 45
Berkeley, 58
Bilingual education, 162
Biology, 9
Boat people, 44
Bo-Chow Hotel, 62
Body, 37, 102
Bookstores, 42
Bordellos, 90
Border, 78
Border-crossing practices, ix, 26, 77, 114, 116, 118, 121
Borderland, 106
Boston, 6
Boundary, ix, 10, 11, 25, 30, 149, 154, 159
Brazil, 21, 72
Broadway, 11
Brown, Margie, xi
Brown, Willie, 126
Brutality, 91–2
Bubonic plague, 61
Buchanan Street, 6
Buddhist temples, 1
Bulosan, Carlos, 91
Burial, 37
Business, 4, 10–12, 14, 16, 19, 21–2, 29–32, 37–9, 42–3, 45–6, 48–50, 54–5, 60–4, 66–8, 70–1, 74–5, 81–3, 87, 90, 93–5, 97, 100, 102, 140–8, 150–1, 156, 158, 161–2

California, ix, 13–14, 114, 132
Cambodians, 45
Canada, 21, 41, 72, 116, 145–7, 150, 152, 156
Canton, 156
Cantonese, 1, 41, 93
Capital city, 2, 4, 6–8, 13, 15, 19, 22–3, 28–31, 33, 36, 47, 49, 63, 145

Index

Capitalism, 77, 129
Casino, Bernadette, xi
Castro District, 20
Cebu, 145
Census, 64, 84
Center of a global process, 118
Centrarchy, 6
Chan, Ada, xi
Chen, Judy, xi
Chen, William, xi
Cherry Blossom Festival, 21, 117, 122
Chestnut Hill, 6
Chiang Kai Shek, 37
Chicago, 60, 145, 160
Chile Town, 1, 4
Chile, 20
China, 15, 29, 33–4, 36–8, 40–3, 46, 52, 156
Chinatown Youth Council, 99
Chinatown, 1–4, 7–9, 11, 13, 15, 22, 26, 28–52, 55–7, 61–3, 66–8, 76, 78–9, 82, 92–3, 94, 100, 102, 108–9, 141, 144, 156
Chinese American, 11, 13, 24, 26, 28–9, 32, 38, 39
Chinese, ix, xi, 2, 5, 7, 26, 29, 37–9, 43, 46, 49, 51–2, 57, 67, 76–7, 80, 82, 87, 92–4, 100, 125–6, 137, 140–51, 158, 166
Chinese in the Bay Area, 137
Chinese businesses, 134
Chinese community, 44
Chinese consumers, 134
Chinese Exclusion Act, 32, 54
Chinese hospital, 32–3
Chinese New Year, 24
Chinese school, 69
Chinese Vietnamese, 44–5
Chinese yellow pages, 134, 138–9
Chinesetown, 5
Christianity, 2
Chu, Elaine Wai-Ling, xi
Chuck, Harry, xi
Chung, Anni, xi
Church, 33, 43, 59, 103, 108, 151
Circumstantial globality, 118
Citizenry, 160
Citizens, ix, x
Citizenship, 82, 89, 91, 103

City, ix–x, 2–4, 8–11, 13, 17–20, 22, 24, 28, 30, 33–4, 47–51, 54–5, 57, 60–9, 75–8, 83–8, 95–6, 102, 143, 145, 150–4, 158–60, 163–6
City government, 12
City Hall, 4, 9–10, 29, 34–5, 45, 50, 92, 108–9, 127
City of Baguio, 149
City-town, 4
Civil Rights Movement, 1, 11, 13, 35, 38
Civil Rights Act, 2, 3, 85
Class, 18, 153
Clientele, x, 11–12, 43, 47, 66, 87, 99, 100–3, 116–18, 122, 124, 130–2, 135, 137, 142–3, 147–9, 151, 164–5
Clients, 141–7, 151
Code, 77
Collapse, 73, 75, 77, 94, 108
Colonial era, 7
Colonial period, 1
Colonialism, 127, 156
Colonization, 7
Colony, 57–8, 67, 77, 84
Commerce, 11, 14, 16, 62, 67–8, 93–4, 99, 101, 149, 151, 161–2
Committee against Nihonmachi Eviction (CANE), 128
Commoditization, 50, 52
Communication, 22, 42, 71, 147, 152, 163
Communism, 13, 33, 40, 46
Community, ix–xi, 2, 5–6, 8, 10–15, 19, 21–2, 30, 35–7, 40, 43–4, 46, 49, 53–9, 60, 62–3, 65–73, 79, 81–5, 92–7, 100, 140–4, 150–9, 163
Competition, x, 31, 69, 140–2, 158
Concentration camps, 53
Confrontation, 9
Congress, 98
Connecticut, 6
Conscription, 76
Constitution, 154
Constructed global space, 130
Consulate, 66, 94, 136, 144
Consumers, 41
Consumption, 10, 12

Index 189

Contract laborers, 76
Control center, 115
Cooked globality, 111, 120, 123
Cooked globalization, 110, 122
Cordova, F., 83
Corporate sector, 127
Corporation, 43, 48, 75, 97, 147, 159
Country, 5–6
Country-town, 4
Covenant clauses, 28, 89
Creativity, 159
Crime, 9
Crown, 8
Cuba, 20
Cuban, 13–14
Culinary traditions, 33, 47
Culture, 144
Customers, 87, 143, 165
Cyclical globality, 118

Daly City, 32, 42, 86, 138
Deconnectedness, 16, 18
Deconstruction, 18
Default, 90
Deglobalization, 53–4, 60, 70–7, 110, 160
DeGuzman, Emil, xi, 100
Delicatessens, 45
Delinking, 53–4, 70–2
Delinquency, 157
Democracy, x, 161, 163
Demography, 2, 9, 15, 61, 84
Demonstrations, 40
Density, 119
Dependent globality, 117
Desegregation, 159
Detention camps, 73, 75
Detention model, 160
Deterritorialization, ix
Devaluation, 90
Development, 9, 30, 48, 58, 95, 161
Dialect, 41
Diaspora, ix–x, 2, 8, 12, 18, 20–2, 24, 52–3, 69, 72, 77, 80, 86, 128, 148, 149–50, 156–7, 161–2, 165
Diasporic businesses, 139
Diasporic communites, 27
Diasporic constituents, 130
Diasporic economy, 12, 112, 164

Diasporic ethnopole, 106
Diasporic invasion, 25
Diasporic niches, 138
Diasporic site, 16, 114
Diasporization, 157
Difference, 18, 157
dim sum, 47
Directory, 141, 145–6, 148
Disaster, 66, 68
Disciplinary mechanisms, 154
Disciplinary control, 92
Discrimination, 2, 7, 78–9, 83, 88–92, 157–8
Disease, 156–7
Dishonorization, 72, 158
Disjuncture, 124
Disneyland, 145
Dispersion, 35, 70, 74, 160
Dispersion model, 160
Displacement, 28, 77, 95
Distribution, 144–6, 151–2
Diversity, 1, 153
Doctors, 140
Drille, Julio, 87
Dynamics of spatial relations, 131

Earthquake, 3–4, 16, 36, 41, 54–6, 61, 63–8
Economic empowerment, 135
Economic model, 162
Economy, 11–12, 18, 23, 38–9, 43, 46, 48–9, 52, 64–5, 71, 79, 82, 86, 148, 161
Education, 65, 69, 72, 85
El Salvador, 20
Elderly, 33–4, 44, 84, 101
Eldorado Street, 93
Elections, 96, 150
Electorates, 150
Elite, 10, 12, 76, 109
Embarcadero Freeway, 41
Emotions, 54
Employment, 63, 66, 79, 80, 82, 87, 161
Empowerment, 5
Enclave ix, x, 1–12, 14–15, 18–19, 24, 26, 29–31, 33, 35, 42, 48, 54, 56–60, 65–9, 79–83, 87–8, 92, 118, 123–6, 149, 151, 153, 156

Enclave city, 11
enclave economy, 12, 132, 135
Endo, Kenneth, xi
England, 6–7
Enlistment, 76
Enterprise, 47–8
Entertainment, 80, 83
Entrepeneurs, 14, 29, 31–2, 54, 68
Environment, 11, 18–20, 33, 48, 103, 159
Epidemic, 156
Equality, x
Ethiopian, 166
Ethnic background, 8
Ethnic businesses, 134
Ethnic clientele, 140
Ethnic communities, 30
Ethnic economy, 12
Ethnic enclave, 12, 132, 138
Ethnic entrepreneurs, 132
Ethnic fair, 151
Ethnic globality, 122
Ethnic groups, ix, 1, 15, 76, 142, 148, 150, 155, 156
Ethnic ideology, 135
Ethnic market, 135
Ethnic minority, 8
Ethnic model, 162
Ethnic newspapers, 132
Ethnic niches, 1, 138
Ethnic place, 159
Ethnic radio, 132
Ethnic solidarity, 135
Ethnic space, 151, 154
Ethnic Vietnamese, 44
Ethnic yellow pages, 129–31; as a localized global site, 131; as a geographical document, 135; as a telephone book, 135; as post-Civil Rights movement phenomenon, 129; advertisements in, 136; as an information resource for monolingual ethnics and new immigrants, 136; as a business directory, 136; as a general information resource on the homeland, 136; bottom-up approach, 132; Chinese, Japanese, and Filipino, 131; in the Bay Area, 137; language of, 138–9
Ethnicity, 20
Ethnography, x
Ethnopole, 2, 11–13, 15–26, 28–33, 37, 43, 47, 49–54, 56, 60–1, 68–80, 81, 83, 86, 109–66
Ethnopolis, 111
Ethnopolitan globalization, 129
Ethnospace, 149–50
Europe, 148
Evacuation, 16, 62, 67, 70–3
Everybody's Bookstore, 99
Exclusion, 69, 77, 78, 102, 107, 158–9
Exopole, 20
Exoticism, 10, 14, 50–2, 93, 112, 157, 162
Expansion, 148
Expatriates, 130, 149
Exploitation, 52, 81
Extinction, 2
Extraterritorial sites, 129, 135

Façades, 48, 93
Factionalization, 35
Family, 32, 37–8, 42, 44, 45, 48, 52, 54, 59, 60, 63, 65, 68–8, 73, 75, 79, 81, 85, 87, 97, 103, 150, 151, 161
Family associations, 44
Family globality, 122
Family reunions, 32
Featherstone, M., 24
Federal government, 25
Fernandez, Grace, 84
Festivals, 1, 20–1, 24, 162
Filipino Americans, ix, xi, 7–8, 28, 76–82, 83–5, 87, 93, 102, 109, 125, 143, 145–6, 150, 159, 161
Filipino business, 92
Filipino settlement, 80
Filipino yellow pages, 133–9
Fillmore District, 56
Fillmore Street, 55
Films, 40
Filth, 9
Finances, 19
Fire, 55, 68

Firms, 11, 52, 147, 164
Fish canneries, 82, 87
Floats, 21
Flower shops, 35
Flows, x
Fong, Joe, xi
Foods, 15
Foreign currency, 162
Foreign policy, 25, 38
Foster City, 42
Four Seas Investment Corporation, 100
Free people of color, 7
French, 1
French Hill, 6
Fresno, 57–8
Friends, 32, 37
Fuat, E. 131
Fung, Betty, xi
Fung, Peter, xi

Gangs, 157
Geary Street, 54, 64
Gender, 72, 75, 152
Genealogy, 2, 13, 30, 37, 68, 70, 81
Generation, 3, 14–15, 35, 40, 56, 60, 70, 71, 140, 153, 160
Generational transnationality, 121
Gentlemen's Agreement, 57, 59, 71, 75
Gentrification, 1, 2, 109, 125, 160
Gentrification model, 160
Gentrified enclave, 126
Geography, 22–3, 145–6, 154, 163
Geography of sites, 135
Germ theory, 156
Germantown, 6–7
Ghetto, 2
Ghettoization, 28, 154–5, 159
Gilroy, 146
Ginsburg, Marsha, 35
Ginseng, 43
Glenn, Evelyn Nakano, xi, 59
Global city, 16, 19, 21–2, 27, 110, 117, 128, 153–4, 159, 164
Global entities, 130
Global ethnic market, 131
Global ethnopole, 128
Global ethnopolis, 119

Global ethnospace, 129
Global family, 117
Global flows, direction of, 120
Global heterospace, 129
Global homecoming, 117
Global niche, 130
Global racism, 15, 52
Global reach, 145–7
Global space, 130, 152, 155
Global spatial infrastructure, 128
Global tension, 126
Globality of products, 130
Globality, 15, 17, 19, 21–2, 25–6, 30, 37, 49, 52, 77, 104, 111, 115–17, 135, 145, 148, 152–7, 163
Globalization, ix–x, 15, 18–19, 24, 26, 29, 37, 52–3, 60, 70, 71, 78, 101–3, 105, 120, 122–8, 152, 153, 163–4, 110, 127, 150
Globalization of gentrification, 125–6
Globalization of homogeneity, 125
Globalized locality, 26
Global–local continuum, 26
Go, Charmaine, xi
God, x
Golf, 147
Gossip, 94
Governance, 10, 11, 33
Government, 4, 8–9, 12, 15–16, 36, 40, 44, 46–50, 58, 61, 66, 68–71, 86, 95, 101, 161
Governmentality, 102
Grant Avenue, 30, 49, 63, 67
Grassroots foreign policy, 25
Grassroots leaders, 12, 31
Grassroots organizations, 10, 20, 33, 150, 163
Greektown, 7, 160

Hanford, Louise, xi
Hannerz, U., 71
Harassment, 9
Harlem, 74
Harvey, David, 24
Hawaii, 61, 76, 145
Headquarters, 12, 21, 29, 35, 40, 46, 49, 67, 114, 116, 117, 127, 130, 147, 148
Health, 9, 43

Hegemony, 5–7, 11, 15, 22, 154, 159
Herbal medicine, 140
Herbs stores, 41
Heterospace, 148–9
Hierarchy, x, 6, 23, 26, 31, 35–6, 77, 151, 154–6
Hiroshima, 62
Hispanic yellow pages, 131
History, 16, 24, 29, 30, 40, 46, 56, 60, 68, 69, 70, 81, 154, 161
Ho Chi Minh City, 8, 13, 22
Hokubei Mainichi, 67
Holidays, 1, 15
Homeland, ix, x, 1, 2, 4, 5, 7, 11, 12, 15, 18, 20–6, 30, 38, 50, 52, 61, 62, 66, 68–72, 77–8, 80–1, 84, 86, 87, 108–9, 117, 132, 134, 136, 138, 144, 148–9, 150, 154, 156–7, 160, 162–4
Homeland businesses, 139
Hometown, 37
Homopole, 20
Hong Kong, 3, 15, 29, 33, 36, 37, 39, 46, 47, 52, 99, 101, 147
Honolulu, 61
Hospitals, 42
Hostility, 16, 58–9
Hotel, 54, 58, 63–8, 84–8, 99–102, 118, 120
Housing, 13, 19, 43, 44, 48, 51, 54, 58–9, 63–4, 77–8, 85, 89, 91, 95–6
Housing discrimination, 76, 155
Housing segregation, 28, 61, 79, 80, 88
Houston, 141
Howe, M., 129
Human rights, 163
Humiliation, 72
Hybridity, x, 88

Identity, 11, 19, 21, 25, 27, 54, 59, 62, 69, 88, 93, 97
Ideology, 35, 38, 40, 77–8, 103, 105, 152, 154
Iki Hotel, 62
Immigrant community, 45
Immigrants, ix, x, 3, 4, 7, 11, 13, 14, 28, 30, 38, 43–7, 54–9, 61–3, 67, 74, 71, 76–9, 80, 83–4, 134–5, 140, 153, 155, 158, 161–2

Immigration, ix, 2, 9, 39, 44–7, 57, 59, 61, 65, 70, 72, 75–7, 81–2, 86, 124–6, 140
Immigration Act of 1924, 59, 70, 72
Immigration Act of 1965, 85
Impact studies, 37
Implementation, 47, 65, 159
Import/export, 21, 36, 43, 68, 74, 147, 162
Incarceration, 70, 72, 155
Inclusion, 80
Inclusion/exclusion, 130
Inclusion advertisement, 152
Income, 82, 84, 99
Incorporation, 2, 9, 27, 68, 155
Incubators, 20
Independence, 86
Individualism, x
Industry, 3, 12, 49, 61, 96, 95, 149
Inflation, 95
Informal urban system, 151
Informality, 28
Information, 93, 145
Infrastructure, 11, 19, 45, 48, 50, 56, 96, 145, 149, 154–5
Inherited space, 131
Institutions, x, 16, 19–20, 22, 30–5, 46, 49, 59, 68, 73, 101, 148, 159–60
Insurance, 140
Integration, ix, 1, 28, 44, 64, 106, 127, 155, 157
Intelligence agent, 81
Interaction, 8, 18, 20, 28, 34, 46, 67, 78, 157, 163
International Hotel, 85–6, 88, 93–7, 159
Internment, 72, 74
Internment camp, 59
Interpenetration, 23
Interpretation, 3, 16, 80, 157
Intersection, 20, 127; people, 127; goods, 127; capital, 127; communication, 127
Intervention, 47–9
Investment, 46, 106
Investors, 21
Involution, 161
Iranian, 166

Isolation, 53–4
Issei, 56, 58–62, 65–70, 75
Italian, 1
Italian quarters, 7
Italy, 148

Jackson Heights, 24
Japan, 5, 21, 22, 58, 72, 62, 65–70, 72, 111–24
Japan Cultural and Trade Center, 124
Japan Street, 63
Japan Trade Center, 112–16, 123
Japanese, ix, xi, 1, 5, 16, 21, 22, 26, 39, 42, 43, 54, 56–9, 62, 64–70, 73, 76, 87, 91, 117, 118, 123, 126, 140, 143, 145–50
Japanese American Democratic Club, 126
Japanese American Religious Federation, 125
Japanese Americans, 5–6, 13, 28, 53–4, 56, 58, 72, 111–24, 120–5
Japanese Brazilians, 118
Japanese Center, 74
Japanese Consulate, 122, 126
Japanese Daily New World, 5
Japanese diasporans, 117, 119, 124
Japanese Government Act of 1885, 62
Japanese government, 126
Japanese internment camps, 120
Japanese Merchants Association, 123, 125
Japanese Peace Plaza, 128
Japanese women, 75
Japantown, 2–5, 8–9, 13, 16, 20–2, 28, 43, 53–75, 94, 110–28, 164–5
Jersey City, 7
Jessie Street, 54–5, 61
Jewish quarter, 7
Jewish synagogues, 1
Jews, 53, 166
Jewtown, 7
Johnson, Lyndon, 92
Jordan, Frank, 126

Kearny Street, 86, 91, 93–4, 96
Keeling, D., 26
Ken, 66, 68
Kibei, 70

Kim, Myoka, xi
Kimono, 21, 117
Kimura, Michiko, xi
King Street, 93
Kinokuniya Building, 62, 113, 122
Kintetsu, 122
Kintetsu Enterprises Company of America, 112–13, 124
Kirk, G., 79
Kitano, H., 58
Kleyman, Paul, xi
Kong, Frank, xi
Kono, Richard, xi
Korea, 33
Koreans, 22, 42, 125–6, 140, 148, 151
Koreatown, 1, 5

Labor, 82
Labor market, 83
Laboratory, 18
Lai, Him Mark, xi
Landlord, 98
Landmark, 51, 97
Landscape, 1, 2, 4–5, 14, 24, 26, 65, 97
Language, 3, 32–3, 41, 47, 57, 59, 68–9, 94, 108, 140–1, 162
Lash, S., 24
Latin America, 14
Latin Quarter, 14
Laundries, 67
Law, 65
Law offices, 35
Lawyers, 33, 140
Le, Ann, xi
Leaders, 6, 10, 14, 35, 38, 40, 44, 112
Leadership, 34–5, 93
Legitimacy, 39
Liberation, 14
Light, I., 66
Little Africa, 4, 7
Little Bombay, 7
Little Brazil, 7
Little Canton, 4
Little China, 4
Little continents, 7
Little country, 4
Little Haiti, 7
Little Havana, 13–14

Index

Little Italy, 1, 3–4, 7, 9, 13, 92, 160
Little Manila, 8, 78, 93
Little Mexico, 4
Little Michoacan, 7, 13
Little Osaka, 7, 62, 67
Little Saigon, 7–8, 13
Little Taipei, 4, 7
Little Tehran, 4, 7
Little Tokyo, 7–8, 56, 59, 79
Loan, 90
Local, 113–14, 118, 128
Local/global space, 135
Local reach, 145
Local tension, 126
Locality, 15, 19, 24–6, 53, 68, 72
Localization of globality, 118
Localization of globalization, 117
Location, 13, 22, 58–62, 67, 72, 76, 80, 84, 145–7, 154
Locke, Cheryl, xi
London, 6, 115
Los Angeles, 3, 5, 8, 14, 57–8, 62, 78–9, 92, 115, 118, 133, 135, 145–8
Lunar calendars, 166
Lynch, Paula, xi

Machida, Osamu, xi
Macroglobalization, 18
Macy's, 143
Maida, Gaetano, xi
Mainland, 39, 41, 69
Mainstream, 52
Mainstream companies, 135
Mainstream economy, 112
Mainstream yellow pages, 132; top–down approach, 131
Major's office, 12
Management, 100, 142
Mandarin, 1, 41
Mangiafico, L., 80
Manhattan, 4
Manhattanization, 88, 97–8
Manila, 7, 13, 94, 133, 145
Manilatown, 1, 3, 4, 7, 8–9, 13, 16, 28, 76–109, 138, 159
Manongs, 82–3, 85, 87, 95–7, 101, 108
Mao Tse-Tung, 38
Map, 9, 16

Marasigan, Bullet, xi
Marcos, Ferdinand, 81
Mardi Gras, 84
Marginality, 78, 105
Marginalization, 77, 80, 101–2, 106–7, 158
Margins, ix, 78
Marin County, 146
Market, x, 37, 42, 45, 47, 52, 65, 95, 140–1, 143, 144, 151–2, 164
Market place, 15
Market target, 131–7
Marketing, 21
Marketplace, 31, 36, 49
Marriage, 58–60, 62, 79, 90
Master plan, 47
Matsushita, Karl Kaoru, xi
Mayor, 34–5, 117
Mayor's office, 10, 15
McClain, Charles, xi
McWilliams, C., 57, 78–80, 82
Media, 157
Medical clinics, 35
Medical doctor, 41
Medicines, 37, 47
Melendy, H., 79
Memory, 15
Merchants, 40, 43, 50, 52, 61, 66, 123, 140, 146–9, 151, 162
Metropole, 4, 19
Mexican Americans, 2, 13, 20
Microchip, 20
Microglobalization, 18, 123
Micromanagement, 48
Microspace, 152
Middle class, 33
Migration, 1, 3, 4, 33, 38, 43–4, 58, 61, 64, 72, 76, 78, 84, 82, 98, 160
Millano, Benito, 86
Millis, H., 57
Milpitas, 36, 42
Milton Meyer, Inc., 100
Miniature, 4
Miniaturization, 156
Minor, 8
Minorities, 2, 90, 98
Minority, 9, 79
Minority status, 8
Minsk, 7

Miscegenation, 90
Mission District, 2, 20, 84, 94
Missionaries, 2, 159
Mobility, 65, 80, 90
Modernization, 50
Monkey, 90–91
Monterey Park, 4
Montreal, 145
Moran, Kathleen, xi
Morgan Hill, 146
Morphology, 2
Mortgages, 90
Motherland, 6
Multiculturalism, ix, 2, 18, 22, 33, 51; municipal, ix; industrial, x; academic, x; congregational x; diasporic, x
Multilocal sites, 129
Multinational, 116
Multinational family organization, 121
Multinational operation, 115
Museum, 15, 50
Mushrooms, 41, 43
Muslim mosques, 1
Muslims, 166
Mutual Benefit Building, 96

National-Braemer, Inc., 112
Nationalism, 33
Nationalist Party, 34
Nationalists, 40
Nation-state, 13, 22
Natural order, 29
Navarre Hotel, 86
Navy, 84, 87
Negotiations, 38
Neighborhood, ix, a, 3–5, 7, 9–11, 18, 24, 31, 45, 47–50, 55, 63, 65, 74–6, 79, 81, 85, 89, 90, 92, 114, 123, 151, 155, 160, 164
New Britain, 6
New England, 6
New Germany, 6
New Jersey, 115
New London, 6
New Year, 151, 166
New Year's banquets, 32
New Year's Day, 24
New York, 4, 6, 7, 115, 146

Newsletter, 40
Newspaper, 12, 36, 38, 47, 50, 54, 59, 67, 88, 108, 141, 143–4, 152
Ng, Alex, xi
Ng, Johnny, xi
Ngo sector, 128, 136
Ngopole, 20
Nguyen, Binh, xi
Nicaragua, 20
Niche, 11, 18–20, 58–9, 66, 68, 141
Nihon-Machi, 5, 58–9, 66
Nihonjin-Machi, 55–6, 63
Nisei, 56, 59, 73
Nisei-Kibei, 60, 73
Nixon, Richard, 15, 29, 37–42, 46
Nob Hill, 6
Nodal globality, 114
Node, 20, 114, 118
Non-profit, 43
Normalization, 38–40
Northern California, 137–8

Oakland, 35–6, 141, 146
Occupational mobility, 59
Oka, Seizo, xi
Okazaki, S., 58, 65, 68
Okazaki, Tomoshige, xi
Okita, David, 112
Olympic games, 5
Omiya Company, 62
Omiya Hotel, 62
Onuma, Michi, xi
Opposition forces, 162
Ordinance, 10, 69, 158–9
Organizations, 34–5, 38, 47, 66, 59
Oriental school, 69
Oriental Warehouse, 62
Orientalist project, ix
Osaka, 21, 111, 117, 163–4
Ottawa, 145
Outreach, 143
Overseas Chinese Committee of the Republic of China, 134

Pacific Bell, 140–4
Pacific Gas and Electric Company, 96
Pacific Mail Dock, 63
Pacific region, 143
Pacifica, 42

Panethnopole, 20
Panethnospace, 151
Parades, 1
Paradigm, 19
Parking, 51
Parliament, 149–50
Partnership, 11
Patriotism, x, 37
Peace Pagoda, 112
Pearl Harbor, 75, 160
Peng, Linda, xi
Pension, 99
Pensionados, 76
People's Republic of China, 39
Performances, 16
Performativity, 15
Permanent globality, 118
Persecution, 95
Peru, 20, 21, 72
Phase of insertion, 9
Philadelphia, 6
Philippines, 4, 13, 33, 76–7, 81, 83, 86, 102, 109, 145–6, 149–52
Physicians, 30, 33
Picture bride, 58–9, 65, 68, 72
Pido, A., 80
Pieterse, J., 24
Pinoys, 91
Planned globality, 120
Planning, 50, 56
Polarization, 11, 35
Pole, 19–20, 23, 37
Police, 10, 48, 64, 91–2, 97, 100
Policy, 2, 9, 11, 12, 25, 38, 50, 84, 92, 98, 101, 161
Political opposition model, 162
Political organization, 34
Political system, 10
Politics, 12, 24–5, 33–4, 40, 43–4, 86
Population, 1, 2, 3, 5, 7, 9–12, 15, 19, 20–3, 28–9, 33–6, 39, 45, 47, 51, 61, 63–4, 69, 74–5, 78, 83–6, 93, 96, 102, 142, 144, 146, 148, 151
Post Street, 6, 73
Postcolonialism, 127
Poststructuralism, 31
Poverty, 3, 9, 84, 92, 157
Power, 7, 77, 143, 157
Power structure, 33

Prejudice, 28, 57–8, 65
Preservation, 97
Presidio, 54
Production, 15–16, 21, 25, 60, 78, 80, 154
Profit, 90
Projected space, 131
Property, 74, 90
Prostitution, 157
Protection, 59
Provinces, 149
Public assistance, 45
Public sphere, ix
Publicity, 10, 52, 143
Puerto Rico, 20

Quarantine, 9
Quarantinization, 156
Quarters, 6, 11, 55, 87
Queens, 24
Quinlan, Tara Lai, xi

Race, 2, 13, 38, 57, 83, 154–5
Racial discrimination, 13, 28, 56, 59, 61, 64, 80, 88
Racial segregation, 3
Racialization, 28, 157
Racism, 9, 11, 28–9, 50–2, 79, 157
Radio, 141, 143–4
Railroad, 61, 62, 68
Ramos, Fidel, 149
Raw globality, 111, 120–2
Raw globalization, 110
Readership, 130
Real estate, 43, 89
Real estate agency, 12
Real estate agent, 21
Recruitment, 61, 68, 76
Red Guards, 40
Refugees, 41, 43, 45, 47
Reglobalization, 53–4, 74, 110–11, 122, 124
Regulation, 34, 49, 158
Relations, 16–17, 21, 26, 31, 37–9, 47, 51, 60, 69–72, 148, 160–6
Relationship, 26
Religious life, x
Relocation, 53, 56
Relocation center, 73

Index   197

Relocation model, 160
Remittances, 25, 68–9, 74, 81, 160, 162
Rent, 45, 55–7, 62, 65, 74, 92, 169
Repatriation Act, 79, 83
Repatriation model, 161
Replicas, 4
Representation, 159
Representativity, ix
Reproduction, 9, 16, 24, 27, 31, 47–8, 50–1, 60, 68–9, 71, 81, 108, 153–5, 157
Reputation, 55
Resentment, 26
Resettlement, 3, 56, 66, 75
Resistance, 11, 26, 77, 159, 162
Restaurant, 32, 35, 43, 45, 47, 67, 87, 91, 94, 144–5
Reterritorialization ix, 80, 156, 160
Retirement, 82
Reunification, 46
Revenue, 4, 87, 143
Richmond District, 1, 7, 32–3, 35, 86
Rights, 9
Rivington Street, 7
Robertson, R., 24
Robles, Al, xi
Roosevelt, Theodore, 70
Roots, 38, 52
Roundtable Pizza, 143
Ruiz, Neil, xi
Rules, 102, 127
Russian, 1, 7
Russian Hill, 3, 6
Russo-Japanese War, 69

Sacramento, 57–8, 86
Safeway, 143
Saigon, 8, 15, 29, 43–4
Salespeople, 141, 143–4, 146
San Diego, 145
San Francisco, 1–9, 11, 13, 16, 18–21, 25, 28–30, 32, 34, 36, 42–4, 49–50, 54–7, 60–4, 69, 72, 76, 78–81, 86–7, 92, 111–18, 122, 125, 128, 133–4, 138, 141, 155, 163
San Francisco Economic Opportunity Council, 92

San Francisco Redevelopment Agency, 6, 112
San Joaquin Valley, 82
San José, 13, 35, 41, 144–6
San Mateo, 36, 41–2
Sandinista government, 25
Sansei, 60
Santa Clara, 36
Sarmiento, Jose, 87
Satellite, 113
Scale, 22, 26, 35–6
School, 10, 25, 42, 59, 68, 108
Sears, 143
Seattle, 57, 76, 82, 92, 141
Secondary city, 6
Sectoral globality, 115
Security system, 72
Segmentation, 71
Segregation, ix, 10, 13, 25, 52, 59, 69, 84–5, 89, 154–5, 157–8
Servicemen, 98
Services, 11, 12, 19, 21
Settlement, 6–7, 9–10, 54, 57–9, 68, 79
Sexual orientation, 20
Shame, 72
Shanghai, 41
Shelter, 95–6
Shin Sekai, 54
Shipyards, 74, 82
Silicon Valley, 22, 145, 165
Singapore, 33, 101
Site, 3, 9–10, 15–17, 19, 20, 22–4, 26, 28–31, 33, 47, 50–3, 55, 57, 62, 68, 72, 77, 79, 97, 116, 130, 142, 145, 148, 153, 157
Site of consumption, 130
Site of production, 130
"Six Companies," 34–5
Skyscrapers, 96
Slaves, 7
Smith, B., 57, 61, 66
Sobriquets, 1, 14
Social formation, x, 157
Social justice, x
Social representation, 157
Social services, 9, 10, 20, 33, 44, 77
Socialism, 40
Socialization, 54, 63

Society, ix–xi, 3, 8, 19
Solar calendars, 166
Solidarity, 159
South Asian community, 45
South Bay, 44, 81
South Korea, 22
South Park, 3, 62, 63, 66–8, 70
Southern Blacks, 74
Soviet Union, 38
Space of difference, 28
Space of representation, 156
Space, 2, 6, 8, 10, 13–16, 18, 22, 24–5, 49, 77, 80, 93, 97, 99, 106, 146, 148–55, 159, 165–6
Spanish, 1
Spanish colonization, 76
Spanish Hill, 6
Spatial globality, 118, 130
Spatiality, 16, 131, 135, 129
Spatialization, 28, 155
Spy, 12
State, 8, 77
Status, 2, 5–6, 8, 23, 27–8, 33, 35, 49, 51, 84, 91, 103, 153, 155, 157, 162
Steiner, Edward, 7
Stevenson Street, 54–5, 61
Stigmatization, 13, 157
Stockton Street, 8, 30, 49, 57–8, 78, 79, 82, 92, 138
Stores, 41, 52, 55–6, 32, 35, 42, 45, 54, 60, 62–3, 66, 93–4, 99, 148–51, 164
Strategy, 143
Street fairs, 24
Strike, 72
Structuralism, 31
Subalternization, 28, 69, 156
Subjects, 77, 103
Subsidiary firms, 11–12, 21, 35, 77, 114–17, 123, 126–30, 142, 147–8, 164
Subsidiary process, 54
Suburbs, 33, 35
Sunset District, 32, 35
Supermarket, 36, 42
Surveillance, 72, 83, 91, 162
Survey, 99
Sustained globality, 118

Sweatshops, 165
Symbolism, 15

Tagalog, 1
Taguma, Kenji, xi
Taiwan, 3, 33–4, 37–40, 46, 52, 147
Taiwanese, 34, 36, 38, 46
Tamura Hotel, 62
Tamura Tokunosuke, 62
Taniguchi, Yoshiro, 112
Tasamak Plaza, 113, 122
Tax, 50, 96
Tax collection, 10
Taxation, 158
Technopole, 20
Telegraph Hill, 6
Telephone, 31, 150, 152
Television, 50, 141, 144
Temple Street, 93
Temporality, 16, 60, 119, 130, 153, 158
Tenants, 98
Tenderloin, 45, 88
Tenderloin District, 43–4, 85
Tension, 39, 45
Tenth Ward, 7
Territory, 2, 13, 18, 76, 106
Thai, Thyrale, xi
Thailand, 33
Thanasombat, Siri, xi
Theme-parkization, 111, 127
Tibetan, 166
Time, 10, 24, 30, 39, 165
Time zones, 166
Tokyo, 21, 111, 156, 164
Tourism, 4, 9, 10–11, 29, 30, 32, 36, 41–2, 47–52, 67, 93, 109, 111, 113, 119–27, 130, 144–5, 147–8, 150, 161
Town, 5–7, 57
Trade, 41, 43, 46–7, 55, 67
Trade lawyers, 12, 21
Trade protectionism, 126
Traditions, 1, 15, 20
Trajectory, 158
Transactions, x, 11, 18, 38, 62, 64, 67, 162, 165
TransAmerica Building, 96
Transethnic economy, 12

Transgenerationality, 121
Transglobalization, 29
Transgression, 10
Transnation, 52, 80, 88, 153
Transnational communities, 26
Transnational economic system, 119
Transnational family associations, 29
Transnational locus, 121
Transnational model, 162
Transnational relations, 11, 22–3, 25, 27, 52, 118
Transnational space, 129–30
Transnational tension, 126
Transnational transactional spatial corridor, 130
Transnationalism, x, 12, 15–16, 19, 21, 26, 60, 66–78, 114, 118–20, 122, 127, 134, 147–50, 153–5, 162, 164
Transnationality, 68, 116
Transportation, 31, 49, 51, 83, 164
Travel, 140, 148
Travel agency, 144
Travel guides, 50
Treaty, 75

Unemployment, 99
Unglobalization, 53
United Filipino Association, 97
United States, 132, 135
Universal Studios, 145
Universality, 157
University town, 76
Urban renewal, 95, 101
Urban system, 23, 25, 31
US occupation, 77, 76, 81, 86, 111, 115–18, 121, 126
US–Japan relations, 119
US–Spanish War, 77

Valverde, Caroline, xi
Van Ness Avenue, 54

Vancouver, 146
Vasquez, Anna, xi
Veterans, 84, 96, 99
Video shops, 45
Vietnam, 8, 33, 39
Vietnam War, 45
Vietnamese, 1, 13, 42–5, 151
Vietnamese Americans, 22
Village, 41–2
Visitors, 49, 145

Wada, Richard, xi
Walnut Creek, 33, 35
Walnut Grove, 58
War, 44, 71, 74, 84, 92
War brides, 68
Warehouses, 37
Washington, DC, 146
Wealth, 3, 6, 155
Weddings, 32
Welfare, 161
Welfare reform, 45
West Coast, 82, 143
Western Addition, 1, 3, 16, 54–6, 62–7, 74, 95, 112, 126
Westminster, 8, 13
Westwood Village, 4
Winnipeg, Canada, 149
Women, 79, 82
Wong, Harvey, xi, 35
World War II, 16, 26, 39, 47, 53, 58, 67, 71, 74, 82, 84, 98, 112, 120

Yamamoto, J.K., xi
Yamaski, Minoru, 112
Yasonia, Alfonso, 88
Yellow pages, 16, 50, 140–52
York, 6

Zoning ordinances, 48